History of Education in America

Third Edition

History of Education in America

Third Edition

JOHN D. PULLIAM
University of Oklahoma

Charles E. Merrill Publishing Company
A Bell & Howell Company
Columbus, Ohio

Merrill's Foundations of Education Series
Under the editorship of
Ray C. Phillips and Robert J. Stalcup

Published by Charles E. Merrill Publishing Company
A Bell & Howell Company
Columbus, Ohio 43216

Composition: Melior
Cover design: Will Chenoweth

Library of Congress Catalog Card Number: 81–84794
International Standard Book Number: 0–675–09820–3
2 3 4 5 6 7 8 9 — 90 89 88 87 86 85 84

Printed in the United States of America

Contents

Preface

This book is designed to give the student of education an overview of the history of American education and to provide a quick reference to the most important persons, dates, events, and movements that shaped the nation's educational system.

The tremendous growth of information and published material each year in the field of education makes keeping up a very difficult task. At the same time, professional growth demands sophisticated knowledge and an understanding of the latest research. Many students of education find that they must reduce their scope in order to keep up with their own special area. At the same time, some understanding of the entire field of education is vital. It provides a foundation for the whole profession and enables the scholar to gain perspective with regard to the role of each specialized field. This book gives a capsule presentation of the basic concepts and most significant events in American Educational history. It contains much more information than the previous editions and the whole book has been updated to include recent developments. Time lines have been provided at the opening of each chapter to guide the reader. Two entirely new chapters have been added, one treating contemporary issues in American education and another dealing with the educational future. A "then to now" section has been included at the end of the chapters to show the relationship between historical events and contemporary problems in education. These sections stress the continuity between the past and issues in modern education. And they show the contrast between present and past as well.

This third edition reflects the same clear organization and writing style of the original book. My goal is to provide a clear yet succinct coverage of the history of American education. Selective chapter and general bibliographies are provided as guides for more extensive study.

I am indebted to Marianne Taflinger and the staff at Merrill for suggesting the third edition and for their work in editing and preparing the format of the book. I also wish to thank my wife, Willie, who helped with the manuscript and provided psychological support.

John D. Pulliam

History of Education in America

Third Edition

Introduction   1

As Alvin Toffler has demonstrated in *Future Shock*, the pace of change and the birth of new information are the most significant characteristics of modern society. As a major social institution, the schools are constantly bombarded with new demands and challenged with alternative ideas about how goals might be achieved and problems solved. In a broader sense education is called upon to provide all members of modern society with the skills, values, information, and attitudes needed to survive in an uncertain world. The very nature of an unknown and dangerous future creates controversy in educational matters. Never before in American history have so many issues involving the social, economic, and political aspects of the culture been so hotly debated. The progressive and dynamic nature of American society has long allowed opposing viewpoints to be passionately expressed, but controversy is more intense today because basic values and the public philosophy are at stake.

In a world marked by war, inflation and recession, a population explosion, careening technology, pollution, racial strife, unemployment, an energy crisis, starvation, ecological suicide and anxiety about the future, education and schooling cannot be taken for granted. The teacher today is likely to be overwhelmed by the

Greek City States	Roman Republic	BC	AD	Roman Empire	Dark Ages
c 900 Homer	Cato			First Century Quintilian	
	Cicero			Tacitus	
Athens					
Sparta			University of Alexandria	360 Julian Revived	
Fifth Century				Classical	
Socrates				Learning	
Plato					
Aristotle				529	
Isocrates				Justinian Closed the Pagan Universities	

number and variety of demands made and conflicting theories about how demands should be met. In a time of information overload it is especially important for educators to have some sort of theoretical base to serve as a map through the labyrinth of facts and opinions. Misconceptions and misunderstandings may often be avoided if teachers and the general public have a sound understanding of the historical forces which served as the foundation for our present culture.

While the history of education does not provide the teacher with a blueprint for classroom practices, it may serve to recall previous techniques and concepts with which others have had success or failure. Much of what is regarded as new or innovative in education has a long historical record. For example, individual instruction, team teaching, open classrooms, schools without walls, alternative schools for secondary students, work-study programs, nongraded schools and competency based programs were all tried in one form or another by the progressive educators of the 1930s. It is incredible that some modern educators have overlooked the progressive experiments which can supply valuable information on proposed educational changes. Without a knowledge of history teachers find themselves "re-inventing the wheel."

An even more vital use for the history of education consists in reassessing educational and cultural traditions as a guide for making judgments about the future. Accepted practice and tradition are simply not good enough at a time when the very survival of the race depends upon educating children who are able to cope with the mammoth problems surrounding us now and future ones which can barely be imagined. Today a critic like Ivan Illich, who advocates deschooling society because he believes that the values carried by formal educational institutions are unwholesome and dangerous, must be taken seriously. In the 1950s Illich would have been the

Middle Ages		Renaissance	Reformation
569–632	776–586	1158	1466–1536
Mohammed	Alcuin	University of	Erasmus and
		Paris	Humanism
800	Chivalry		
Learning		1225–1274	1517 Luther's
Revived by		Thomas Aquinas	95 Theses
Charlemagne			
		Scholasticism	1509–1565
Monasticism			Calvin
		Growth of the	
		Universities	1550
			Knox and English
			Puritans

object of ridicule. The concept of "culture lag," central to William F. Ogburn's *Social Change*, is now so much a part of reality that it is taken for granted; but school planners must still find ways of keeping education from falling hopelessly behind. The age of electronic communication, computers, cybernation, and mushrooming scientific discovery is upon us.

It follows that teachers must have an appreciation of the culture in which schools operate if they are to influence programs and choices of curriculum. To understand problems in a world of exponential change, educators need to know how problems have arisen, what dangers and opportunities are linked with them, and what future developments may reasonably be predicted. A teacher who has excellent techniques for communication with and stimulation of students may achieve great success in teaching. However, *what* is taught may be vital or useless to the student, depending on the state of the culture and the rapidity of change. Many American high school students now receive training for jobs which all indicators show will not be needed in the future.

Education locked into a rigid pattern with few alternatives is a blueprint for disaster. To deal with an issue of this kind, educators must understand the culture — the social, political, and economic forces at work. To this end, the history of education should be treated as social and intellectual history. It is the significant forces, movements, ideas, and conflicts which shaped the American school system that are vital to a comprehension of the present.

Professional educators need to understand the close functional relationship between theory and practice. This requires more than accuracy in reporting events, authenticity of records, and credibility of sources (although all these are vital). While the historian must attempt to determine the meaning of the record, that record must always be interpreted and there is always the possibility of bias. The author of this book takes responsibility for the validity of the material presented and for efforts to show relationships, evaluate trends, and understand context. Interpretation, however, assumes the active participation of the reader, who must draw upon his or her experience in addition to the historical facts.

It is not possible to give a complete history of American education in a book of this length. Many excellent treatments with more detail and depth are available, most of which are included in chapter bibliographies. An adequate historical reassessment of our cultural and educational foundations requires examination of the documents upon which history is based. The object of this work is to give an outline of the most significant educational events and movements which shaped the American schools. It is designed to provide a sound historical base from which to evaluate and judge modern educational theory and practice. The level of information provided is about what most American universities expect graduate students in education (not majoring in educational foundations) to know about the field. The book may therefore prove useful to those studying for preliminary or general examinations.

The broadly chronological organization of this book is justified by the ease with which the novice may find topics and grasp the material. Time lines, section headings, a glossary, and an index are included for the same reason. Nevertheless, it should be remembered that events, dates, laws, and administrative structures are less important than evaluating, understanding, and criticizing the historical material.

HISTORY AND PURPOSES OF EDUCATIONAL HISTORY

As subjects of study or "disciplines" go, the history of education is relatively new. In a general way it has been included as part of the field of history, but intellectual and cultural history (of which the history of education is a segment) is much more recent than military and political history. Systematic study of the history of education has developed in America largely within the past seventy-five years, although there were many earlier accounts of the training of particular individuals or unique groups. Thus, literature contains some history of education, as in the case of the life of Lycurgus in Plutarch's The Lives of the Noble Grecians and Romans, which provides considerable information about the training of boys in the ancient Greek city-state of Sparta. Biography is obviously a rich source of information about educational practices in times past, since authors nearly always attempt to account for character development by describing childhood experiences, schooling included. Historians have also been attracted by customs or practices which they considered rare or bizarre, so that atypical educational systems often have been described in some detail.

Modern history of education received its greatest stimulation from the theory that teachers should have a knowledge of the development of at least their own national school system as part of their professional equipment. Obviously, this belief was dependent upon some sort of formal training for teachers — something which did not occur in the United States until after 1825, and then only to a limited degree. The common assumption that educational historiography started in the nineteenth century is largely true, even though one may point to numerous efforts to trace school development in earlier times. Quintilian, the Roman educator of the first century, included some history of education in his *Institutio Oratoria*, while Robert Goulet's book on the origins of the University of Paris, published in 1517, could be considered educational history. Professor Harry Good identifies Claude Fleury's *Treatise on the Selection and Methods of Studies* (France, circa 1700) as the oldest systematic history of education. There were numerous histories of institutions of higher learning and some efforts to describe higher education generally, such as that of the Puritan minister Cotton Mather who wrote about New England college programs around the year 1700.

Nevertheless, the history of American education was hardly a field for systematic study until Ellwood P. Cubberley of Stanford University published his *Public Education in the United States*, followed by books of readings in the history of education and critically annotated bibliographies on the subject. Cubberley, who produced his books just after 1900, was a widely respected educator and scholar who had considerable influence upon the inclusion of the history of American education among standard subjects in teacher-training programs. Since normal-school education had become common by the beginning of the twentieth century and education departments were by then established in many of the nation's leading universities, courses dealing with history of education in the United States sprang up all over the country. Historians who were not also educators continued to avoid the field; but scholars such as Paul Monroe and I. L. Kandel contributed vastly to our knowledge.

History of education was identified by its broad area of coverage as compared to other kinds of history. The emphasis of historians who were also interested in teacher preparation and school improvement was not simply on the development of the public system of education, but also upon the social factors which gave rise to the system. In this sense, the history of education may be called the earliest systematic treatment of cultural and intellectual factors affecting the American people. No full understanding of the current educational situation in a nation is possible without a knowledge of the evolution of the school system, together with the practices and theories which contributed to its growth. Thus, the educational historians do not limit themselves to a single field of knowledge but draw upon information from such disciplines as economics, sociology, anthropology, and psychology in an effort to get a true conception of educational development. For this reason, their approach should be considered interdisciplinary.

Differing Points of View.   Leading historians of education have been more interested in the application of their studies to professional improvement of teaching than to the study of "pure" history for its own sake. This fact and the educators' point of view have led to disagreements between modern historians of education and professors of history who are interested in studying education. Both groups add to the existing body of knowledge about education. The historian contributes special skill in the detailed study of limited periods, geographical areas, and special topics. Educational historians are usually interested in interpreting broad cultural trends in order to clarify the goals and aims of education, as well as intensive work on specific topics related to schooling.

Historians of education have differed on the interpretation of the facts, especially since the field was entered by scholars with a strong interest in sociology. Bernard Bailyn is an example of an author who feels the schools have generally supported educational equality, while Michael Katz argues that they have served the special interests of the dominant middle-class whites. Much of the current historical literature in education is directed to one side or the other of the interpretation of the role of education in American culture.

Influence of Recent Changes.   A number of changes have taken place in education during the past few years which have had a marked influence upon the study of the history of education. Among the more important developments are the following: (a) rapid increase in scientific activity and the accumulation of knowledge, together with an extension of average time spent in school and a major increase in adult education and training by private industries;

(b) substantial involvement of the federal government in educational matters, especially after the success of the Soviet space effort in 1957; (c) growth of graduate work in education due to a much larger demand for teachers with advanced degrees, bringing many more scholars to the field of history of education; (d) an increased interest in foreign school systems, the role of education in emerging nations, and the problems of social class, racial integration, and poverty in America; (e) the work of critics of the school system in the United States who have taken issue with the organization, methods, and especially the curriculum of our public schools.

The history of education is therefore a developing rather than a finished area of study. It is concerned with building a full understanding of the current educational situation through the study of the evolution of educational practices, ideas, and institutions in social context. An excellent definition of the subject was given by William W. Brickman in the 1964 lecture to the Department of Education of Johns Hopkins University. He described educational history as that branch of history which deals with the development of thought, practice, materials, personnel, administration, organization, and problems of schools. The subject also includes institutions and organizations which instruct both the young and the mature, the mass media, and other learning experiences.

INTELLECTUAL BACKGROUND

American education is western education and therefore the intellectual roots for it extend back to ancient Greece and Rome. Plato and Aristotle formed the basis of the school curriculum and also laid the foundation for educational theory. Classical studies especially stressed Latin and the culture of the Greeks and Romans. Humanism in the age of Erasmus looked back to Cicero and Quintilian for models of literary style. Leaders of the American Revolution were familiar with writings of classical antiquity and often quoted the ancient writers.

Force of Medieval Tradition. With the decline and fall of the Roman Empire, an intellectual and social stagnation began in Europe that continued until the several revivals of learning known collectively as the Renaissance. Feudal patterns of social structure and economics developed in this era, while philosophy and learning were handmaidens of the Church. Education was at a low ebb, the monasteries and a few cathedral schools being the chief instruments of instruction. Charlemagne made an effort to revive learning at the end of the eighth century, but theological questions continued to occupy the minds of the learned elite while the great bulk of the people remained ignorant in an "otherworldly" society.

A reintroduction of ancient classical learning, especially the Arabic translations of Aristotle in the thirteenth century, gave rise to the higher level scholarship of Albert the Great and Thomas Aquinas. Medieval universities and the scholasticism of Thomas eventually provided a basis for working out of the traditions of the Middle Ages. Nevertheless, medieval influences were still very strong at the time of American colonization. They are to be found in the social structure, the dominance of religion, superstitions, and other beliefs widely held by settlers from all parts of Europe.

Impact of the Renaissance. The Renaissance, or rebirth of learning, began in the 1200s and lasted through the Reformation of the 1500s. There are many aspects of this movement which had some influence on American development. The Renaissance replaced a religious point of view with a secular one, making man rather than God the focal point with reference to art, literature, and the government. Humanism, as it is sometimes called, was based partly upon the transfer of wealth and political power from the Church to laymen and nation states. The Renaissance also included a revival of interest in the ancient classical culture of Greece and Rome. Humanists studied and imitated the manuscripts of the great writers of the past. They also examined the ancient social order (especially of Rome) and made critical comparisons with their own time. Classicism protested against the narrow religious nature of education in the Middle Ages. Erasmus made editions of the New Testament in Latin and Greek and also criticized the ignorance of the clergy and the injustice of society. Renaissance emphasis on the development of the individual helped to purge ignorance and encourage education.

Significant new inventions made rapid progress in learning possible. As the Renaissance swept through Europe, a great desire for books developed that hand copying or block printing could not satisfy. Johannes Gutenberg developed his technique for using separate pieces of raised metal type in a press about 1440. The resulting revolution in the production and availability of printed information had a profound impact on education in the Western world. The availability of books at a low cost allowed many more members of society to read and think for themselves, instead of accepting everything on the authority of scholars. Growth of cities, revival of trade, exploration, and increased mobility of scholars helped to spread information and expedited the exchange of ideas.

Impact of Scientific Thinking.   From 1500 to 1700 significant changes were taking place in Europe such as geographic exploration, religious revolution, the growth of nationalism, and the discovery of science. While the classical humanism of the Renaissance period continued to be the dominant educational force, commercial interests and cultural diversity gave rise to the growth of scientific facts and methods.

Around 1500, Leonardo da Vinci called attention to the importance of observation and experimentation in learning. Francis Bacon (1561-1626) popularized the scientific technique in *Novum Organum.* The astronomical discoveries of Copernicus, Kepler, Galileo, and Bruno challenged traditional conceptions of the universe. William Gilbert made studies of electricity, Robert Boyle examined the chemical properties of gases, and Isaac Newton published basic laws of physics and mechanics. Mathematical support for science was found in the contributions made to calculus and analytical geometry by Leibniz, Descartes, and Newton.

Science was still suspect when the American colonies were founded. Very few learned people accepted the materialism and the concept of a machine universe expounded by Thomas Hobbes or Pierre Gassendi. Nevertheless, the scientific method of thinking did provide a challenge to established beliefs and laid a foundation for the enlightenment of the eighteenth century. William Harvey's theory of the circulation of the blood was discussed at Harvard while that institution remained a theological college strongly opposed to science.

Significance of Religious Revolutions.   Probably no single movement so greatly affected colonial America as the Protestant Reformation and the Catholic Counter-Reformation. The tremendous impact of the Reformation on social, economic, and political life was of paramount importance in the formation of the United States, and some of the influences are still felt today.

In 1517, when Martin Luther posted his Ninety-five Theses on the church door in Wittenberg, Germany, the Catholic Church was the most important educational agency in the world. At the close of the Thirty Years' War, all institutions and every aspect of the culture had been affected. Most of the Europeans who came to America were Protestants; but there were many denominations. Lutherans from Germany and Scandinavia settled in the middle colonies, especially

Pennsylvania. Followers of John Calvin were represented by Puritans, Presbyterians, Huguenots and several smaller sects. Anabaptists (followers of Zwingli) were persecuted by both Catholic and Protestant authorities and therefore sought freedom in the New World. Much of the struggle known as the Reformation centered upon efforts to capture the minds of men and therefore great emphasis was placed upon the written word. Obviously, schools were needed by both sides to foster the growth of each denomination or sect.

Luther's doctrine of the "priesthood of all believers" made it necessary for boys and girls to learn to read the Scriptures. Educational programs which were intended to give the masses the ability to read the Bible in the vernacular were started by Protestant groups in Germany and wherever Luther's concepts spread. While the schools were often rudimentary, they offered universal education for all children regardless of wealth and were supported by both church and state. Protestants also provided secondary education of higher quality for the elite destined to enter positions in the government or the Church. While Catholics played a substantially smaller role in colonial America, they were very much part of the Counter-Reformation. Catholics in Maryland were influenced by leaders such as Jean Baptiste de la Salle and Ignatius Loyola.

In England the break with the Catholic Church came when Clement VII refused to annul Henry VIII's marriage to Catherine of Aragon. By the Act of Supremacy in 1534, Henry became head of the Church in England and proceeded to break up the monasteries. The English Church remained very much the same during Henry's time with the Reformation really starting under Edward VI. Catholicism was briefly restored by Mary I, but during the long reign of Elizabeth, Anglicanism was firmly established. Anglicanism is a moderate form of Protestantism which preserves most of the organizational structure of the Catholic Church. English Calvinists who wanted to change or purify the Anglican Church became known as Puritans and were very important in the settlement of New England. Other dissenters from the Anglican faith included some called Separatists, who denied the establishment of religion and held that each man must be free to worship as he thought fit. Followers of Knox in Scotland (Presbyterians), Quakers, and Catholics tended to move to America when the political tide was against them in England. For example, the great Puritan migrations took place in the 1630s because of the persecution directed by Anglican Archbishop Laud.

Conservative Traditions. Students sometimes get the idea that the Renaissance and the Reformation were entirely progressive

movements. In fact, they were often reactionary. Humanism looked
to the past rather than the future for its model. The Reformation had
a tendency to make religion once again the dominant intellectual
interest of mankind. There were, however, other forces which
tended to counteract the importance of the Reformation and the
Renaissance. The American colonies were an integral part of a great
English colonial empire. They were not isolated outposts or temporary communities but a portion of a larger capitalistic scheme brought
about by a strong middle class for the purpose of material gain. The
rise of capitalism was one of the strongest factors in the development
of this nation. American civilization, from the first, was profoundly
affected by economic motives and interests. Even the New England
Puritan, who came to a "stern and rockbound coast" in order to
escape religious oppression was not without economic concern. The
soil in New England was shallow and unproductive. Pilgrims and
Puritans soon turned to timber cutting, ship building, fishing for cod,
manufacturing, and trade in order to make a livelihood.

In addition to capitalism, the parliamentary form of government
was brought by the colonists to America. The New Englanders especially supported Parliament against the King. They wished to substitute their own body politic for the authority which had been vested
in the crown. Thus, the effort of the Pilgrim fathers in making the
Mayflower Compact, which served as a constitution and defined the
responsibilities of the people as well as centering authority in the
people, could hardly have occurred without the struggle for parliamentary supremacy which had taken place in the mother country.

Many other potent forces played a part in the intellectual climate
out of which American educational institutions developed. The rise
of science, British empiricism, the forces of rationalism, and the
movement toward greater intellectual discovery all had their effect
on the birth of American schools. The point to be made is that
American educational and intellectual foundations have roots
which run very deep into the European past. While many of the most
conservative ideas, such as the evil nature of man, were preserved in
America, there were also factors tending to develop an attitude of
change.

THEN TO NOW

The casual student of history may not immediately see the relationship of the remote past to the age in which we live. Nevertheless,
connections do exist between the world of today and those past traditions which were once dominant. A better understanding of modern

attitudes and ideas can be gleaned from an analysis of historical forces. Consider, for example, the curriculum of present schools and colleges. Medieval universities offered studies which had been derived from ancient educational interests reaching back to Aristotle. These were the seven liberal arts which scholars believed to be essential to the life of the mind and the education of men. The basic or tool subjects were grammar, logic, and rhetoric. Advanced studies consisted of arithmetic, geometry, astronomy, and harmony. Although the names have sometimes changed (music for harmony and language arts for grammar) it is obvious that these medieval curriculum offerings are still found in the schools. It is also true that modern groupings into natural sciences, social sciences, and the humanities are based on these early subjects and that we still speak of a liberal arts curriculum in reference to such studies. There have been many modifications and additions but the curriculum of the universities of the Middle Ages has not disappeared. The whole idea of a university stems from the medieval organization of a guild of teachers and a guild of students. The modern master's degree is named after the guild practice of awarding master craftsman status for those who had demonstrated excellence in their work. Our most modern research universities still have deans, lecture halls, student organizations and rectors (presidents) all of which were part of the early universities.

The rebirth of learning known as the Renaissance has never really ceased. Ideas from the classical past together with the humanism of scholars like Erasmus produced a new desire to understand the forces that shape human society. When modern sociologists attempt to analyze the actions of groups of people, they are involved in the spirit of inquiry that was the heart of the Renaissance. Educators today still debate the role of humanistic studies in an age of scientific research and specialization. Likewise the invention of the printing press led to improved production and distribution of information which is still accelerating. Modern telecommunications, electronic media, and computer-based research are current aspects of the revolution started by Gutenberg. It should be obvious also that the secular scientific thinking started by Bacon, Galileo, Gilbert, and others has continued to grow and expand at a rapid rate. The study of the history of science in many universities and popular television programs like Connections illustrate the need for understanding the past in order to cope with the present. Current issues over tax support for religious schools may be linked to the struggles of the Protestant Reformation and the Catholic Counter-Reformation.

While we are able to get a better picture of the forces that shaped values and attitudes in historical times than we are today, currents of opinion and climates of thought are difficult to isolate in any age. It is easy enough to mark the founding of the English settlement on the American seaboard with Jamestown in 1607 and the first major school law with the "Old Deluder Satan Act," but it is another matter to trace the cultural forces that shaped the minds and deeds of the colonists. Nevertheless, whatever light can be cast on the intellectual, social, ethical, and philosophic forces which created colonial culture will be useful in helping to gain a better understanding of our own times. Just as the Puritan ethic of early America still casts its shadow over modern educational theory and practice (as in the case of Bible reading and prayer in public schools), so the Puritans themselves were influenced by mainstreams of thought going back at least to medieval times. As difficult as the task may be, cultural and intellectual history must try to identify main currents of thought and influential values that set the parameters of basic cultural beliefs. In this way, history can be a most useful tool in helping us to understand ourselves and the times in which we live.

Because we tend to think in a contemporary time frame, it is important to recall that many of the movements considered in this book required many years. The Protestant Reformation and the Catholic Counter-Reformation were not single events like those reported every day on the CBS News. They were revolutions of many facets of society which took centuries to develop, decades to complete, and their aftermath continues to be felt in contemporary society. Due to the brief treatment given to colonial history in the common school history courses, it is easy to make the error of thinking of the colonial period as brief. Actually the years between Jamestown and the American Revolution cover almost half of the time that has elapsed since 1607. In the passing of nearly two centuries, changes occurred in colonial America that were dramatic and vast, even though they took place at a slower rate than modern transformations. The revolt against England and the birth of a new nation could hardly have taken place in the conservative climate of opinion that existed in the beginning of the seventeenth century.

Educational development in colonial America and its influence on the schools of later times can only be appreciated against the backdrop of an earlier Old World culture. What is happening in education today must also be evaluated in terms of changing world conditions. For the first time in all history, all of the school age children in mainland China actually attend school. Mass starvation in East Africa makes it impossible for children there to reach their full potential or to achieve educational goals. The American economy can be altered by oil production in Arab nations, the production of automobiles in Japan, or the wheat harvest in the Soviet Union. All people living on earth are affected by the ways in which natural resources are used and all are demanding more human services, education included. An airport or a computer is much the same whether it is found in New York, Manila, or Buenos Aires. Our educational history began with influences from many areas and traditions; the future of education also depends on events and developments that are global in nature.

Many causes were at work in the settlement of the American colonies. Adventure, money, love of God, and a desire to convert the Indians gave rise to the colonies. Many wished to escape oppressive governments and the hard times in Europe such as the English depression of 1595. The first settlers were Europeans, dominated by English traditions. Modern society in the United States has been greatly modified by the influx of other people and ideas, but the Protestant religions and the English language remain dominant today. This dominance, like that of middle-class values in schools, creates a major educational problem in equal treatment of students whose first language is other than English or who represent religious backgrounds other than Protestant Christian.

Most of the time and effort of teachers and administrators in schools is spent in dealing with contemporary needs and problems. It is all too easy for us to think of events in the remote past as having no relevance for modern educators, if we think of such events at all. This is a fundamental mistake which may prevent us from making the best decisions for the well-being of our students and their communities. Religious conflicts starting with the protests of Martin Luther are still evident in current arguments over prayer in public schools. Attacks by the "moral majority" on "secular humanism" can be clarified by an understanding of conservative theology, Renaissance humanism, and laissez faire politics. Several states have passed or are considering a law requiring schools to give equal time to the Biblical theory of creation and to the theory of evolution. It is not enough to link this with the work of Darwin or with the Scopes trial of 1925. The educator needs also to consider it in the light of the opposition to scientific knowledge in the time of Copernicus and Bruno. Historical knowledge is vital to placing current issues into perspective and to making decisions that will stand critical analysis.

BIBLIOGRAPHY

Barrow, Robin. *Plato and Education.* Boston: Routledge & Kegan Paul, 1976

Brann, Eva. *Parodoxes of Education in a Republic.* Chicago: The University of Chicago Press, 1979.

Curtis, Stanley and M.E.A. Boultwood. *A Short History of Educational Ideas.* 3rd. ed. London: University Tutorial Press, 1964.

Gross, Richard. ed. *Heritage of American Education.* Boston: Allyn & Bacon, 1962

Gwynn, Aubrey. *Roman Education from Cicero to Quintilian.* rev. ed. New York: Teachers College Press, 1966.

Holley, Raymond. *Religious Education and Religious Understanding.* Boston: Routledge & Kegan Paul, 1978.

Meyer, Adolphe. *Grandmasters of Educational Thought.* New York: McGraw-Hill, 1975.

Mulhern, James. *A History of Education.* 2nd. ed. New York: Ronald, 1959.

Pounds, Ralph. *The Development of Education in Western Culture.* New York: Appleton-Century-Crofts, 1968.

Rusk, Robert. *The Doctrines of the Great Educators.* Rev. ed. New York: MacMillan, 1969

Wood, Norman. *The Reformation and English Education.* London: University Tutorial Press, 1931

European Heritage and 2
Colonial Influence on
American Education

The first American educational theory and practice tended to reflect European patterns, but the instances of transplantation without modification were few. Early but relatively slight in influence on later developments were the settlements of the Spanish in Florida and the French in the Mississippi Valley — settlements in which European institutions, including schools, were copied as closely as the new environment would allow. This was true in St. Augustine which was founded by Pedro Menendez in 1565 and in the French settlements at Montreal, Quebec, Kaskaskia, and New Orleans. Spanish monasteries were educational as well as religious institutions and the duty of teaching Indians the Spanish language was required by royal order in 1643. Convents and schools founded by French and Spanish Catholics reached much of North America, including California where Father Junipero Serra was active.

British colonials, on the other hand, began to incorporate distinctive new features in the models they took from their homeland. The apprenticeship system, elementary reading schools, the Latin grammar school, and even Harvard College were not exact duplicates of their English counterparts. The Reformation had suggested the principle of universal education, but in England it had also caused church property to be used for secular purposes, nearly

Protestant Reformation			Glorious Revolution
1601 English Poor Law	1620 Plymouth Colony		1664 New Amsterdam became New York
1607 Jamestown	1636 Harvard College		1688 William and Mary
1619 Black Slaves in Virginia	1642 Massachusetts Compulsory School Law	1647 Old Deluder Satan Act	1689 English Act of Toleration

destroying elementary schools. Philanthropists, therefore began endowing British charity schools, while the middle-class children attended schools taught by private masters for fees. In America, charity education provided by such agencies as the Society for the Propagation of the Gospel in Foreign Parts (SPG) became popular. The SPG was an agency of the Anglican church which provided money, books, teachers, and physical facilities for American children who otherwise would have had no opportunity to attend school. Of course philanthropic education usually had special interests attached, such as furthering the cause of a particular religion or fostering a set of values esteemed by those who contributed funds. The English pattern of high quality private schools catering to the children of the well to do and supported by tuition was not followed to a great extent in the colonies. Secondary educational institutions modeled on Westminister, Eton, or other English "public" schools were uncommon in America. Private venture schools tended to offer practical courses such as surveying, navigation, or bookkeeping. In those areas where religion was the driving force of a community, education became an instrument for social control through transmitting and preserving the beliefs of the sect. Such efforts had often been discouraged by the authorities in England. All schools underwent changes, sometimes slight, often dramatic, as a result of cultural forces in the colonies and the experience of coping with the American wilderness.

COLONIAL MELTING POT

Some alteration may be attributed to environmental difficulties, such as the struggle to produce food, the communication problem, disease, isolation, and hostile natives. Economic stresses and strains have always played a part in education. Other changes were caused

French and Indian War		Boston Massacre

1690 New England Primer		1762 Rousseau's *Emile* Published in France	1765 Stamp Act
1693 William and Mary College in Virginia	1751 Franklin's Academy in Philadelphia	1763 Treaty of Paris Ended the French and Indian War	

by the new intellectual climate illustrated by the many nonconformist or religiously dissenting settlers and the shift of the center of civil authority represented by the signing of the Mayflower Compact. Of course, the colonists remained Englishmen and the crown retained sovereignty until the American Revolution, but local control and some degree of political independence began to emerge quite early. Dissatisfaction with conditions in the homeland caused the migration of thousands of individuals who were not anxious to restore the agencies of their grief and oppression. The availability of free land and the desire of the English to encourage settlement made it possible for almost every group of people to find a place where they could practice their own religion and follow their own life style. Quakers sought freedom from restraint on their religious activities, while indentured servants wanted freedom from bondage and social advancement.

It must be understood, however, that European schools themselves were not the objects of attack by dissatisfied groups. The fact that educational facilities in the homelands were often decadent, and offered very limited opportunity for the children of many who stayed behind, did little to harm their reputation in America or undermine the attempt to imitate them. In an effort to preserve the European civilization of which they were a part, the colonists tried to copy the educational institutions they knew best. English textbooks and school methods were widely accepted in all the American colonies. Nevertheless, schools in the colonies were not merely transplanted but also revolutionized in spirit and sometimes in form. While the colonies were never a melting pot in the sense of mixing all the people together into one homogeneous mass, cultural diversity and the presence of many different religious denominations had a considerable influence on colonial schools.

Colonial legislatures, royal governors, proprietors, and stock companies were delegated educational authority along with political powers by the British crown. However, the degree to which civil governments took an interest in education differed greatly from one colony to another. Established churches and European governments exchanged mutual support in seventeenth-century culture. This alliance was also found throughout the colonies, although the nature of established churches differed considerably from Puritan New England to Anglican Virginia. Some degree of religious toleration developed in Rhode Island, Pennsylvania, New York, and Maryland.

RELIGIOUS SECTARIANISM

Religion played a very important part in colonial schools and colleges, both in the conduct of the institutions and in the curriculum. Although Bible reading and prayer continued to be a major part of common school practice well into the national period, control of education gradually shifted away from sectarian authorities. Just as the several states in modern America delegate authority to local school boards, so the colonial governments allowed private individuals and religious groups to establish schools of their own. In part, this was caused by the failure of governments to support schools with tax revenues and, in part, it was due to the rise of numerous religious sects which demanded the freedom to educate children in their own way. As a general rule, the central civil government did not engage in close supervision of schools which were built and financed by local or church agencies. This was true throughout the colonies in the eighteenth century and was especially obvious in frontier settlements.

In a very real sense the desire for greater religious freedom contributed to the doctrine of separation of church and state. Roger Williams was driven from Massachusetts partly for supporting such separation and he made it a policy in his Rhode Island settlement. The various sects eventually obtained freedom of worship and since there was no consensus concerning religious principles to be taught in schools founded by civil authorities, the various denominations conducted and controlled their own schools. In New England the selectmen of a town, the General Court, or the ministers constituted ultimate educational authority. Royal governors and towns gave charters for schools in the Middle colonies. In the Anglican South, the Bishop of London was responsible for licensing teachers.

SOCIAL CLASS IN THE COLONIAL ENVIRONMENT

English feudal structure was not equally superimposed upon all parts of the American colonial culture, but social class stratification was marked. Southern plantations usually contained every social class from slaves to owners of estates. Virginia reflected British class divisions almost exactly and even feudal practices such as primogeniture (passing an estate to the eldest son) and entail (making sale or exchange of real property unlawful) were found in that colony. Indentured servants and at least a few slaves lived in all of the colonies. New England had no gentlemen-planter class, but ministers and magistrates had great prestige and Puritan emphasis on work and frugality soon produced wealthy merchants. Middle Colonies like Maryland had a well-developed middle class consisting of artisans and skilled workers; but the middle classes grew everywhere as trade developed and the population increased. Scarcity of labor, and especially of skilled labor, made it easy for the ambitious man to improve his social status through hard work. It was difficult to prevent a servant from becoming an independent frontier farmer.

While social class mobility was a feature of colonial society, the schools long remained class-centered. Latin preparatory schools and theological colleges favored the upper classes. For many years, Harvard College class roles were arranged by social rank. Public demand for new skills resulted in a special school — the academy — which catered to the practical requirements of the commercial class. Nevertheless, many students obtained only rudimentary education and many of the earlier settlers of the lower classes could not read or write. Even in New England where schools were in operation by 1636, the level of instruction was low and not all children could attend. Before American independence, there were trends toward a more flexible and democratic school pattern, but the rigid class system and the strong religious atmosphere continued to influence education until comparatively recent times.

Few experiences in England fitted colonists for the difficulties of sustaining life in a wilderness. Nor were the colonies similar in climate, landforms, or population so that quite different life styles emerged. Thus the South concentrated on agriculture and created great plantations with a social system resembling that of England, while economic complexity in New England led to towns and villages sufficiently dense in population for the maintenance of schools. Each colony also had different community patterns. Land was too cheap to sustain the feudal privileges of southern planters, and soon a new breed of small farmers and hunters emerged. These rough and ready pioneers were not at all like the gentlemen who owned large estates planted in indigo, rice, or tobacco. They were not cultured or highly educated and they had little leisure time to pursue the intellectual graces commonly acquired by wealthy slaveholders, but they soon became a political and economic force. This new class of independent people had little use for the classics or the Latin grammar schools, but they wanted their children to have the basic skills of reading and writing. In England the sons of working men and farmers seldom had an opportunity for formal schooling. In America the possibility for a better life in the future for children of all classes created a demand for some sort of schooling in every community.

THE SOUTHERN COLONIES

Of the English colonies on the eastern seaboard, Maryland, Virginia, the Carolinas, and Georgia most closely resembled the British home-land in cultural and social patterns. Economic factors were respon-sible for most of the migration of English gentlemen to the South. They were not dissatisfied with conditions in the homeland, and therefore expected to replicate English institutions in America with-out substantial change. Southern planters devoted their energy to business and the development of their estates. They remained loyal to the Anglican church and the values of the British landed gentry. Plantation owners emphasized the enjoyment of the cultured life which included gambling, dancing, literature, music, art, books, and the breeding of fine horses. Religion was reverently practiced by prayer and church attendance, but it did not become the dominating force of life as in New England. There was no Puritan zeal for having every person taught to read the Bible for himself. The clergy was responsible for interpreting scripture and clerical authority was vested in the Anglican hierarchy. Educational matters also rested with the decisions of the Archbishop of Canterbury or the Bishop of London. Since both church and state favored the landed gentry and large estates were the rule, social equality did not develop in the South. Those not favored by conditions of birth and wealth were expected to be satisfied with their station in life and the decisions made for them by their "betters." In 1671, Governor Sir William Berkeley of Virginia held that every man should instruct his own children according to his means. He said:

> ... I thank God, that there are no free schools nor printing, and I hope we shall not have them these hundred years, for learning has brought disobedience, and heresy, and sects into the world, and printing has divulged them, and libels against the best govern-ment.

Berkeley no doubt spoke for many Virginians, but some free schools did develop in spite of the opposition. Occasionally a parish built and maintained a school which was open to children who could not pay tuition. There were numerous endowments for schools such as those provided in the wills of Benjamin Syms (1634) and Thomas Eaton (1659), both of whom gave land and goods for the maintenance of an "able schoolmaster" to teach poor children. Nevertheless, free schools remained rare in Virginia and large areas of the South had no formal education of any kind.

The planters did devote a good deal of time to intellectual pursuits beyond the instruction of their children. The art of writing letters was highly developed and many newspapers were circulated. Even the remote plantations usually had a good collection of books from England and other European nations. Some private libraries were excellent: that of William Byrd contained some four thousand volumes. An excellent account of the intellectual and social life of the colonial South is found in the diary of Philip Fithian. Fithian was a graduate of Princeton and served as tutor to the Carter family of northern Virginia.

Leading elements of the social order attempted to copy the customs and mores of wealthy Englishmen in everything, including schools. Southern educational institutions reflected more English ideals than schools in other parts of the colonies, and every planter who could afford it wished to send his son to Oxford, Cambridge, or the Inns of Court (London law schools) for training.

Rigid southern social class distinctions allowed few opportunities for the indentured servants, the slaves, and the poverty-stricken freemen to engage in cultural pursuits or to improve their minds. The persons lowest in social rank were entirely dependent upon the wealthy and powerful for what little education they received. Skills needed to operate farms and plantations were not taught in schools, nor was education very clearly related to success patterns of nonprivileged southerners.

Gentlemen thought of themselves as natural political leaders, as well as guardians of refined manners, learning, justice, hospitality, and religion. No effort was spared to initiate sons of the planter class into the intellectual pursuits of their fathers. They were given generalized readings in the Greek and Roman classics. French was widely taught along with English literature and the Bible, and studies such as painting and architecture were commonly included.

No single educational pattern developed in the Southern Colonies, making it difficult to generalize. While diversity of educational practice was at a maximum in the South, public interest in education was at a minimum. Virginia had money earmarked for education as early as 1618, but the revocation of the charter for the Virginia Company seven years later stopped these funds. From that time until 1660, Virginia passed laws which required children to be taught religion, although public financial support was lacking. Since southern leaders came from the upper classes of England, the Anglican church was dominant and exercised considerable influence over the existing educational programs. Schools, however, were only indirectly controlled by law or the church because education was considered a private matter left in the hands of individual citizens. Exceptions were apprenticeship education, which was carefully regulated by law, and efforts of philanthropic or religious societies in behalf of the poor, the Indians, and the slaves. Attempts to save souls of native red Americans met with slight success, but continuous appeals were made for giving slaves the rudiments of a religious education, especially by suggesting that Christianity would make them more content and harder working.

Plantation Schools.   Plantation schools existed throughout the South, although they varied widely in form. Very wealthy planters hired learned tutors to train their sons and frequently their daughters as well. When there was time and interest, such a tutorial system was also used by others attached to the plantation, such as the sons of foremen or managers. Teachers were often Anglican ministers who served churches in the proximity of the estate, but private schoolmasters were also employed to teach. Sometimes it proved cheaper or more expedient to buy the services of an indentured servant for teaching. Many well-trained Scots who knew Latin and Greek were included in the shiploads of indentured persons entering southern ports, and their time could be purchased at a lower rate than that of skilled labor. Private plantation schools were sometimes sufficient to prepare boys for college in England. The curriculum was usually classical, but practical subjects such as surveying and mathematics were by no means excluded. Girls were instructed in French, music, dancing, and polite manners by their tutors, and for them the instruction was terminal. Boys who had mastered Lilly's *Latin Grammar* were often sent to one of the private preparatory schools (great public schools) in England.

Travel was considered to be a major part of education even for boys who did not attend Latin grammar schools or colleges in England. High standards of scholarship were maintained by such educational leaders as James Blair and the Reverend Thomas Bray of

Virginia. The universal employment of tutors indicated a greater interest in education by American planters than by their English counterparts.

Other Southern Colonial Schools.   Schools for those not favored by birth were limited in the Southern Colonies. Early efforts to provide endowed schools for all children, including Indians, failed. Some laws required education for pauper children but little was actually done. Like England, the southern governments made an effort to keep the poor from starving and to see that children of paupers learned a trade, but the Virginia law requiring training of "bound" boys was not passed until 1705. Virginians saw nothing odd in imposing requirements upon parents and ministers for religious instruction without giving financial aid to education. Teachers in private schools were seldom examined on their qualifications beyond the ability to read and write, but were expected to prove their orthodoxy in religion.

Meager efforts were made to establish chartered or publicly aided schools in the Carolinas. Maryland fared a little better with a provision in 1671 for a "School or College" and a system of secondary county schools founded in 1728. Duties on tobacco and fines for crimes were used to support such schools, but only a small proportion of the population had access to them. Maryland had a quasi-public corporation made up of church and government officials to make policy and secure funds for schools in each county. Georgia was the last Southern Colony to be settled and little progress toward an educational program was made there before the Revolution.

Old Field School.   One southern innovation was the old field school. This was a local elementary school built by members of a community on one of the fallow "old" fields which had lost its productivity through over-use. Sometimes Anglican ministers taught in these schools as they did on the plantations, but the masters were often persons with very little education. Old field schools were usually maintained by private subscriptions with some sort of scholarship or other provision for poor scholars. Control of the schools, including the securing of teachers and materials, was in the hands of the local community. These schools were similar to later ones established in frontier towns during the national period. They commonly were in operation for only a few months each year.

Dame School.   In most colonies including the South dame schools were found. These were not really schools at all, but consisted of rudimentary instruction given by a woman in her own home, usually while she carried on household duties. The lessons were limited to the alphabet, counting, prayers, the catechism, and perhaps reading a few sentences from the Bible. A standard instrument in the dame school was the *hornbook*, which consisted of a single printed page attached to a wooden paddle, covered with a transparent film made by boiling down the horns of cows. Hornbooks often were inscribed with the alphabet, numerals from one to nine, and the Lord's Prayer. They were a means of keeping "letters faire from fingers damp" and were used throughout the colonies. Dames who offered instruction were often barely literate themselves. One is recorded as saying, "T'is little they pays me and little I learns em."

Secondary and Higher Education.   Plans for a Latin grammar school were made in Virginia before 1630. Property bequested by Syms and Eaton apparently was used for such classical schools. Thomas Jefferson graduated from a Latin school before entering William and Mary College. Nevertheless, due to preference for sending sons to preparatory schools in England and the sparse early population, few secondary schools developed. Some towns were able to maintain academies. Those in Charleston were supported by a combination of fees and grants. Some academies were classical schools for college preparation and some taught only practical or commercial subjects. William and Mary was the only institution of higher learning in the southern region during the colonial period. It began granting degrees in 1700.

Charity Education.   Other educational measures were taken by philanthropic societies, most of which were organized by religious institutions. The Anglican church encouraged slaveholders to teach their charges Christianity. Charity schools were operated in England and this idea soon spread to America for the training of orphans and paupers. By far the most active group was the SPG of the Anglican church, which raised funds in England and used the money to send out teachers and to buy textbooks for the colonies. Many able instructors (often young ministers) brought their knowledge and missionary zeal to the colonial schools for the poor. The best charity schools, and also the most numerous ones in the Southern and Middle Colonies were provided by this Anglican society. It printed and distributed books on history, agriculture, and mathematics as well as religious tracts.

Perhaps the most conspicuous thing about education in the South before the American Revolution was the lack of public interest in schools. Several factors contributed to this attitude, some of which continued to affect public schools in the national period. It was strongly believed by the dominant planter class that each man was responsible for the education of his own children. Further, it was against the prevailing custom to tax one person for the education of the sons of others. Southern Colonies had widely scattered populations not concentrated in cities and towns. Even if the people had wanted one, physical remoteness made an educational system almost impossible. Secondary schools of either the Latin grammar or practical academy type did not develop. The classes most interested in education could afford to hire tutors or to send their sons to England, while many of the smaller landowners and pioneer hunters were more concerned with the practical skills necessary for survival than with formal schooling. Also, the southern attitude toward religion failed to bring about the New England emphasis on education as a means of salvation, hence one of the most important duties of every Christian man. Southern colonial education remained very much like education in England. Nevertheless, many of the most learned and able leaders in the revolutionary period were from the South.

THE MIDDLE COLONIES

Diversity and parochialism are perhaps the best words to describe the colonial settlements of Delaware, New Jersey, New York, and Pennsylvania. Settlers from Holland, Germany, Sweden, England, Wales, and Scotland came to the Middle Colonies in large numbers. Disparity in religion was even more pronounced than differences in nationality so that the colonies became a potpourri of faiths, languages, and ethnic cultures. It is said that thirteen languages were spoken in Dutch New Amsterdam before it became New York in 1664. So many different religious denominations were represented in the region that toleration soon became a necessity. The Quakers of Pennsylvania were theoretically opposed to persecution. Commerce and trade worked better in an open society, and no single religious sect had the numerical power to force its will on the others. Although the Catholics in Maryland had been protected in Lord Baltimore's time, religious freedom was limited there after 1654. Other Middle Colonies and Rhode Island thereafter became the haven for all persons escaping from any form of religious persecution. It was this freedom that attracted the Pietist scholar Francis Daniel Pastorius

(1651–1720), who was the best educated man in America at the time. Pastorius wrote a primer called *The True Reading, Spelling, and Writing of English*, published in New York in 1697. New York, like Philadelphia (the largest British city in America during the eighteenth century) was a center for intellectual activity.

Mennonites, Quakers, Lutherans, Calvinists, Moravians, Huguenots, Separate Baptists, and Episcopalians established educational practices of their own. Small numbers of Dunkards, Jews, disciples of John Hus, and other minor sects emigrated to America and set up schools. In short, the Middle Colonies were the ones with the largest number of national and religious groups; therefore, they tended to develop many kinds of schools. There was also a considerable urban growth in this area and constant communication with the most sophisticated centers of Europe. Intellectual freedom (and tolerance) was possible in the central coastal cities to a degree unheard of in New England or the South.

From its very beginning the Dutch West India Company accepted its obligation to provide schools, and it demanded careful records showing every expenditure down to and including paper and ink. All nine villages chartered in New Netherlands probably had schools. The schoolmaster was not only a teacher but also a minor church official. He was picked for his orthodoxy and had other duties such as reading Scriptures on Sunday, digging graves, and acting as church sexton. When the English became dominant, Dutch schools continued to exist very much as they had before; but they became parochial institutions supported by local church congregations or private schools supported by towns.

Except for insisting on the right to license teachers, practically no laws were made concerning schools. The SPG of the Anglican church was responsible for the majority of the common schools in New York, which were intended for the poor and thus were charitable institutions. These enjoyed the favor and support of the governor and his offices but were seldom entirely free, each student paying what his family could afford. This system of charging different amounts was known as the "rate bill" and was widely adopted. Private instruction was sometimes similar to the plantation schools of the South, but individual tutors were rare.

Private venture schools in towns sometimes taught such practical subjects as bookkeeping, geography, and navigation. Each denomination was permitted to set up its own school system, and therefore schools were nonpublic in nature and intolerant of individuals representing other views. Nevertheless, religious differences kept the schools out of the hands of the central civil government and made them the responsibility of the churches. It was common, therefore, in the Middle Colonies to have many sectarian schools together with a considerable number of charitable institutions for education.

Where the Quaker faith was strong, there was much support for primary education. Pennsylvania, with its Quaker commonwealth, had many laws regulating morality; they included punishment for such offenses as drunkenness, dancing, gambling, and profanity. Nevertheless, jailing for debts was abolished and a great deal of freedom of speech and religion was allowed. Since the colony was open to all creeds, Pennsylvania attracted Mennonites, Moravians, Lutherans, and Anglicans in addition to the large numbers of Quakers.

Denominational Influence.   Dissenting factions in Pennsylvania caused many Quakers to fear for the unity of their church and to be suspicious of college education; but they remained active in their support for elementary schools. Quaker schools were excellent in quality. They taught reading, writing, arithmetic, and probably bookkeeping as well as religion, and they were not closed either to the poor or to girls. Quakers teachers received an apprenticeship training, the first teacher education in America. That some control was used is shown by the record that one Thomas Meking was rebuked by the Council of Philadelphia for teaching in a Friends public school without a license. The first American education for freed Blacks was provided by Quaker schools. Smaller religious sects known as "dissenters" also established schools and colleges. The "log college" opened by Presbyterians in 1726 trained boys for the ministry. In Philadelphia, the William Penn Charter School taught both the classics and an English curriculum. The German scholar Francis Pastorius taught there. Baptists and Moravians set up denominational schools that were also open to the public. Governor Nicholson set aside land for a free Catholic school in Maryland.

Academy.   Vocational education was more significant in the Middle Colonies than elsewhere in colonial America. English poor laws of 1562 and 1601 proposed the establishment of working schools as well as forced apprenticeship for the poor. William Penn was influential in bringing the idea of trade training for pauper children to Pennsylvania, and John Locke's concern for practical subjects was well known in the colonies. The academy, a terminal secondary school which prepared students for a vocation, did not become highly significant until the national period. Nevertheless, both elementary and secondary schools in the Middle Colonies offered such practical subjects as merchandising, navigation, trade, and mechanics. Benjamin Franklin's academy in Philadelphia opened in 1751 and became a model for others. While it was organized in part as a Latin school, the academy was intended for the heterogeneous population of Pennsylvania. Franklin was particularly interested in training teachers for rural schools and officials for the government. The seeds of the American comprehensive high school were planted in the private and parochial schools of the Middle Colonies which offered vocational subjects.

Latin Grammar Schools.   Secondary schools of the Latin grammar type were necessary for college preparation. New York, Pennsylvania, New Jersey, and Maryland had such schools. Higher English schools and Latin schools existed together in Quaker Pennsylvania and denominational support for both was common.

The teachers were usually ministers who had no church to serve and the purpose was college preparation, leading eventually to political or church positions. Latin secondary schools and colleges were strictly for men. The curriculum often included Juvenal, Ovid, Vergil, Caesar, Cicero, and Horace, with perhaps some Greek grammar.

Religious sectarianism was a major force in Middle Colony education even though freedom of choice was respected. Schools were used for propaganda and there was often bitter condemnation of other groups, especially Catholics.

Common Schools.   Private education in Pennsylvania was largely the prerogative of the upper classes. However, there were some accommodations for sons of workmen and artisans of the middle class. A *night school* teaching writing, arithmetic, and some mathematics was opened in Philadelphia in 1731. Navigation, surveying, and mathematics were taught in another night school in the same city. Later in the eighteenth century, *private evening schools* for accounting, mathematics, and modern languages were advertised in many cities. Public lectures on natural science, astronomy, and mechanics attracted large crowds. Private circulating libraries were available for a fee. Journals, books, and newspapers were numerous in larger cities. Philadelphia continued to be a major center for learning throughout the colonial era. Although New England led in universal education during the colonial period, there was a great deal of school activity on the elementary level in the Middle Colonies.

Higher Education.   The Middle Colonies also had their share of denominational colleges as well as the College of Philadelphia (1755) which was the only nonsectarian institution of higher learning. The College of New Jersey (Princeton) was established by Presbyterians in 1746. King's College (Columbia) was an Anglican effort of 1754, and Queen's College (Rutgers) was founded in 1766 by the Dutch Reformed Church. The College of Rhode Island (Brown) was created by the Baptists in 1764. Of the nine colonial colleges in America, five were in the Middle Colonies.

The cultural variety which characterized the Middle Colonies made education quite different from both the North and the South. Particularly significant were the early influences of settlers from Holland and the later emigration of large numbers of Germans. There was no one single powerful ruling church, and therefore no establishment of religion. Tolerance was greater than in New England or in the South and many more sectarian schools developed. Class differences in the Middle Colonies were less distinct than in the South, and the central colonies became a melting pot for many nationalities and many social positions. Pennsylvania probably had the most divergent cultural pattern and also the greatest amount of freedom of religion. But by and large, less interest was shown in educational development in the Middle Colonies than in New England.

THE NEW ENGLAND COLONIES

In many ways, education in New England was most significant for the growth of later American schools. The influence of parliamentary rule and the Christian duty of educating each child caused the theocratic governments in New England to take great interest in schools. The Puritans wanted a state church ruled by congregations rather than by bishops, and a government which substituted the authority of the people for the divine right of a king. New England colonies made laws requiring education of the children, but left details to local communities — thereby creating the traditions of local autonomy and the district system. These colonies provided both for universal elementary education and for the training of ministers, which tended to perpetuate the English dual system of education. But it is wrong to assume that Puritan efforts fostered religious freedom or democracy.

Puritan Philosophy.   Part of their educational interest stemmed from a concept of the nature of man which is found in the Calvinistic creed. It was assumed by the Puritans that man is by nature evil, having fallen in the sin of Adam. Not only is man bad, but he also has an active nature which must be controlled to prevent the Devil from becoming his master. It is this notion of man's being bad and active which gave rise to the establishment of schools which should prevent idleness and show mankind the way to overcome the evil in his nature. Assuming that man is depraved, there must be an effort to bring him to salvation. This, together with the Protestant notion of the priesthood of all believers, made it mandatory that the New England Puritans establish elementary schools.

In Massachusetts, New Hampshire, and Connecticut, Puritans were determined to build their own religious orthodoxy in the way Calvin had suggested. They established theocracies in which the church and state ruled by means of public disapproval, whipping, banishment, and fines. It was common for them to use the General Court and the authority of the minister to enforce conformity both in behavior and in belief. Such positive support of religion required not only that schools be created, but also that every child be able to read and understand both the Scriptures and the capital laws.

There were numerous Puritan ministers who wrote works in theology and philosophy which reinforced this educational theory. In his book, *A Family Well-Ordered,* Cotton Mather dwelt upon the duties of parents and the obligations of children. John Cotton reflected the same view and even the learned Jonathan Edwards (1703-58) made his idealism the servant of a narrow Calvinistic theology. The views of these Puritan theorists are clearly seen in the religious nature of textbooks like the *New England Primer* of 1690 which included:

In Adam's Fall
We Sinned all

. . .

Thy Life to Mend
This Book Attend

. . .

The Idle Fool
Is Whipt at School.

As previously stated, in New England the farm land was not especially fertile, and people turned early to such occupations as shipbuilding, manufacturing, and trade. A merchant class developed which had need of people who could take care of business accounts and work with all sorts of business documents. It was therefore an economic necessity to have large numbers of people, able not only to read and write, but also to cast accounts. Even so, the New England schools were primarily established for the propagation of the Gospel and the control of new generations. It was usual for children to spend only a few years in the common school. There were, however, Latin grammar schools established for the use of the elite.

The Pilgrims insisted that education be taken care of by the parents. As early as 1642, however, the General Court of Massachusetts came to the conclusion that many parents were neglecting the training of their children. The court therefore ordered that the selectmen of every town should require that all parents and masters undertake the education of their children. After a short time, it was found that this provision was not working well. In 1647, therefore, the General Court passed its famous Old Deluder Satan Act. This law required that every town set up a school, or that it pay a sum of money to the next larger town for the support of education. A precedent was thus made for requiring the towns (or townships) to take the responsibility for establishing and maintaining schools. The theocracy not only required education, it also set both the curriculum and the standard procedures for operation. These early efforts of Massachusetts were soon picked up by other parts of New England.

The first tax on property for local schools was in Dedham, Massachusetts, in 1648. New Hampshire required towns to support elementary schools as early as 1693. Taxes were used to pay the wages of teachers and to build school buildings, but tuition fees were universally charged in the New England colonies. The curriculum of the early New England schools was almost entirely religious, for these institutions were viewed officially as being indispensable to the stability of Puritan society. Such books as the Bible, the New England Primer, and the catechism were widely used in schools. Education was for salvation as well as for getting along in life. It was a primary duty of parents to bring their children up according to the orthodox religious beliefs of Puritan society.

The Puritans feared to leave an illiterate ministry to the people. For this reason they established Harvard College (1636) almost as early as the town schools. The college was primarily for the education of ministers of the Gospel, though after a few years students preparing for professions such as law attended Harvard. Once the college had been established, it was necessary that Latin grammar schools be provided so that the boys wishing to enter Harvard could get the necessary preparatory studies. The first of these schools was established in Boston. A famous teacher, Ezekiel Cheever, taught for many years in the Boston Latin Grammar School with considerable influence on the prestige of the teaching profession in the New England area. Almost no curriculum choice was offered in any of the colonial schools and the methods were both fixed and harsh. It was ordained that school masters be examined and certified by the minister of the town or the adjoining towns where the school was to be held. Education was generally narrow, limited, elementary, and moral in character. In Massachusetts it was common for masters who failed to carry out their responsibilities adequately to be fined and sometimes even thrown out of their jobs.

Educational Conditions. In the lower schools there was normally one master for a room full of children of various ages. Supervision of the school was provided by the local minister and the "selectmen" of the town. Buildings were of the log cabin or clapboard variety, furnished with benches, a fireplace, shelves around the walls for writing, and a few small windows. The master usually had a chair and lectern, but the meager equipment seldom included blackboards or maps. A whipping post was commonly erected by the school door. Severe floggings were administered for misbehavior or breaking the rules, since Puritan philosophy called for literally beating the Devil out of the child. Massachusetts law allowed children to be confined in stocks for some offenses, and fathers had a legal right to execute their children if they could not be controlled, although this extreme was never practiced. There are records of pupils who were tortured by having a stick of flat wood (whispering stick) placed like a bit between their teeth, pupils made to kneel on hard pebbles, or made to wear heavy wooden yokes. The school in colonial New England was not a pleasant place, either physically or psychologically. Great emphasis was placed on the shortness of life, the torments of hell and the fear that one's behavior might not be acceptable for salvation. Children in dull and grim schools memorized passages such as:

I in the Burying Place may see Graves shorter there than I;
From Death's Arrest no Age is free, Young Children too must die.

Oh God may such an Awful Sight Awakening to Me be,
That by Early Grace I shall, For Death Prepared be.

The elementary curriculum consisted of the three R's: religion,
reading, and writing. Arithmetic was added later but never received
the emphasis placed on the other studies. Boys and girls entered the
school at the age of six or seven. They began with the hornbook or a
similar instrument printed on stiff paper called a battledore. Next
they were given the New England Primer, a crudely illustrated
reading text that included the Westminister Shorter Catechism, a
picture of the martyr John Rogers being burned at the stake in
England, a dialogue between Christ, a youth, and the devil, and John
Cotton's Spiritual Milk for American Babes drawn from Both Brests
of the Testements for their Souls' Nourshment. Many children remained in school only three or four years and did not progress
beyond the primer. For those who remained longer, there was the
Psalter (Book of Psalms) and the Bible. Paper was scarce and of very
poor quality. It came in large unlined sheets and had to be folded,
sewn together, and marked with pieces of lead in order to make a
tablet for the children. Hornbooks, crude slates, and quill pens were
provided by the students themselves. Often the masters would can-
vass the community to determine the availability of books, and
whatever they found would be used as reading material for older
pupils.

The school normally operated six days each week, except in the
summer. There were long periods of prayer and Bible reading both
morning and evening. Most of the subject matter was memorized by
the student and tested in a cue and recitation session before the
master. There were no group activities or mass assignments. Students were not encouraged to express opinions or to ask questions.
The word of the master and the text were regarded as absolute
authorities. Teachers had no pedagogical training as such, but in
New England the school masters were often among the best educated members of the community. The pay was extremely low and
many communities required masters to "board around" in order to
save money.

Latin School and College Programs.   Boston had a free Latin
grammar school and many other New England towns developed
secondary schools supported by tuition. These "higher track"
schools for the social and intellectual elite were intended to prepare
boys for college and were always taught by college graduates —

often ministers. Boys usually entered the Latin school at the age of eight after having learned to read English at home or in a lower school. The curriculum consisted of three years of Latin grammar "accidence" and practice in parsing Latin sentences. Thereafter, the scholars began to "make Latin" and to translate Latin literature into English. The program continued from six to eight years and included some Greek and Hebrew in the last two years. All the students in the Latin grammar school hoped to be admitted to a college for that was the entire purpose of such schools. Entrance requirements for Harvard College indicated the curriculum of that institution:

> When any Schollar is able to understand Tully, or such like classical Latine Author *extempore*, and make and speake true Latine Verse and Prose, . . . and decline perfectly the Paradigm's of *Nounes* and *Verbes* in the *Greek* toungue: Let him then and not before be capable of admission into the College.

Since the first Puritan ministers were graduates of Oxford and Cambridge, colleges in New England closely copied those English institutions. Until 1653, Harvard was a three-year college with a fixed course which offered one subject at a time, so that all classes could be taught by the president. Classical and theological studies were the mainstay of the program. Aristotelian logic and physics, arithmetic, geometry, astronomy, grammar, rhetoric, dialectic, etymology, syntax, and prosodia were taught for the purpose of disciplining the mind. Upperclassmen studied Greek and Hebrew grammar and there were occasional lectures in history and natural science. Students were expected to declaim once a month and great stress was placed on study of the Bible. For a degree the student had to present evidence of his ability to read the Scriptures in Latin and to resolve them logically, "withall being of godly life and conversation."

Yale College was founded in 1701 and Dartmouth in 1769. All three New England colleges were Congregationalist and similar in curriculum. They were theological seminaries, not schools for professional men in other fields such as law, medicine, or science.

Religious Cycles.   Education in New England during the colonial period was highly influenced by religion, but the degree of religious activity varied greatly. Harvard and the early town schools of Massachusetts were established during the time of religious enthusiasm of the great Puritan migration. Economic interests and secular views soon created apathy which caused a decline of educational zeal. Between 1661 and 1681 enrollment at Harvard dropped steadily and the district schools had difficulty obtaining support. But in the first half of the eighteenth century, there occurred a fervent religious revival known as the *Great Awakening*. While the movement was largely evangelistic, it also sparked renewed interest in schools at all levels. Yale opened at the beginning of that period of new religious enthusiasm and produced the most famous preacher of the time, Jonathan Edwards. Edwards was an eloquent speaker, well known for his fiery "Hell and Damnation" sermons. He was also a learned scholar and the author of many pamphlets widely used in schools and colleges. The Great Awakening and the efforts of Edwards caused numerous conflicts, such as the issue over predestination that split the "Old Lights" from the "New Lights"; but it also caused a major revival of educational activity. The new demand for ministers led Eleazar Wheelock to found a school in Connecticut in 1754, which was later moved to New Hampshire and renamed Dartmouth College. The College of Rhode Island, founded by the Baptists, was also a product of the Great Awakening.

New England schools were crude in form, narrow in curriculum, and poorly supported, but the significant fact remains that they existed in quantity. Long before the United States became a nation, traditions of education, including the ideas of universal schooling and public support, had been formed. Americans had already started to demand what was to become standard — better education for children than their parents had enjoyed.

THEN TO NOW

Life in pre-Revolutionary colonial American culture seems to bear very little direct relationship to present conditions, at least at first glance. Educational institutions such as dame schools, academies, old field schools, and Latin grammar schools have long since disappeared. Of course, the New England pattern of district schools, compulsory education, taxation, and distinct educational levels continues to exist in highly modified form. More important than the schools themselves, however, is the vast heritage of beliefs, values, and attitudes inherited from the Puritans. Modern citizens are more highly influenced by the colonial past than they might imagine because systems of value tend to persist over generations. As the theory of culture lag suggests, materialistic and technological inventions occur rapidly while concepts of proper conduct and ideas about the good life tend to remain constant. Alteration of values is likely to be slow and evolutionary while changes in material aspects of the culture are quick and revolutionary.

This is obviously important because schools have a major role in transmitting the core values from one generation to the next. Teaching values or value clarification is always difficult but it is even more complicated in a multicultural society where some children come from families more influenced by the Puritan ethic than others. Choosing and reinforcing values for survival and maximum realization of the human potential in the present and the future is central to the socialization function of education. It can hardly be accomplished without a basic understanding of the Puritan ethic of old Massachusetts Bay Colony. Puritan beliefs about the evil nature of the child and their support for corporal punishment are no longer popular, but the basic values are found in the "pioneer spirit," the work ethic, and middle-class values.

Since the Puritans held that God allowed his elect to prosper and that idle hands did the work of the devil, they stressed productive work and striving for economic improvement. Today, justification of one's existence through hard work and social service is supported by schools. Puritans were not supposed to display their wealth and therefore they invested in land and various commercial enterprises. Frugal life style, saving money, preparing for the future, and investing were New England values that proved useful to business and commercial interests. These values are not limited to the Puritan tradition (they are practiced also in Japan) but they are central to the American cultural core.

Socialization requires that the most important aspects of the culture be taught. Using models of accepted behavior and sanctions, schools attempt to get students to accept and internalize values cherished by the institutions and the leaders of the dominant culture. Some of these values which can be traced to the Puritan heritage are:

Respect for authority
Postponing immediate gratification
Neatness
Punctuality
Responsibility for one's own work
Honesty
Patriotism and loyalty
Striving for personal achievement
Competition
Repression of aggression and overt sexual expression
Respect for the rights and property of others
Obeying rules and regulations

Without making a judgment about these values, it may be pointed out that teaching them creates certain problems. Ours is a multicultural society in which minority and ethnic groups differ in the emphasis they place on traditional values of the majority culture. Contemporary American society is also stratified and the various social classes do not exhibit the same esteem for all behaviors prized by schools. For example, American Indian and Hispanic cultures have had a more casual attitude toward time than the middle-class Caucasian society. As a result, they cherish punctuality less and their children may not understand the school's demand that homework be turned in on time. Lower-class youngsters seldom have the future orientation which is the ordinary time frame of the middle class. Living for the immediate moment and letting tomorrow take care of itself is an attitude sure to be in conflict with schools that require planning and a postponement of rewards. Competition may be discouraged by some ethnic groups even when it is encouraged by schools. Urban Black youngsters are not apt to appear neat to White teachers, even when their appearance is quite acceptable to their parents and peers. The "macho" image many lower-class boys need to create for peer acceptance makes them seem rude and loud in school. Expression of sexual interest may be tolerated and encouraged in a lower-class environment in ways likely to be unacceptable and punished in middle-class schools. Extreme concern about respect for property and the need to be still while others speak may be more difficult for students with no experience in valuing such behavior. Puritans were not tolerant of any violation of their social norms. They were quick to condemn and punish any who dared to challenge the authority of their institutions or to break the rules. Modern versions of the Puritan ethic may be insisted upon by middle-class teachers but many of the students find that ethic incompatible with their own cultural backgrounds. The critical literature on contemporary education indicates that children of ethnic groups and minorities are more likely to fail in school if the school attempts to teach values foreign to them.

Of course it was not the case that the Puritans believed in democracy, whereas modern education must attempt to promote democratic values in order to deal constructively and creatively with the confusions and conflicts of the modern world. They also had the church, the family, and the local community in absolute support of their educational efforts while contemporary schools exist in an environment of special interests and conflicting beliefs.

Not all middle-class people from the dominant culture support the traditional values of the schools. Sociologists say that there are emerging values in American culture that are in conflict with the traditional ones. The family is no longer the major socializing agent, but if that duty is passed to schools, the schools need support. Many families now stress hedonism, materialism, living the good life, social interaction, and the value of leisure. These are examples of emergent values in conflict with traditional ones. The peer subculture of American adolescents is unconcerned with older traditional belief systems. Rock and roll music, experimentation with drugs, and permissive attitudes toward sex dominate the interests of teenagers. Another potent force in value formation is the mass media. Television especially fosters values in conflict with those of traditional schools and the Puritan ethic. Television urges people to gratify their every desire, to "buy now and pay later," and to enjoy life without concern for future consequences. No one viewing television gets the impression that hard work, striving, and deferring to authority are necessary for success or the good life. Many members of the modern society have no faith that honesty really is the best policy or that patriotism is a higher value than individual gratification.

Many educators also disagree with transmitting an enduring cultural heritage as an educational function. They want to allow children to develop their full potential without the restrictions of an older ethical system. Transmitting an authoritative body of knowledge has been undermined by the rapid explosion of knowledge and there is disagreement about what values the young should be taught. Many educators now are concerned about a "relevant" curriculum while others do not want the school to impose values on children. Still others feel that schools should work for diversity, tolerance, open-mindedness, and the development of a sound self concept.

It remains to be seen just how effective the schools will be in supporting traditional values or in teaching emerging ones. It may be that some of the Puritan values are not at all appropriate for a future learning society where leisure and cooperation are more important than work. Schools tend to be quite conservative but there are many other institutions that carry cultural values. In Puritan America, the family and the church supported values taught in schools. Contemporary society finds the schools often in conflict with such agents as the mass media and advertising. At present, the moral majority is trying to win support for the values of the Puritan ethic while others push for diversity, free choice, and multiculturalism. Regardless of the position, educators need to understand the historical link with the colonial past and the Puritan heritage if they are to understand the present culture and prepare for a viable future. Beliefs of the early settlers of colonial New England still cast a shadow over values in the modern American society. Those who do not appreciate this historical fact are ill-prepared to understand the value conflicts that are central to so many modern educational issues.

BIBLIOGRAPHY

Butts, R. Freeman and Lawrence A. Cremin. *A History of Education in American Culture.* New York: Rinehart and Winston, 1953. Chapters 1-3.

Church, Robert. *Education in the United States: An Interpretive History,* New York: The Free Press (Macmillan), 1977.

Curti, Merle. *The Social Ideas of American Educators.* Patterson, N.J.: Littlefield, Adams, 1959. Chapter 1.

Edwards, Newton and Herman G. Richey. *The School in the American Social Order.* Boston: Houghton Mifflin, 1963. Chapters 4 and 5.

Good, Harry and James Teller. *A History of American Education.* 2nd. ed. New York: Macmillan, 1973.

Havinghurst, Robert and Daniel Levine. *Society and Education.* 5th ed. Boston: Allyn and Bacon, 1975.

Miller, Perry, ed. *The American Puritans: Their Prose and Poetry.* Garden City, N.Y.: Doubleday, 1956.

Morrison, Samuel Eliot. *The Intellectual Life of Colonial New England.* New York: New York University Press, 1956.

Potter, Robert. *The Stream of American Education.* New York: American Book Company, 1967. Part 1.

Rippa, S. Alexander, ed. *Educational Ideas in America: A Documentary History.* New York: David McKay, 1969.

Warren, Donald, ed. *History, Education, and Public Policy.* Berkeley, Calif.: McCutchan, 1978.

The Period of the   3
American Revolution

Before the time of the Revolutionary War, the population of the
American colonies had grown to more than two and one-half million
people. An expanding frontier fostered perseverance, ingenuity,
self-confidence, and a defiant individualism among the western
settlers. This frontier character was unique to America, as was the
mixture of nationalities and religions found in the Middle Colonies.
The district system with its decentralization and local control continued to dominate New England schools before and after the Revolution, and the idea of free, compulsory, universal education was
central to the ideal of self-government there. While schools varied
widely in number and quality in the New England Colonies and later
in the New England states, America looked to Massachusetts, Rhode
Island, and Connecticut for educational leadership. Religious denominational or parochial schools remained common in the Middle
Colonies until the country became independent, but such sectarian
schools were weakened by the withdrawal of English financial support and by the separation of church and state.

1776	1780	1785
Declaration of Independence	English Sunday School Founded by Raikes	Northwest Ordinance Land Grant
Thomas Paine's *Common Sense*	1781 Battle of Yorktown	1787 Constitutional Convention
Adam Smith's *Wealth of Nations*	1783 Treaty of Paris Ended War with England	1789 Constitution Accepted without Mentioning Education

DEMOCRATIC IDEALS

The rising tide of democracy threatened a dual system of education in which the elite enjoyed good schools and the masses were largely ignored. This factor accounts for the shrinking influence of Latin grammar schools and the vast growth of the academy. The revolutionary period saw academies, with their emphasis on practical subjects such as bookkeeping, navigation, and surveying increase in popularity. Town schools in the most populated areas and even crude schools of the remote frontier settlements became more numerous as the eighteenth century closed, and such educational institutions did not cater to an aristocracy. Southern educational patterns altered little during the revolutionary era except that students did not study in England and many of the charity schools were closed.

CHANGES IN COLONIAL CULTURE

American capitalism was providing general growth and prosperity in the economic order and in intercolonial trade before the Revolution. New York, Boston, Philadelphia, and Charleston had become large cities with sophisticated populations interested in all sorts of European ideas. There was a diffusion of culture between the various parts of the colonies, as well as much travel and correspondence. Colonial intellectual life was stimulated by newspapers like the *Boston News Letter* and other periodicals such as *Poor Richard's Almanac* published by Benjamin Franklin. At the outbreak of hostilities in 1775, there were thirty-seven newspapers in regular publication.

French Revolution		War of 1812
1791 Bill of Rights Ratified	1798 Lancaster and Bell Start Monitorial Schools	1805 New York Free School Society
Philadelphia Sunday School Society	1802 West Point	1806 New York Monitorial Schools
	1803 Louisiana Purchase	1812 State Superintendent Appointed in New York

College, private, and city libraries were found throughout the colonies, although many did not permit the circulation of books. Subscription libraries were available at a small fee. Only a few Americans published books before the Revolution, but British volumes were for sale in most large towns. Bookstalls had the works of Bacon, Locke, Boyle, Newton, Swift, Milton, Hume, Voltaire, and Addison, among others. Learned professions like law and medicine made progress in the late eighteenth century and gained in respect. Experiments in science and medicine were as popular as speculation in philosophy. The American Philosophical Society, which developed from a proposal by Franklin, brought Americans into contact with the learned world of Europe. Not many colonial minds were on a par with the cosmopolitan Benjamin Franklin or the theologian-philosopher Jonathan Edwards, but there were well educated, widely read, cultured Americans before the Revolution. Leaders in public life like Patrick Henry, John Adams, and Thomas Jefferson were much influenced by intellectual changes in Europe.

THE SHIFT IN THE COLONIAL MIND

Dissatisfaction with conditions in Europe was one reason for the first American settlements, but this feeling shifted to dissatisfaction with English colonial policies such as mercantile capitalism. The American Revolution was a combination of native efforts and contributions from foreign thinkers and movements. The rationale for the American experiment in self-government was provided by political philosophers like John Locke and Jean Jacques Rousseau, philosophers whose effect on education was both direct and indirect.

Locke's Influence. The English philosopher John Locke (1632-1704) not only provided a theoretical basis for the Declaration of Independence, but also contributed to American educational thought. Locke's political ideas concerning the inalienable rights of man and the contract relationship between a people and its government were accepted almost without qualification by Thomas Jefferson and other leaders in the movement for independence. The high reputation Locke enjoyed among Americans caused his philosophical writings to be widely circulated in the colonies and later in the United States. Locke had severely altered the direction of educational thought through his denial of the existence of innate ideas and his insistence that the mind at birth is passive and like a blank tablet (*tabula rasa*) upon which experience writes. He believed that all our ideas come from experience and that the measure of the truth of an idea is its correspondence with concrete, objective, common-sense reality (empirical principle). Emphasis on experience, good study habits, a utilitarian curriculum, and sense-realism aided the scientific and practical elements in American education. Franklin's belief in self-education for practical utility, his broad interest in empirical science, and his desire to provide educational opportunity for anyone who wanted to learn were all in keeping with Locke's theories. The emergence of a strong middle class with large numbers of lawyers and merchants was an event of the late colonial period which helped to support the ideas of Locke. Franklin and Locke emphasized the secular aspects of education as opposed to the ecclesiasticism of the schools supported by religious organizations. While sectionalism, a lack of money, disunity, and religious sectarianism prevented any common educational program in colonial America, the theoretical foundation for free, universal, and public schools was laid.

Comenius.   An outstanding spokesman for the power of education in improving the human condition was John Amos Comenius (1592-1671). Born in the village of Nivmitz in Moravia, Comenius became bishop of the Moravian Brethren, a Hussite religious sect persecuted by both Lutherans and Catholics. In spite of exile, the murder of his family, and the destruction of his library, Comenius managed to develop a philosophy of education and to write some of the most influential school books produced in Europe. His *Great Didactic* and *Door of the Languages Unlocked* (an introduction to Latin grammar) were produced while he was rector of the gymnasium at Lissa, Poland. Influential Englishmen invited Comenius to present his plan for universal knowledge and a world university to Parliament, but the English Civil War of 1642 prevented his appearance. For six years he wrote textbooks for Latin schools in Sweden and later established a school at Sanosptak, Hungary. There, Comenius developed his idea of schools in graded order from "the school at the mother's knee" to the university. In 1658, while living in Amsterdam, he published his *Orbis Sensualism Pictus*, the first popular illustrated textbook for children. Cotton Mather claimed that Comenius was invited to become president of Harvard in 1654. He was a highly respected educator whose ideas fell on fertile soil in America.

While the religious background of Comenius caused him to accept the doctrine of original sin, he agreed with Locke that ideas come from experience and that our sense organs are our teachers. This sense realism lent support to empirical investigation, practical education, and the potential of science. Comenius believed that war could be prevented if scholars were brought together to work out solutions to international problems. To this end he proposed a pansophic university with functions faintly similar to those of the United Nations. He felt that universal education could improve civilization through the discovery and dissemination of practical information on subjects such as economics, medicine, agriculture, and sanitation. Although a linguist himself, Comenius believed that primary instruction should be given in the vernacular. He encouraged the publication of dictionaries, textbooks, and encyclopedias in order to simplify instruction. He thought a science of education was possible and that teachers could be trained to practice that science. Comenius influenced American education through his textbooks, his support for science, and his belief that education must be practical. The growth of the academy and the concept of self-education made popular by Franklin were also part of the educational theory of Comenius.

Impact of European Movements.   The sense realism of Comenius, the empiricism of Locke, and the scientific movement in Europe paved the way for new conceptions of man and society. The verbal or humanistic realism of John Milton advocated encyclopedic studies and general education. In place of the narrow religious view and conservatism of the New England Puritans, Englishmen were substituting a secular, realistic, liberal world view.

The life of the mind in the American colonies varied from theological arguments in the early Puritan settlements to broad scientific and secular issues addressed by men like Franklin in the urban centers of the Middle Colonies. The scientific revolution of seventeenth century Europe reached America by degrees and had a major impact after 1750. Findings of the Royal Society of London for Improving Natural Knowledge excited American interests and stimulated discussion, especially of the physical sciences. Empiricism, sense-realism, and scientific discovery foreshadowed the movement of the late seventeenth and early eighteenth centuries known as the Enlightenment.

The Enlightenment was a rationalistic, liberal, humanistic, and scientific trend in thought which vastly altered the climate of opinion in Europe. It was grounded in the naturalistic and social theories of Comenius and Locke, but found new expression in the works of Diderot, Voltaire, Rousseau, Hume, Paine, and Kant. Kant described the Enlightenment as the liberation of man from his self-caused state of minority. It was a protest against authority which insisted upon man's ability to understand the universe without divine revelation. It held that men as individuals have worth and dignity and that they are able to judge truth for themselves. It fostered belief in a universe governed by natural law which reason could penetrate. The Enlightenment was a protest against both the authority of Christian dogma and absolute monarchs. Its leaders sought a balanced social order free from the control of a single powerful class. Enlightenment thought favored autonomous economic enterprise and parliamentary forms of government. It created an attitude of distrust for despotic monarchs and all other forms of strong centralized government. British mercantile capitalism, which exploited colonies as sources of raw materials and dumping grounds for surplus manufactured goods, was attacked by the theorists of the Enlightenment. Scottish economist Adam Smith, with his ideas of value placed on labor, *laissez-faire*, and a free market, appealed to leaders of the Enlightenment.

Humanism looked to the past through a study of classics for solutions to problems of the world. Great interest was shown in the social and governmental arrangements of ancient Greece and Rome. Men like Jefferson used classical models for the new republic and for institutions such as the University of Virginia. Sense realism placed man (not God) at the focal point and sought knowledge through ordinary experience or scientific observation. American revolutionary leaders were much influenced by books written by liberals like the humanitarian, Montesquieu. Cultural changes of the Enlightenment helped to plant the ideas which grew in the fertile soil of a comparatively free society and became the timber of revolution. It should also be remembered that more than one hundred and fifty years of colonial growth and development before the Revolution provided ample time for a major alteration of values and beliefs. The intellectual climate of 1776 was far different from that of 1650.

COLONIAL LIBERALISM

By no means were all of the colonial settlers conservative and narrow in their beliefs, in spite of restrictions imposed by Puritan and Anglican authorities. James Oglethorpe proposed colonization of Georgia as an experiment in humanitarianism after he had visited English prisons. The Quakers of Pennsylvania were not only tolerant of other religious beliefs, but also were concerned about the dignity and worth of all persons without regard to color, creed, or social position. Catholics in Maryland brought a different tradition to America and they were hardly in a position to resist religious freedom.

The Puritans were outspoken in their opposition to secular authority that overran the "just bounds" which they defined as God's word and the common interest, although they were not willing to grant religious freedom. Even so, Roger Williams, Thomas Hooker, Jonathan Mayhew, and John Wise were Puritans who dissented from church authority with considerable success. Puritan schools were dominated by orthodox teachers like Ezekiel Cheever, who was praised by Cotton Mather as much for his preaching as for his pedagogy; but tolerance and liberalism became widespread ideals before the Revolution.

Other systems of thought had considerable influence on the cultural climate before the United States emerged as a nation. The Puritan theologian Jonathan Edwards was hard pressed to defend his religion against science. Samuel Johnson was attracted to the idealism of Bishop Berkeley, while deism (the belief that God created the world and then withdrew to let it operate according to natural law) was popular with many intellectuals. The naturalism of Rousseau and his concept of government were known in America, although his influence on education was severely curtailed by the conservative reaction that followed the war for independence. Adam Smith's Wealth of Nations appeared in 1776 and became the basic economic theory of the new nation. Thomas Paine was one of the great champions of the American Revolution because of such writings as Common Sense which had an enormous circulation and which proclaimed independence. But later Paine's Age of Reason was considered radical in the conservative period that followed the Revolution, and its author lost his influence in the United States.

EDUCATIONAL CHANGES IN THE LATE COLONIAL PERIOD

Several of the colonial colleges were founded in what may be called the revolutionary era. King's College, the College of Philadelphia, the College of Rhode Island, Queen's College, and Dartmouth were all founded between 1750 and 1776. Some of the political leaders in the movement for freedom from England were products of the colonial colleges, but they were basically conservative institutions. The total enrollment of the nine colonial colleges operating on the eve of the Revolution was about 750 students.

On the secondary level, Latin grammar schools declined in importance with respect to the academy. Academies were more democratic in organization and far more geared to the needs of an expanding economy. Franklin's first effort at Philadelphia in 1751 was secular, practical, and widely copied. Courses in Latin and Greek were included in some academies but modern languages, including French and German, were more popular. Gauging, drawing in perspective, merchant's accounts, logic, chronology, astronomy, and rhetoric were added to the older subjects of history, geography, bookkeeping, writing, surveying, and navigation.

Academies and some private venture secondary schools flourished in the larger towns in the decades before the War. As colonial interest shifted from religion to shipping, commerce, and agriculture, civil town governments became more important in education. Many efforts were made to obtain town schools in which children without means could receive rudimentary training, and town schools often had secondary departments for those who could pay.

Elementary schools continued to operate with crude instruction and equipment. Several factors led to the decline of certain kinds of schools, but the educational tradition continued. The early New England writing school, which had never been in great demand, expired before the Revolution. In Pennsylvania, the SPG gave up in disgust after 1763, while the decline of New England theocracies made schools more difficult to support. Massachusetts, Connecticut, and Rhode Island did not abandon efforts to educate all the children, but some towns were without schools and many provided them for only a few winter months. Denominational efforts such as the Reverend William Tennant's Log College (a classical secondary school for training Presbyterian preachers) declined after 1742. Nevertheless, elementary education was provided for most colonial children who could pay a small fee. A larger and more prosperous population gave rise to more schools in the Middle Colonies than had been the case earlier.

THE WAR AND AFTER

The Revolutionary War directed men's energies away from education and science, as De Witt Clinton observed years later. Illiteracy increased because rural schools had to close their doors and even the larger town Latin grammar schools were crippled. British occupation of New York caused schools to be abandoned there. New England schools continued to operate but they suffered from a lack of funds and teachers.

Higher education was restricted in part because many talented teachers were Loyalists. Books were scarce since they came from England and colonial printers could not maintain their presses without outside supplies. Yale College was broken up into groups centered in different towns, while Harvard's buildings and those of the College of Rhode Island housed provincial troops. Dartmouth had neither money nor books, and classes had to be discontinued at the College of Philadelphia. The College of New Jersey and William and Mary also suffered but were not closed.

British support, as in the case of the Anglican SPG, was cut off and never revived. Lack of money and the interruption of the normal economic process made the operation of educational institutions almost impossible. Teachers and scholars joined the fighting forces while school buildings were converted into barracks. Tory or Loyalist teachers were turned out of their schools. Sometimes the schools were burned and libraries scattered or destroyed. Nevertheless, the conflict was restricted to certain parts of the colonial territory and areas that escaped destruction continued with education. Peace allowed for a restoration of many schools even though the money was scarce and authority uncertain.

Sway of Independence.   The Revolution dealt harsh blows to intellectual life in America, but it also provided the seeds for intellectual activity independent of Europe. So long as the colonists were tied to the value system of the mother country, it was almost impossible for the native culture to rival the established and sophisticated English life of the mind. But the Revolution broke those ties and stimulated considerable literary activity, expressed in antimonarchical and prodemocratic pamphlets and books. Further, the heroes of the Revolution were elevated to a dignified and popular social and political status in the new nation. Their ideas gained immediate support. Many revolutionary leaders attempted to put ideals central to the struggle for liberty, such as natural rights, freedom, equality, patriotism, and resistance to tyranny, into the laws. A free press and freedom of speech called attention to the need for schools if the new government of the people was to be successful.

EDUCATIONAL EFFORTS OF THE FOUNDING FATHERS

Many of the men who contributed to the birth of the new nation had plans for schools or other educational institutions. Few of these were actually realized for a variety of reasons including the national debt of seventy-five million dollars (which seemed a staggering sum at the time) and Federalist conservatism.

Freedom of Religion.   Patrick Henry first became involved in the struggle for religious freedom in 1763 when he defended a group of Virginia farmers against Anglican ministers who were suing for their back pay. He lost the suit but the jury fixed the pay of the ministers at one penny which was a victory for the opponents of established religion. James Madison and Thomas Jefferson carried the banner of freedom of religion during the war. They offered a bill in 1776 to exempt dissenters from paying the church tax. In 1779 Jefferson sponsored a bill establishing religious freedom but it was unsuccessful. Patrick Henry proposed a law in the Virginia legislature which would have provided tax support for Teachers of the Christian Religion, without regard to denomination. Madison feared the creation of a "multiple establishment of religion" and in 1785 he managed to push through Jefferson's earlier proposal. Virginia became the first state to have a law guaranteeing freedom of religion. Jefferson returned from his mission in France in 1787. Finding no constitutional guarantees for individual rights, he refused to support ratification of the Constitution without the series of amendments known as the Bill of Rights.

The First Amendment specifically prevented Congress from making any law respecting the establishment of religion or prohibiting religious practice. Connecticut, Maryland, Massachusetts, and New Hampshire did have constitutional provisions for tax-supported religion but these were abolished by 1833. While the long range effects of disestablishment and religious freedom were beneficial to public schools, the immediate result was to take away public funds which had been used to support church-related schools. Separation of church and state also gave rise to educational problems which persist today, such as the issue over prayer and Bible reading in public schools. Nevertheless, sectarian control over public education was broken by the provision for religious freedom.

National University.   James Madison and Charles Pinckney attempted to include a provision for a national university in the Constitution. Although it failed, interest in the idea was expressed by several national leaders including Washington. His farewell speech to the army emphasized the need for the promotion and diffusion of knowledge. Several times Washington attempted to get Congress to establish a national university and he left part of his estate to the proposed institution. John Jay, James Monroe, and John Quincy Adams shared the desire for a national university with Washington, Jefferson, and Madison. The university was never built, partly because Congress failed to act and partly because of legal and financial arguments.

Plans for a National System.   Despite the omission of education from the Constitution, a number of proposals for a national school system were made by revolutionary statesmen. In 1795 the American Philosophical Society offered a prize for the best essay on the subject of a national system of education. Many plans were submitted including those of Benjamin Rush, Noah Webster, Samuel Smith, Samuel Knox, and Du Pont de Nemours. Knox and Rush shared the prize. All these plans were founded on the theory that a public system of education is necessary for a free and self-governing republic. Consideration was given in the plans for public control, public support, a practical curriculum, compulsory attendance, and all levels of schools including a national university. The plans differed: one in particular designed by Rush, offered a very extensive system with supervision of schools and academies for teacher training. Support for an American school system also came from essayists such as Robert Coram of Delaware and Revolutionary War officer Nathaniel

Chipman. In spite of the interest, all plans for a national system were rejected by Congress.

REVOLUTIONARY PERIOD EDUCATIONAL LEADERSHIP

Many men aided the cause of schools during the period of the American Revolution. Benjamin Franklin lent his great prestige to all intellectual and cultural causes, although he supported practical self-education more than public schools. Benjamin Rush, a signer of the Declaration of Independence, wrote numerous essays on education in addition to his plan for a national system. Perhaps the most important influence of the era came from Noah Webster and Thomas Jefferson.

Noah Webster.   Known as the "Schoolmaster to America" because of the popularity of his textbooks, Noah Webster (1758-1843) was a major educational force for many years. His *Compendious Dictionary* (1806) was the first of a series of dictionaries and lexicons which made his name a household word in the United States. While keeping a classical school in New York, Webster began his *Grammatical Institute of the English Language,* of which the first section, often revised, became the famous "blue-backed speller." It is estimated that this book had sold nineteen million copies by the time of Webster's death, and by all measures it was the most successful textbook ever produced in America. He also wrote books on grammar, reading and history, all with a strong patriotic and nationalistic flavor. As a young man, Webster was caught up in the liberal ideas of the Enlightenment and the Revolution. He supported free schools, a national language as a band of union, and separation of church and state.

The French Revolution shocked Webster and he repudiated his earlier republican principles in favor of conservative federalism. His later works stressed religious morality, respect for government and a patriotism that sometimes bordered upon the fanatic. He believed that all books, schools, masters, and programs for the schools of the republic should be strictly American and even suggested that the first word taught to an infant should be "Washington." Webster called for strict teaching and supported traditional methods of instruction, but he was against corporal punishment. He wanted education for girls because they would be the mothers of future citizens and the teachers of youth. Webster felt that no legislature should ignore the need for free schools in which all American children could learn the virtues of liberty, just laws, morality, hard work, and patriotism.

Thomas Jefferson.   Jefferson's contribution to education would constitute ample material for an entire book. He provided the ideology for extending educational opportunity to all citizens and argued that no democratic society is safe without an educated population. For more than fifty years, Jefferson was personally active in efforts to put his educational theory into actual practice. As a young man he worked to reform the schools of Virginia, while much of his old age was devoted to building the University of Virginia. The basic theme of Jefferson's educational policy was academic excellence with equality of opportunity for all. He was not, like Hamilton, a supporter of strong federal government and therefore his efforts to improve schools were on a local and state level. Jefferson did not agree with the schemes for a national system of education, although he did not oppose a national university.

Jefferson's Bill for a More General Diffusion of Knowledge in Virginia was widely circulated and used as a model. The plan called for a state system of free elementary schools with local control. Secondary schools were to be tuition institutions, with a provision for scholarships to meet the needs of poor but gifted boys. A state university was to crown the educational system. Jefferson submitted three bills to the Virginia Assembly but he was not successful in passing any of his proposals except that for the University of Virginia. His effort to overcome the danger of an ignorant populace was very modest; the Bill called for only three years of public schooling. His organizational pattern with decentralized control and localization of financial responsibility became popular even though Virginia failed to adopt the plan. For example, Edward Coles became governor of Illinois in 1818 and promptly submitted a plan for a school system in that state which borrowed many of Jefferson's ideas.

After attempting to reform the College of William and Mary, Jefferson became convinced that an entirely new university was required. Few institutions have reflected one person's views as closely as the University of Virginia reflected those of Thomas Jefferson. Not only was he the driving force for the creation of the university, he organized the curriculum, hired the faculty, planned many of the buildings, purchased and catalogued the books for the library, and generally supervised the entire operation. In 1825, Jefferson saw his creation open with forty students. The University of Virginia became the first state university and one with a "modern" curriculum.

EARLY GOVERNMENTAL PROPOSALS

It was the prevailing view of the founding fathers that while knowledge was the best guardian of liberty, education did not belong in federal hands. James Madison wanted a general tax for schools, and Samuel Knox argued that private schools were subversive in a republic, but such reasoning did not convince the Constitutional Convention. The Constitution, therefore, contains no reference to education, although state control and nonsectarian public schools are assured by the First and Tenth Amendments. Other measures significant in the development of education came out of the early national period.

Early National Legislation.   In 1785 the Congress outlined regulations for the national territory west of the Alleghenies, north of the Ohio River, and west of the Mississippi River. This Northwest Territory was to be laid out in townships consisting of thirty-six sections. By the Ordinance of 1785 (also called the Northwest Ordinance) the sixteenth section (one square mile) in each township in the territory was reserved for the support of schools within the township. A second Ordinance two years later authorized not more than two full townships in each new state to be reserved for a university. The act contained a statement that schools and education should forever be encouraged for the benefit of human happiness and good government. These acts became a precedent for land grants to the states for public schools and colleges. By later acts, most new states entering the Union received federal land for educational purposes.

In 1802 Congress established the national military academy at West Point. This was the first of many federal acts which created special educational institutions with specialized functions. West Point had the first American training center for engineers.

State Efforts.   Seven of the state constitutions adopted before 1800 mentioned education. Those of Pennsylvania, North Carolina, and Vermont called for the establishment of schools in each county with some public financial support. The Pennsylvania Constitution, accepted in 1776, became a model for several others. It required that the state pay salaries of teachers in public schools. New Hampshire and Massachusetts stressed the need for wisdom and knowledge as a means of preserving liberty, but their constitutions did not require schools. Massachusetts legalized its traditional local district school system and in 1789 admitted girls to district schools. New York made public lands and certain other funds available to free schools.

Before 1812, the Union had grown considerably with the purchase of the Louisiana Territory in 1803 and the admission of the new states of Vermont, Kentucky, Tennessee, Ohio, and Louisiana. The constitutions for these states all indicated some concern about education, and several set up a system of schools in law. As the nation grew, each new state adopted a constitution modeled after those which were admitted earlier. The tradition of having educational provisions in the state constitutions became common.

OTHER EDUCATIONAL MOVEMENTS

Lacking public school systems and the ability to obtain laws for education, a number of leaders tried to support schools by other means. Many church-related institutions continued to offer charity education as they had in the colonial period.

Monitorial Schools.   Monitorial schools originated in England through the work of Joseph Lancaster and Andrew Bell. This type of school provided for inexpensive education that could be given to the masses by a minimum teaching staff. Students of ability were selected as monitors or student teachers, and these monitors were instructed by the master. The monitors, in turn, taught the lessons they had learned to small groups of pupils. Simple lessons were memorized and slates or chalk boards were used. The Lancasterian monitorial system allowed one teacher to instruct hundreds of children. One of these schools appeared in New York City in 1806 and the idea spread. Lancaster himself came to America in 1818, where he promoted his mass education program until 1830.

Sunday Schools.   Another English educational plan introduced in America was the Sunday school. Its champion was Robert Raikes of Gloucester. Raikes wanted to rescue children of factory workers from their filth, ignorance, and sin. Since the children worked in the mills all week, schools could be provided only on Sundays. Several religious groups, especially Methodists, supported the Sunday school with money and teachers. Children were supervised and given instruction in rudimentary principles during their free time on the Sabbath.

In 1791, a Sunday School Society was organized in Philadelphia. American Sunday schools developed in most of the major cities. They were primarily for the poor, but were not confined to factory or mill workers. Generally, the schools operated from six to ten o'clock on Sunday morning and again from two to six in the afternoon, leaving time for worship. Many children learned to read in these institutions, although they could hardly have provided more than the bare fundamentals of education.

Free School Societies.   School societies were organized to develop Monitorial schools, Sunday schools, and free public schools in certain areas. The Connecticut school societies were authorized to be district school authorities, while the New York Free School Society promoted several types of education. Schools for girls and for the poor were founded by the New York group which later became the Public School Society of New York. It was assumed in this period that students who could afford private schools would attend them, and indeed they did. Public schools and free schools carried the stigma of poverty because they were charity institutions.

SCHOOL IDEAS AND THE CURRICULUM

Independence brought about the development of a native American culture and a set of national institutions. Education was a reflection of this new spirit, as were self-reliance, optimism, individualism, and democracy. Farmers wanted more schooling for their children in order that they might gain the full benefit of the democratic society, for schooling was a mark of achievement and a step up the social ladder. The population of the new nation grew rapidly, increasing more than tenfold in a single century after the Revolution, and much of this growth came through immigration from European nations other than England. For these new citizens, education was the means of becoming "real Americans."

Improvements in transportation brought about social consciousness that was lacking in isolated colonies. It fostered an exchange of ideas and a national feeling which aided schooling. The start of the American industrial revolution shifted many people from rural to city areas, especially in the Northeast. Factory workers created special needs for free elementary education on a much larger scale. Doctrines of freedom and equality gave rise to free speech and a free press, which in turn fostered democracy.

But there was also a conservative reaction to the War for Independence. Liberals who fought for a free public system on the national level were opposed by those who feared the education of the masses and federal control. Lack of money and opposition to direct taxation prevented the building even of a national university. Yet there was interest in education, expressed in state constitutions, land grants, school societies, state universities and philanthropy. The start of American interest in free public schools for all the people can be found in the period before the War of 1812.

Separation of church and state did not take religion out of the schools. Both sectarian and public schools of the revolutionary era continued to use textbooks that were religiously centered. The Bible and the New England Primer were by no means expelled. Cheever's Accidence, the Westminster Catechism, and the Psalter continued to be used in New England schools after independence.

New Materials.   Changes did occur, however, in fields like mathematics, commerce, history, geography, and English grammar. Lindley Murray's English Grammar and the Universal Geography of Jedidiah Morse appeared before 1800. Samuel Goodrich wrote texts in reading under the pen name of Peter Parley, while Nicholas Pike's A New and Complete System of Arithmetic appeared in 1788. Noah Webster entered the field with his Grammatical Institute of the English Language in 1783.

In 1812 New York provided for a superintendent of common schools, but later abolished the office. Supervision was almost nil in the revolutionary period, except in Monitorial schools and in those operated by school societies. There was little effort to train teachers. Methods remained as crude as they had been earlier, with memorization the central concern. Liberal ideas from Europe and the frontier brought about changes in textbooks but not in the conduct of the schools, for it was still believed necessary to keep strict discipline by means of corporal punishment. Difficult subjects were learned for their value as a "discipline" to exercise the faculties of the mind. A more enlightened theory of learning was not to develop for more than fifty years.

THEN TO NOW

Anyone interested in describing an educational system must look for answers to several fundamental questions. Among the most important are: Who will be educated? What institution will control education? Who will provide the financial support? The colonial era was a period of transition from European educational patterns to ones more appropriate for life in the American environment. As we have seen, southern planters retained the English family-supported tutorial system while New England towns adopted a district system with some tax support. By the time of the rebellion against the British, no uniform educational policies had been established. Sectional differences in attitudes toward public schooling continued in the states as in the colonies. The great liberal leader Thomas Jefferson understood the need for citizens of a republic to be educated, but he did not believe in a federal system of schools. His Bill for the More General Diffusion of Knowledge proposed to the Virginia legislature in 1779 was a very modest plan which combined elements of an aristocratic attitude with a desire to broaden the educational opportunities of poor but able students. Even so, Jefferson's ideas were too liberal to gain the support of his colleagues from the South. Far-reaching plans for a national system of education such as those designed by Robert Coram, Benjamin Rush, and Noah Webster met with even more opposition. Yet the question of whether education should be public or private, supported centrally or locally, and managed by parents or governmental agencies, is still debated.

Although the fifty state systems of public schools have been operational for many years, Americans are still divided on numerous educational issues. An example is the argument over tuition tax credits for parents who send their children to private schools. These credits and the debate over the various voucher plans constitute significant support and control disputes about which many modern Americans obviously disagree.

Many of the founding fathers of the United States feared that leaving education in the hands of private families, churches, local communities, or philanthropic societies would not guarantee the survival of a democracy. Nevertheless, they were unable to promote a national system of education at any level. Considerable effort was made to obtain a national university but even that modest proposal was finally defeated. No educational provision was made in the Constitution so that the power to create schools fell to the states by default. This is very important today because there continues to be conflict over what powers rightfully belong to the federal government, to the states, and to local school boards.

One of the major current issues in American education centers on the influence of political and governmental forces on community educational practices. The states were very slow in passing educational laws even though the right was stated in the enabling acts incorporated in the several state constitutions. The original states did not begin to legislate for education until the 1830s, while new states added to the union lagged even further behind. Revolutionary and early national practices allowed religious organizations, free school societies, and Monitorial schools to fill the void before state systems were developed. Early laws provided for a great deal of autonomy to be delegated to local school boards while funding came largely from local property taxes. Under these conditions, it was natural for the district school authorities to consider themselves all powerful and without much control by the state. Leaders in the early national period like Horace Mann and Henry Barnard built their respective state school systems without taking away the policy making power of boards of education. The tradition of local autonomy has resulted in considerable conflict with state legislatures since World War II. State governments and state departments of education now take a more active role in teacher certification, establishing lists of approved course materials, and even mandating the curriculum. Federal pressure on local schools comes through court-ordered plans of desegregation, laws for equal educational opportunity (including the handicapped, disadvantaged, and non-English speaking children), and regulation of programs supported by federal taxes. There exists a great deal of resentment over the involvement of the central government in matters many consider to be the business of local boards. School boards and parents often feel that the bureaucrats in Washington have no understanding of local conditions and needs. Perhaps the most negative feelings have been generated by busing children away from neighborhood schools in order to achieve better racial balance in the classroom environment. Public sentiment for getting the federal government out of the schools and restoring local control was clearly demonstrated in the Reagan victory in the election of 1980.

Two points need to be made here. The history of the early national period clearly indicates that education is a state function even though the states have traditionally permitted a high degree of local control. Secondly, although the federal Constitution did not deal with education, there has been a long tradition of federal aid to the states and to local schools as well. People who are trying to understand the current issue over local, state, and federal control of education should remember that all three levels have had input into educational policy since the founding of the nation. Granting federal land to the states for educational purposes began with the Northwest Ordinance of 1785. This practice was continued with the Morrill Act of the Civil War era, which used federal land grants to create universities. Congress also established a number of schools for specific purposes and encouraged vocational education through legislation such as the Smith-Hughes Act. Recent federal acts such as the National Defense Education Act, the Elementary and Secondary Education Acts of 1965, the Equal Opportunity Act, and Public Law 94-142 are merely current extensions of federal involvement in education reaching back to American historical beginnings.

The mood of the nation has often been reflected in political activity which has a direct bearing on education. The history of the United States Office of Education is an example. As we have seen, many of the founding fathers wanted to establish a federal system of education. In 1829, Congressman Joseph Richardson proposed a federal Committee on Education to coordinate the state programs. This was squelched by Congress but the idea kept emerging. Charles Brooks of Massachusetts (a Unitarian minister and school reformer) devoted thirty years to efforts at getting a national system. Although he failed, he stimulated educators to form communications networks to gather data and influenced Congress to consider federal aid to the South after the Civil War. Following the War, the National Association of School Superintendents proposed a bureau of education. In somewhat reduced form, the Bill creating a Department of Education was passed and signed into law by President Andrew Johnson in 1867. Henry Barnard, who had also lobbied for such a department, became the first Commissioner. Barnard was not popular in Washington and the Department was soon reduced to a Bureau. General John Eaton, Barnard's successor toned down the office and made its function mainly one of collecting information. For almost a century after its creation, the United States Office of Education kept a low profile and concentrated on statistics. Then, in the 1950s with the Black revolution, and the Civil Rights Movement, latter-day reformers found the Office a useful instrument for implementing the reforms of the Great Society. In the Kennedy-Johnson years, the Office gained great power and status. It was authorized to distribute vast sums of money to compensate for the inequality of educational opportunity and to stimulate plans for school integration. The Office was placed in the Department of Health, Education, and Welfare and its staff grew to enormous size. Under President Carter, it became a separate cabinet-level Department of Education. The administration of President Reagan, however, took a very dim view of social engineering through federal spending and reduced both the budget and the influence of the department. All through history, the progress of education has been linked to the whims of politics and public attitudes. It should be remembered that the reason we do not have a federal system of public schools in the United States is because of the political climate at the time of the writing of the Constitution.

Another example is furnished by attempts of politicians to control higher education. During the American Revolution, criticism and attacks were directed at conservative colleges because they were considered to be insufficiently patriotic. William Smith, president of the College of Philadelphia, was an Anglican minister accused of Tory sentiments. In 1776, the College was investigated by the legislature. The board of trustees was dissolved and the faculty dismissed. A new institution called the University of the State of Pennsylvania was created by the legislature with a new board. The old college continued to function without legal status and finally, in 1789, the two institutions were joined to form the University of Pennsylvania. The case of the College of Philadelphia is similar to that of Dartmouth College which will be treated in the next chapter. The point to be made is that political influence over education is nothing new in American history.

It should be obvious that periods of political unrest foster attacks on institutions of education. Notable modern examples include the investigations by Senator Joseph McCarthy following World War II and the controversy over loyalty oaths for teachers (*Wieman v. Updegraff*) in the 1950s. It is also clear that while education is legally a state function, all levels of government are involved in educational matters. The arguments over control and support of education that began in the period of the Revolution are very much alive today and may be expected to continue into the future.

BIBLIOGRAPHY

Arrowood, Charles Flinn. *Thomas Jefferson and Education in a Republic.* New York: McGraw-Hill, 1930.

Best, John Hardin, ed. *Benjamin Franklin on Education.* Teachers College, Columbia University Bureau of Publications, No. 14. New York: Columbia University Press, 1962.

Butts, R. Freeman and Lawrence A. Cremin. *A History of Education in American Culture.* New York: Holt, Rinehart and Winston, 1953. Chapters 3-6.

Davis, David. *The Problem of Slavery in the Age of Revolution, 1770–1823.* Ithaca, N.Y.: Cornell University Press, 1975.

French, William M. *America's Educational Tradition, an Interpretive History.* Boston: D. C. Heath, 1964. Chapters 2-4.

Gutek, Gerald. *An Historical Introduction to American Education.* New York: Thomas Crowell, 1970.

Hansen, Allen O. *Liberalism and American Education in the Eighteenth Century.* New York: Macmillan, 1926.

Hofstadter, Richard and Wilson Smith. *American Higher Education: A Documentary History.* Chicago: The University of Chicago Press, 1961.

Ketcham, Ralph. *From Colony to Country: The Revolution in American Thought, 1750–1820.* New York: Macmillan, 1974.

Perkinson, Henry J. *Since Socrates: Studies in the History of Educational Thought.* New York: Longman, 1980.

Thayer, V. T. *Formative Ideas in American Education.* New York: Dodd, Mead, 1965.

Ulich, Robert, ed. *Three Thousand Years of Educational Wisdom.* 2d ed. Cambridge: Harvard University Press, 1963.

Woody, Thomas. *Educational Views of Benjamin Franklin.* New York: McGraw-Hill, 1931.

American Education 4
1812-1865

Before the War of 1812 education was virtually a religious enterprise, with the exception of some academies and free school societies. The period from 1812 to the Civil War was a transitional one during which educational leaders such as Horace Mann, James G. Carter, and Henry Barnard forged the first links in what has evolved as a free, public school system, supported and controlled by the state. The rise of nationalism and Jacksonian Democracy, the Industrial Revolution, and the forces of westward expansion, immigration, and population growth provided impetus to the concept of universal education. There was a rebirth in the growth of the elementary or common schools. The academies supplanted the elite-oriented Latin grammar schools and they flourished to a peak about 1850.

More important in this era was the birth of the American high school, an institution that would, in time, become the vital force of secondary education. This period saw the passing of the Morrill Act and the subsequent establishment of land grant colleges. European ideas were transplanted by innovations such as those of Victor Cousin, Joseph Lancaster, and Mrs. Carl Schurz. The curriculum was expanded. The sectarian stronghold gave way to a more secular orientation, and the concept of teacher training was realized in the establishment of the first normal school in 1839.

1817	1821	1827
Gallaudet Established School for the Deaf in Boston	First American High School, Boston	Massachusetts Required High Schools
1818 Robert Owen's Infant School	Emma Willard's School for Girls	1832 New York School for the Blind
1819 Dartmouth College Case	1825 Froebel Published *Education of Man*	1837 Calvin Stowe's Report on Prussian Schools
University of Virginia		Horace Mann Made Secretary of Massachusetts School Board

SOCIAL, POLITICAL, AND ECONOMIC TRENDS

The period of time from the War of 1812 through the Civil War is often referred to as the age of the common man. This is true in part because of the impact of Jacksonian Democracy and the social, political, and economic developments of the nation. Throughout the land, the advancement of the common man carried the banner of education as a basic right and opportunity that should not be denied any citizen.

Common School Ideal. The doctrine of equality of all citizens demanded mass education and made a system of separate schools for the elite social classes unacceptable. Equality led to the belief that all should read in order to participate in government and to have the opportunity to improve. The idea that schools could provide a ladder by which one might climb socially and economically was widespread. There was a demand for general education and for vocational skills as well. The attitude supported local control with no federal regulations. It was felt that common schools should be public in curriculum and tax supported. Separation of church and state was upheld, but no restrictions were placed on nondenominational religious instruction in public schools.

Impact of the Industrial Revolution. The Industrial Revolution began in Europe and spread to America a few decades later. Its beginning in the United States occurred in the eighteenth century, but its development continued through the nineteenth and twen-

Missouri Compromise		Civil War
1839 First American Normal School, Lexington, Massachusetts	1848 Attempt to Teach Idiots in Boston	1855 German Speaking Kindergarten
1840 Rhode Island Compulsory Education	1849 New York General Tax for Schools	1860 English Kindergarten in Boston
1846 Laboratory Sciences in Colleges	1852 Mass. Compulsory Education Law	1861 M.I.T. Founded 1862 War Begins Morrill Land-Grant College Act

tieth. One effect of the change from an agricultural to an industrial economy was the demand for a terminal secondary school to train boys for the work for which they were destined. From 1830 to the Civil War, considerable pressure was generated for the expansion and improvement of public schools. The industrial working class became a political factor. Workers in urban areas could not afford to send their children to school at private expense. They wanted a better opportunity for their sons and daughters than they themselves had enjoyed. Therefore, the demand for universal free education became more pressing. In the East, the vast growth of cities and factories tended both to increase the desire for schools and to decrease the opportunity many children had to attend them. The factory system employed whole families. Some youngsters began working at the age of eight. The severity of this problem is evident in the fact that in the 1830s two-fifths of New England's working force was composed of children under sixteen years of age. This was also a period of geographical mobility. The labor supply was made up largely of immigrants and transplanted farmers. Vast improvement in industrial processes increased the wealth of the nation, but it also created slums, urban blight, and new social problems. Many reformers hoped to use education as a means of overcoming the difficulties produced by the Industrial Revolution, such as child labor, crime, drunkenness, and extreme poverty.

Public School Support. Throughout this period there was an increase in the political power of the ordinary man and aristocratic birth came to be a political handicap. Private philanthropy, even by such a popular organization as the Public School Society of New York, could not really provide the answer, and increased agitation for tax-supported schools became commonplace. Bands of factory workers in cities formed working men's societies which tended to give their support to public education. Because they were important politically, the working men's societies had considerable effect.

The theory behind the taxation of every person for the education of all children was eventually accepted in most parts of the country, and the belief that schools must be both free and tax supported developed into general public policy before the Civil War. This did not mean that all states had established their school systems before 1865, nor that all resentment of tax support for education had disappeared, but the American people had generally accepted the notion of public support for common school education.

There was some feeling, particularly expressed by the *New York Working Men's Advocate*, that the public schools ought to board children so that those from poor families would not feel inferior to the sons and daughters of the rich, and equal educational opportunity would be a reality. This argument of 1830 serves as a reminder of some of the present controversy over civil rights legislation. It was also held that the curriculum ought to be the same for all students and that the classics should not be the basis, but a practical education which included the rudiments of the English language should be required.

Today the population explosion has manifest implications for education, but even in the early national period demographical changes had their educational impact. From 1820 to 1850 the centers of commerce, especially cities like Boston and New York, jumped vastly in population. Rapid growth of the cities and the subsequent surge of poverty and slums made reform and public concern with educational matters much more important. By 1845, the flow of people from foreign countries was so pronounced that cities like Boston had as many as one-third foreign-born residents. The nation's population exceeded thirty million in 1860.

Nationalization.   Many immigrants had customs and languages different from those of the native born population; therefore, the schools became a major instrument in the transfer of the American culture to the foreigners. One aspect of this "Americanization" was not limited to the newcomers. The two wars with England and the rapid growth of America had nurtured a growing nationalism. This resulted in an educational principle that the schools should pursue the inculcation of patriotism — a love and respect for America, its ideals, its history, and its potential. Frontier equality aided public education because of the belief that the people ought to have equal educational opportunity without the stigma of charity. Hence, the new states with large frontier communities tended to provide for education as they provided for universal suffrage.

Frontier Impact.   Frederick Jackson Turner became famous for his study of the impact of the frontier on American history. Other historians challenged Turner's ideas; but it is certainly true that free land, westward expansion and the constant development of new outposts of civilization, were significant factors in making the United States. While it is true that there was a certain amount of anti-intellectualism on the frontier, it is also the case that most pioneer farmers wanted their children to have the rudiments of an education. The frontier towns were raw and unsophisticated; but never dominated by only one class of people. Doctors, lawyers, and well-educated ministers were present along with farmers, ranchers, prospectors, and scouts. Pioneer virtues of thrift, hard work, self-reliance, and independence were often reflected in attitudes toward social institutions such as schools. The theory of minimum public education for every child found wide acceptance on the frontier, but getting tax money for schools often met with a good deal of opposition. The egalitarian view that one man was just as good as any other without regard to wealth, family, or social status became common-place on the frontier and in American schools. The frontier fostered individual freedom and lack of governmental restraint — values that often made it difficult to support and regulate schools. There was also a general distrust of classical or "foreign" education on the American frontier, reliance being placed on practical wisdom and basic skills like reading.

The first quarter of the nineteenth century was remarkable in many ways because it brought about, in the various states of the country, the beginning of the school systems which still exist in one form or another today. This was the time of common school revival in which the older colonial educational programs which had developed in Massachusetts and the other New England states were re-established. Of course, there was widespread opposition. Many newspapers were against taxes for the support of schools, and it was not possible to raise revenues with the speed necessary to develop a really good school system. But well before the Civil War, all the states had given at least some attention to the question of developing a system of public schools for the children of all the people.

First State Programs.   It was not thought necessary by the founders of the American common schools to guarantee a democratic system of education for all the people. The earliest state provisions usually created an ex officio superintendent of schools who also had other duties, such as being secretary of state. It was also common to empower local groups interested in education to establish an educational corporation for the purpose of building school buildings, hiring teachers, and whatever else seemed necessary to the making of a school. But the states moved slowly in the passage of laws which set up their various educational systems. The state superintendent of free schools or common schools, or the state superintendent of public instruction, as the officer was sometimes called, often had very feeble powers. Even when the states passed laws necessary for a real school system they tended to be very slow in the enforcement of those laws. For a long time it was difficult to collect school taxes and nearly impossible to insure compulsory attendance, even when such attendance was a legal requirement. Hence, the development of the state school systems varied as the interest of the people tended to wax and wane. Educational progress was hindered by the old tradition that children should be educated first by their parents and second by the church. However, in the long run frontier democracy overcame the prejudices against public schools.

THE AGE OF THE COMMON SCHOOL REVIVAL

Educational historians often refer to this period as the age of common school revival. It was during this time that the old New England demand for universal common education became an ideal for the American people. The common elementary school was established in the North and West, and it had the task of building social, political, and moral character needed in a democracy. In addition, it was concerned with the teaching of basic skills. The battle for free public education, supported and controlled by the state, was centered around the common school.

As the curtain rose on the nineteenth century, the condition of elementary school education was most depressing. The SPG withdrew its efforts after the split with England, and there were few schools which were for the benefit of the masses. Most existing schools required tuition, although some scholarships were available. Education was traditional, discipline was harsh. In the few public schools, most of which were in New England, the teachers' work loads were heavy and only the fundamentals were taught. For the most part school buildings and equipment were very poor, even in the private schools and academies. Textbooks, blackboards, and all working materials were in extremely short supply. Buildings were not kept up, lighting was not adequate, and quite often one poorly trained teacher was in charge not only of one school but of an entire district.

Teachers who possessed only an elementary school education were frequently hired. Of course, teachers in the Latin grammar schools and academies were educated; but there was certainly no formal teacher training system. There were some teachers of ability, but frequently men who were dreamers or who could not succeed in other professions became school masters. Perhaps people of better quality and training would have been attracted to teaching if the pay and conditions could have been improved, but this was beyond the capability of the settlers in most of the newer areas of the country. It is true that even on the frontier some well-educated and excellent teachers were to be found, but in most cases the quality of teaching was extremely low and the children could expect to gain little learning in return for the brief time and small fees which were required of them.

State Funds and State Laws.   Permanent school funds had been set up by a number of states during the early national period. Connecticut used the money from the sale of its Western Reserve for this purpose in 1795. New York and Virginia also had provisions for standing school funds before creating their state systems in law. While much educational support came from these funds, the tendency to rely on them probably retarded efforts to get real tax support.

One of the first acts commonly passed by states for education was a provision that local districts might tax themselves to support schools if the people in the district agreed. Such a law was passed in Pennsylvania in 1834. While no district was required to provide schools, more than half of the Pennsylvania districts did so. There was a great deal of opposition to school taxes in Pennsylvania, especially among Catholics and German-speaking farmers. Accordingly, the state senate voted repeal of the 1834 law and it was expected that the house would agree. At this point, one of the most unusual developments in the history of American education took place. An appeal was made to Thaddeus Stevens to support the repeal. Instead, Stevens made one of the most eloquent appeals known for free public schools. He offered a substitute law which would strengthen the public schools rather than repeal their support. Stevens used the common man ideal, the need for equality and the argument that public schools cost less than jails or welfare programs. Stevens was able to carry the day, and Pennsylvania accepted his substitute bill. Three years later Massachusetts passed a school law which established the right to use tax money for public schools. Other states soon passed similar legislation.

Curriculum Improvement.   Changes in the curriculum came gradually. Development was slow partly because most states could not afford teacher education or schools that offered much beyond the basic "R's." English grammar and spelling gained a place in school programs in the early national period. In western frontier towns, spelling sometimes was stressed more than reading and writing. American history was offered in some form to boys and girls who remained in school beyond three years. Geography was introduced into many of the elementary schools before 1825. Arithmetic was much improved by the addition of new texts and materials, but many pupils were taught only addition and simple multiplication "to the rule of three." As in colonial schools, reading, grammar, spelling, and later history and geography were treated orally by the recitation method. In 1836 William Holmes McGuffey began to publish his readers which sold over 120-million copies by 1920. These readers stressed individual virtue, literacy, hard work, and moral development.

Graded Primary Schools.   It had been the custom for mothers to teach their children to read and write before sending them to school, and therefore primary education was not considered the responsibility of the state. In Boston in 1818 primary schools were set up to take over this function. They were taught by women and eventually were consolidated with grammar and writing schools; this succeeded in forming the eight-year elementary school, a structure that is still prevalent in many areas today. Grading was not uniform, but the start of a graded elementary school can be traced to 1818 when the Boston Primary School was organized into six classes with the grammar or secondary school forming the seventh. In 1823 the grammar school was also divided into reading and writing sections. Many of the town schools had two rooms. Children were placed in the primary or the advanced room according to age. The person in charge of the older students was called the "principal teacher," which eventually led to an administrative distinction. Of course, many schools remained with no grades or divisions, especially in rural areas. In 1850, forty-five percent of the nation's youngsters attended school and half of the states had established their school systems before the Civil War. Quality remained poor in most schools. The typical common elementary school of 1860 was a crowded one-room institution with poor lighting, bad ventilation, inadequate furniture, and no special equipment. Poorly educated and untrained teachers had no program to follow and much of the time was spent in individual recitations. Severe discipline and corporal punishment stifled creativity and imagination. Nevertheless, schools were growing in number and the principle of direct tax support for elementary education had been generally accepted.

BIRTH OF THE AMERICAN HIGH SCHOOL

Secondary education in the early national period consisted of the Latin grammar school, the academy, and the high school. Latin grammar schools were strictly for the preparation of the college-bound elite and high fees were charged. Academies also charged tuition but some had scholarships for poor students. A booming economy and the religious revival known as the Second Great Awakening contributed to the development of academies. Many were boarding schools which provided a protected moral environment for students. By 1860, one-quarter million students were enrolled in six thousand academies. However, a growing demand for terminal secondary education with free tax support was made by the middle class and many workers. Increasing urban growth and industrial expansion also contributed to the birth of the public high school.

In 1821, Boston opened the English Classical School and renamed it the English High School in 1824. This first American high school was established to meet the needs of boys who did not plan to attend college. Boys as young as age twelve were admitted by examination and very few poor or working-class youngsters were involved. English, mathematics, history, science, geography, philosophy, bookkeeping, and surveying were taught. Massachusetts passed a law in 1827 which required towns of four thousand or more to create a high school, but not all towns complied.

At first high schools grew slowly. There was competition from well-established academies and opposition to taxation for secondary schools. Still, the idea of a free secondary school or a "college for all the people" appealed to the middle class and grew in popularity. In 1826 Boston opened a female high school under the direction of

Ebenezer Bailey. So many girls applied for admission that the school was closed for lack of funds. In 1855, Boston established another school for girls that included teacher training in a "normal" department.

There were no electives in these high schools. Students were expected to take all of the courses offered but there was a choice between an English, classical, or commercial curriculum. Entrance requirements and standardization of courses varied. There were arguments over whether or not high schools should be terminal institutions only. When the Civil War began, there were over three hundred high schools, one third of which were in Massachusetts.

HIGHER EDUCATION BEFORE THE CIVIL WAR

Except for the College of Philadelphia, all the colonial institutions of higher learning had been church related. In spite of efforts to make them democratic, most colleges remained sectarian and aristocratic. Classics, theology, and mathematics dominated their curricula. Control was vested with religious leaders and with the wealthy. It was possible to prepare for college in a low cost academy, and some students worked their way through college by teaching school during vacation periods. But only a small fraction of the population attended college. A majority of the students were preparing for the ministry or for a life of leisure which their families could provide.

Dartmouth College Case.   The struggle over the question of public or private control of colleges came to a head with the Dartmouth College issue. Dartmouth had been founded through the efforts of Eleazar Wheelock, who was succeeded by his son John. A dominant figure, John Wheelock came into conflict with the trustees of the college. In 1815, the board removed Wheelock from the presidency of Dartmouth, but in 1816 the successful Jeffersonian Democrats converted Dartmouth into a state university and restored Wheelock. As a result, the students and faculty rebelled and the trustees filed suit to recover the college. In 1818 the case reached the Supreme Court of the United States. John Marshall wrote the decision which held that a private educational institution could not be taken over by a state against its will. This decision clearly established the right of private as well as state colleges to exist and to solicit gifts or grants for support.

State Universities.   State universities were chartered first, where no institution of higher learning existed. They reflected the theory of

the Enlightenment that education should promote social improvement and individual happiness. The University of Georgia was
created in 1785 and opened in 1800. North Carolina chartered its
university in 1789, Vermont in 1791, and South Carolina in 1801.
There was also Blount College in 1794, which later became the
University of Tennessee. None of these colleges grew rapidly. They
were state universities in name, but all were under the control of a
private board and the curriculum included a large measure of classical studies. The best known of the early state universities was that of
Virginia, which was dominated by Thomas Jefferson. There was a
degree of academic freedom there: professors could select their own
textbooks and they held tenure. The curriculum was also much more
liberal than at other colleges. Jefferson called for professors of ancient languages, modern languages, mathematics, natural
philosophy, natural history, medicine, moral philosophy, and law.
This was the first attempt to include such professional studies as law
and medicine in a university program and the students could select
(or elect) the program they wished to follow. In September of 1825,
there were over one hundred students attending the University of
Virginia.

While the new program at Virginia was getting underway, an
effort was made to reform Harvard. George Ticknor, a professor of
modern languages, proposed a series of changes based upon European universities which he had visited. Among his reforms were
departmentalization of the university, strict examinations, teaching
by the lecture method, and student election of some subjects. These
reforms would have created a university similar to those of Germany, which had very high standards of scholarship. The reforms
were unpopular with faculty members and Ticknor was forced to
resign in 1835.

Resistance to change was also demonstrated by the Yale Report of
1828. This report placed stress on the status quo, emphasizing classical languages and theology as a means of gaining discipline over
the mind. It put little faith in science and held that the foundaton of
a superior education is grounded in traditional subjects. The Yale
Report called for recitations rather than lectures and placed stress on
the "superintendence" of the faculty over all student activities. It
supported the idea that traditional studies are a good foundation for
all vocations including the learned professions. The Yale Report was
a clear statement of the conservatism which continued to dominate
most colleges until after the Civil War.

In addition to Harvard and Virginia, Union College in New York
and Brown University began using the elective system. The major

growth in higher education before 1860 was in the private and denominational colleges. Private and church-related colleges accepted the principles of the *Yale Report* and rejected the elective system. In 1810, there were about thirty private colleges, but more than fifty in 1830. Eastern missionaries were especially active, founding colleges in western states like Ohio, Indiana, and Illinois. After the act which united Presbyterian and Congregationalist efforts, even more western denominational colleges were established. Methodists were also active. Many graduates of Princeton and Yale believed that creating new colleges was a way of reforming society and expressing religious beliefs. There were 182 American colleges in operation before the Civil War, although some of these may have offered only secondary instruction. Many of them ceased to exist before 1900.

State universities were also set up in the areas of westward expansion before 1861. In 1837 the University of Michigan was authorized to begin offering literary, scientific, and practical courses. There was also a branch for the education of primary school teachers. Indiana, Kentucky, Missouri, Mississippi, Iowa, Wisconsin, Minnesota, Louisiana, and California chartered their state universities prior to 1860. Many of these institutions did not reach university status until later.

Technical and scientific education began to increase with the foundation of Rensselaer Polytechnic Institute in 1824. The Lawrence Scientific School at Harvard opened in 1847, and Yale created the Sheffield Scientific School in 1852. There was a great demand for people trained in scientific and engineering skills long before most universities developed professional schools. West Point-educated engineers were too few to meet the need and there were no universities where one could study agriculture. By 1850 considerable pressure for the establishment of scientific, agricultural, and engineering colleges was felt.

An adult education movement developing during the early part of the nineteenth century gave considerable attention to public schools as well as the educational improvement of older citizens. In 1826 Josiah Holbrook of Massachusetts organized the first "lyceum" which was an association of men and women for cultural advancement. By 1832, a national lyceum movement had been organized for the improvement of useful knowledge and the advancement of public schools. Lyceums especially encouraged female teachers and invited them to participate in local educational movements for better support of and higher quality in common schools. Lyceum meetings were similar to county institutes. The nonsectarian character of the lyceum provided common ground for persons of divergent religious persuasion to discuss educational matters.

Other literary and cultural activities helped to give indirect leadership to the school cause. Ralph Waldo Emerson and Walt Whitman idealized the common man. Transcendentalism supported raising the educational level of the whole people as a means of social improvement. Newspaper editorials and publications of workingmen's societies, such as the *Mechanics' Free Press*, continued to urge free schools throughout the nation.

Morrill Act.   In 1857 Justin Morrill, congressman from Vermont, offered a bill for the grant of public lands to the states for colleges which would offer agriculture and the mechanical arts. The precedent of federal land grants of large size for schools and colleges had been established by the Ordinance of 1785. Morrill had the support of the farm interests in the South and West, but there was fear that it might cause the federal control of education. The Senate passed the bill, but it was vetoed by President Buchanan. Congress passed it again when Lincoln became president, and it became law in 1862.

The Morrill Act granted thirty thousand acres of public land to each state for each one of its senators and representatives. The land was to be used for the endowment and maintenance of at least one college in each state for the teaching of agriculture and the mechanical arts. Military science and tactics was also required, but the states retained control of the administration of the colleges and the remainder of the curriculum. Some states used the money to develop existing colleges, while others created new A. and M. universities. The actual development of these state institutions did not occur until after the war years. Congress made a number of supplementary cash grants to these colleges in later years.

AMERICAN EDUCATIONAL LEADERSHIP

Political Leaders.   Political support for educational reform came from many parts of society. DeWitt Clinton of New York was a political leader who showed great interest in educational matters. He often urged that the legislature establish tax-supported common schools and institutions for teacher training. In 1827 Clinton was largely responsible for creating a fund for aiding academies and promoting teacher education. He promoted the creation of the first office of superintendent of schools in New York, to which Gideon Hawley was appointed in 1812.

Governor Wolf of Pennsylvania charged in 1833 that his state had failed to meet the constitutional requirement which charged the legislature to provide poor children with free education. Thaddeus Stevens helped put Pennsylvania at the forefront of the fight for common schools. Archibald Murphy in North Carolina, Calvin Stowe in Ohio, and Edward Coles in Illinois called for complete educational programs in their states. Governors and influential political leaders in all parts of the nation attempted to persuade the various legislatures to pass school laws and provide tax support. Of course, there was opposition and not many political figures had the success of Horace Mann and Henry Barnard; but many were trying.

Literary Support. The *Connecticut Common School Journal* published by Barnard, William Russell's *American Journal of Education*, and the *Academician* which appeared in 1818 are examples of early educational journals which aided the common school cause. The mission of the Western Literary Institute was to create favorable public opinion for free schools according to John Prickett, who founded the organization in 1831.

Professional Educators. Cyrus Peirce, Samuel Hall, Edward Sheldon and Henry Barnard pioneered the normal school movement. Catherine Beecher, Emma Willard, and Mary Lyon were among the promoters of education for women. Caleb Mills in Indiana, John D. Pierce in Michigan, Calvin Wiley in North Carolina, and John Swett in California were important early educators. Probably the greatest influence was exerted by James Carter, Horace Mann, and Henry Barnard.

Carter. James G. Carter (1795-1845) was a pioneer educational reformer who worked his way through Harvard University by teaching in the Massachusetts district schools. He is often called the "father" of the Massachusetts school system and of normal schools. Carter was largely responsible for the passage of the Massachusetts school law of 1827 which provided for public secondary schools in that state. He made an effort to get Massachusetts to establish public normal schools for the training of common school teachers and he helped to set up the state board of education in 1837. Carter wrote essays on popular education in which he attacked the anti-democratic character of the private schools which existed in the early national period. He feared that private education, and especially private academies, would give rise to a differentiation between the classes of citizens which would be detrimental to America. Hence, in addition to his direct work with the schools, which included not only his efforts to pass school laws but also some personal experiments with private schools, Carter contributed vastly to the belief in democratic education for all people without regard for social class or wealth.

Mann.   Horace Mann (1796-1859) was perhaps the best known of the important leaders in developing the American public school system. Mann worked with Carter to persuade the Commonwealth of Massachusetts to establish a board of education and then Mann resigned from the legislature in order to become secretary of that board. During his twelve years as secretary, he was the most active leader of the movement for common school education in the country. The *Common School Journal*, of which Mann was editor, was circulated throughout the nation and in foreign lands as well. Mann often received letters from educational reformers and others interested in the schools beyond his own state, and he himself made many lectures and public appearances in the cause of education. Mann became the acknowledged leader in American school organization and he created a revival in Massachusetts which spread throughout the land.

The twelve annual reports published during his period as secretary of the board contained much information about how the schools could be improved. Mann was an enemy of the old district schools of Massachusetts, and he believed that education should be little influenced by private or religious societies. He succeeded in obtaining the support of the state legislature for liberal taxation which increased educational opportunities through better salaries for teachers and new buildings. From 1839 to 1840 Mann organized three of the first normal schools in the country. He also created fifty new high schools and had a marked effect on increased attendance in public schools at all levels. He worked, too, for improvement of teaching methods and for a better curriculum for the common schools. He attempted to use the schools to improve social conditions as well as to provide an opportunity for those who were on the bottom of the economic order.

Mann's work was so respected that his influence was very great throughout the United States, and his system for Massachusetts was widely copied as the development of common schools and high schools progressed in the rest of the nation.

Barnard.   Henry Barnard (1811-1900) played a role in Connecticut and Rhode Island similar to the role played by Mann in Massachusetts. He was secretary of the board of education in Connecticut, principal of a normal school there, and became the state superintendent of Rhode Island in 1845. Barnard's major contribution came through his editorship of educational publications, particularly the *American Journal of Education* published between 1855 and 1870. Barnard initiated the teacher's institute movement in 1839 and became a popular disseminator of information about better schools. A member of the Connecticut legislature, in 1838 he sponsored successful legislation similar to the Massachusetts bill of 1837 which created a state school board. He became the first secretary of the board of education and stirred much interest in education, although the legislature soon abolished his own office.

Next, Barnard moved to Rhode Island where, after a two-year campaign to awaken the citizens to the problems of the schools, he managed to get a law passed creating public schools, which he administered as commissioner until 1849. Connecticut made some efforts to reverse its previous error in firing Barnard by setting up a normal school and inviting him to be its principal. He held both positions for a number of years, and during this time he also produced many letters, articles, and educational studies. Barnard was also chancellor at the University of Wisconsin, president of St. John's College at Annapolis, and the first U.S. commissioner of education from 1867 to 1870. His greatest success lay in democratic philosophy and his ability to rouse public interest through the dissemination of information about education. Barnard is sometimes called the "father of American school administration."

EUROPEAN INFLUENCES

While it is true that American education was formed and molded by many factors that were uniquely American, the importance of transplanted European movements should not be underestimated. In the period from 1810 to 1865, the influence of European ideas was quite evident in the evolution of American preschool institutions.

Infant Schools.   The infant school of England, originated by Robert Owen and modified by Samuel Wilderspin, ministered to toddlers from the age of three. Owen's version encompassed a sort of informal education centered around health, physical training, and spontaneous activity; Wilderspin defined the school's function in more traditional terms, and his schools have been described as "intellectual packinghouses." In 1818 Boston made provisions for the first American infant school with an allocation of five thousand dollars. Dubbed the "primary school," this institution catered to children who had attained their fourth birthday. Within a decade similar schools had sprouted in New York, Philadelphia, and Providence. The American infant or primary school was influenced by both originators, but the Wilderspin format enjoyed the greatest development.

By mid-century the primary school had been absorbed into the common elementary schools. Infant schools were started to help the children of the poor factory workers; but they did not satisfy the demand for free public schools.

Kindergartens. European educators instituted the kindergarten as the proper foundation for education. The "garden of children" nurtured growth with the concept of activity, accenting the importance of play, songs, and stories. Froebel's educational ideas formed a complex and sophisticated philosophical position, but the kindergarten movement in America only encompassed the outward manifestations of his theory. Strangely enough, the kindergarten met with stern resistance in Froebel's homeland of Germany, and its greatest development was in the United States.

In the midst of a wave of German immigration following the Prussian Revolution in 1848, Mrs. Carl Schurz, a former pupil of Froebel, established the first American kindergarten. Formed in Watertown, Wisconsin, in 1856, Mrs. Schurz's school was really a German kindergarten on American soil, with German language as the means of communication. The growth of American kindergartens was considerably fostered by Elizabeth Peabody, who in 1860 established in Boston the first English-speaking kindergarten. In 1873, the kindergarten was brought into the realm of the public schools, due to the efforts of Superintendent William T. Harris in St. Louis. The movement was expanded in the private arena with contributions of philanthropic societies.

The kindergarten has become a stable part of the modern educational system with more than ninety percent of America's five-year-olds enrolled. Many of the ideas made operational by the progressives in the twentieth century trace their roots to Froebel and the kindergarten.

European School Model.   If the American schools were not al-
together adequate, there was at least an awareness that better programs for education were available in other parts of the world. The
influence of reports on European education can hardly be overemphasized, and the most influential of the lot was by Victor Cousin.
His detailed monograph on Prussian schools was first published in
1831 and translated into English in 1834. It was widely circulated in
America, and its impact can be judged from the fact that shortly after
it gained prominence, a number of important educators journeyed to
Europe with the intent of studying the European systems and
Prussia's in particular. Calvin Stowe's visit resulted in his treatise,
Elementary Education in Europe (1837). Mann made the trip in 1843
and gathered material for his famous Seventh Annual Report to the
Massachusetts Board of Education. While he disapproved of Prussian purposes, Mann found great merit in their efficient methods,
universality, high quality buildings, broad curriculum, and signifi-
cantly effective teacher training. Almost all the American educators
who had an opportunity to visit schools on the European mainland
returned with favorable impressions. They used German or Prussian schools as a model for making the American educational program more uniform and efficient.

European Educational Theory.   While some of the advances
made in European schools were the result of national or political
forces, there was also a new philosophic basis for change. In addition to Comenius and Locke (discussed in chapter 3) major educational concepts were developed by Jean Jacques Rousseau (1712-78),
Johann Basedow (1734-90), Johann H. Pestalozzi (1746-1827),
Johann Herbart (1776-1834), and Friedrich Froebel (1728-1853).
    Rousseau was a critic of conventional civilization, which he
viewed as depraved and artificial. Rejecting the doctrine of original
sin, he held that the basic nature of man is good and only social
institutions, such as governments, churches, and schools, cause evil.
Rousseau demanded a return to nature and an opportunity for the
child to pass through natural stages of development without being
molded by degenerate social forces. Although better known for his
Social Contract, Rousseau's Emile became a major educational classic. In it, he advocated emotional, intellectual, and educational freedom for children. Distrusting books and standard pedagogical techniques of his day, Rousseau believed that children should learn
directly from experience. Thus, physical activity, field trips, learning by doing (including manual or vocational experiences), freedom

to pursue natural interests, and play were advocated as means for developing the latent potentialities of the child. Rousseau suggested that people be aware of "negative education," by which he meant protecting the student from the influences of superficial social institutions. Rousseau's attack on formalism and support for natural interests had little direct influence on American education until the period of John Dewey and the progressive educators. His effect on European educators and schools had an indirect bearing on American schools at an earlier date.

The German educator Johann Basedow attempted to put many of Rousseau's ideas into operation in his Philanthropinum. This school was open to all students, regardless of wealth or class. It stressed natural development, teaching through conversation and sense experience, play, physical activity, and object lessons. Basedow included health, sex education, vocational training, and "world citizenship" in his curriculum, and wrote a book on his theories, *Elementary Work*. He also advocated teacher training. One of the teachers at the Philanthropinum, Christian Salzmann, later created his own school. Salzmann required his students to learn gardening, pursue gymnastics, and develop vocational skills; but there was also time for play, nature study, and formal classes. Other disciples of Basedow, such as J. H. Campe and Johann Guts-Muths, developed German children's literature and the physical education program for the German states.

The Swiss educator Johann H. Pestalozzi experimented with some of the more practical ideas of Rousseau's *Emile* and applied many of his own theories as well. Pestalozzi's major books included *Leonard and Gertrude, How Gertrude Teaches Her Children, Book for Mothers*, and the *Evening Hours of the Hermit*. Pestalozzi conducted schools at Neuhof, Stanz, Burgdorf, Hofwyl, and Yverdon. Starting with his own son's education, about which he kept a careful diary of observations, Pestalozzi developed educational programs for impoverished children and methods that were useful for teaching the children of the common people. Pestalozzi looked upon the child's mind as a union of separate moral, physical, and intellectual faculties. He believed that education was the natural, progressive, and harmonious development of the natural faculties and powers. He trusted children's natural instincts and thought they should provide the motives for learning. Instead of threats and corporal punishment, Pestalozzi believed that cooperation and sympathy could produce discipline in a home-like atmosphere. He saw education as a mutual effort by the student and the teacher which produced mutual respect. Like Rousseau, Pestalozzi believed that the child unfolds or develops through various natural stages, according to the principle of growth. He thought that sense impressions were the foundation of all knowledge. Pestalozzi wanted to develop each child's potential to the maximum and therefore spoke of educating the "hand and the heart," as well as the "head." Moral education and vocational training were just as important to Pestalozzi as intellectual subjects.

For Pestalozzi education was based upon actual observations rather than on books and theories. He relied on object lessons to develop the child's senses of sight, touch, and sound. Plants, animals, music, tools, and the natural environment were important in his education. Unlike the earliest sense realists, he did not view the mind as a passive receptor of sense impressions. He insisted that the mind is active in perceiving, analyzing, and selecting. Pestalozzi believed that society could be improved through adequate educational opportunity for all. Teachers from all over Europe came to observe his methods, and Pestalozzi offered them training. He believed that the basis for teaching should be close observation of the attitudes and activities of children.

In England, the ideas of Pestalozzi were made popular by Charles Mayo. American followers included Joseph Neef, who wrote *Methods of Instruction*, and Edward Sheldon, who created the Oswego movement (see chapter 5).

Froebel.   Since the advent of the kindergarten, educational leaders have been much influenced by Friedrich Froebel's theories concerning education of the very young. Froebel became a follower of Pestalozzi while teaching at a small private school at Frankfort, Germany. In 1816 he opened a school of his own and six years later published *The Education of Man*. At Blankenburg, Froebel finally was able to establish his educational institution offering programs for children between the ages of three and eight. (The German term for his school was *Kleinkinderbeschaftingungsanstalt* which was later reduced to kindergarten.)

Froebel was basically an idealist who looked upon the child as the agency for the realization of God's will in human nature. A mystic, Froebel believed that the spirit of the child could be linked with the absolute through the unity of experience and divine nature. From a practical standpoint, the significance of Froebel was in his conception of the educative process as something which must begin with a child of only three or four years of age. Early childhood educational activities centering on play, music, and physical activity made him famous. Froebel created new respect for the child, especially for his individuality and for the dynamic and active qualities of his nature. Constructive use of objects, story-telling, and cooperative social activities were supported in Froebel's program. Children were also to be free to express themselves and to build good relationships with others in the kindergarten. While later educators often disagreed with Froebel's mystical concepts, his efforts to create early childhood education had a profound effect. Froebel greatly influenced both Maria Montessori and John Dewey.

Growth of Academies.   The age of the common school revival was also a time of expansion for academies. Those which developed in colonial times were terminal private venture schools with practical programs. Many of those in operation before the Civil War offered college preparatory courses. Some were denominational, while others were governed by a local board or city government. Most academies charged tuition, but several enjoyed some sort of private endowment as well. Various schemes for public support of academies were tried, and a large number did benefit from some degree of public finance. The curriculum of the academy was never fixed; many offered a wide range of courses. Reading, writing, grammar, arithmetic, and higher mathematics were usually offered. Chemistry, botany, mineralogy, logic, moral philosophy, and natural science were sometimes in the program. Many academies offered modern languages and music. Some claimed to prepare students for teaching and other professions. A large number of academies admitted girls and some were designated as "female seminaries" or schools for girls only. After 1860 academies declined in number, due largely to the vast increase in public high schools. The census of 1850 numbered 6,085 private schools and academies in the United States. New York had over 800 incorporated academies. Both Ohio and Virginia chartered more than 200 before 1860. The majority were located in eastern states; but there were frontier academies in newly settled regions as well. Many academies closed after a few months because of lack of support. Some were only elementary schools and others largely vocational; but most American communities had access to some sort of academy for those who could afford tuition.

Normal Schools and Institutes.   Private academies for the training of teachers did not satisfy educational leaders like Mann, Barnard, and the Reverend Charles Brooks. Brooks began a campaign for state normal schools in Massachusetts in 1835, using the Prussian model of teacher education as a guide. Brooks had some influence on the school board and in 1838 when Edmund Dwight offered ten thousand dollars for educational improvement, three normal schools were founded. The state matched Dwight's grant and used the funds for salaries and operating expenses of the teacher-training institutions. In 1846 the normal school at Bridgewater got its own building. The name "normal" school came from the model or practice school in which the standard or normal curriculum and methods were observed. Cyrus Peirce, the first principal of the normal school at Lexington, stressed the review of common subjects and practice teaching under his own observation.

New York created a state normal school at Albany in 1844; but state money was also used to subsidize private academies for teachers. David Page, principal at Albany, wrote *Theory and Practice of Teaching* which became a standard text for teacher education. Only twelve normal schools were created in the United States before the Civil War. Many districts were satisfied with the untrained young ladies they hired as elementary teachers.

Henry Barnard started the teacher's institute. This was a meeting of a group of teachers for instruction and usually lasted only a few weeks. County superintendents of schools often conducted institutes for teachers in summer months. This was the only professional training many teachers were able to obtain.

Educational Opportunity for Women.   The growth of academies provided a much greater opportunity for secondary and higher education for women. A few girls' schools in colonial times offered courses in ornamental needlework, polite manners, music, French, and other subjects deemed proper for females. The curriculum was expanded by the many academies for young ladies in operation before 1860. There was some opposition to teaching girls Latin, logic, and the sciences; but all other courses were offered in at least some of the schools for girls. Coeducation was rare; most academies admitted one sex or the other, but not both. Employment of male teachers only, except in the Dame schools, ended during the early national period. Horace Mann and other educational leaders encouraged women to teach in elementary schools. It became common for many academies to offer courses in "schoolkeeping" for girls. Preparation of common school teachers was largely confined to a review of the common branches and a series of highly moralistic lectures on the "duties" of teachers; however, it was often the only teacher training available. Samuel Hall's *Lectures on Schoolkeeping* was the basic text for teacher training at the time.

Catherine Beecher, Mary Lyon, Almira Phelps, and Emma Willard were leaders in the movement for girls' secondary education. In 1821, Mrs. Willard opened the Troy Female Seminary, while Mary Lyon founded Mt. Holyoke Female Seminary in 1837. Catherine Beecher founded the American Women's Education Association and Almira Phelps wrote a series of *Lectures to Young Ladies*. The efforts of these women educators helped to establish the first coeducational college program at Oberlin in 1838.

Minority Education.   Very little progress was made in providing educational opportunity for minority children before 1861. Early Indian schools which had been established by missionaries were largely unsuccessful because the teachers misunderstood native American culture and attitudes. An occasional Indian learned to read English; but formal schooling was almost nonexistent for the American Indian population.

In the colonial period, many slave owners permitted Blacks to read. Some felt it was their duty to teach slaves something about the Bible and the tenets of religion. A few free Blacks made their way into Quaker schools in the North, which were open to all. In 1833, a Quaker teacher named Prudence Crandall was criticized for admitting Black girls to her school in Connecticut. In 1846, Benjamin Roberts of Boston filed suit because his son was forced to attend a segregated school for Black boys. The Massachusetts Supreme Court held that the school committees had a right to keep schools segregated. However, by 1857 Massachusetts passed a law preventing discrimination. The school laws in most states before the Civil War did not provide for Black scholars. Those of Indiana and Illinois specifically required schools for White children.

Even in the South, Blacks were occasionally educated. John Chavis was a teacher and a licensed Presbyterian minister until North Carolina passed a law against Black preachers in 1832. Most southern states prohibited the teaching of Blacks after Nat Turner's rebellion of 1831.

THEN TO NOW

The age of the common school revival was a period in which equality of educational opportunity was stressed. Horace Mann was a great champion of education for all. He and Henry Barnard believed that the schools had the power to unite the United States into an integrated national community. Economic, social, racial, ethnic, and religious diversity were to be subsumed under one democratic system of education which would unite all the people into a single indivisible nation. Education was to be used as the chief instrument for assimilating the foreign born into the mainstream of American life and culture. Schools did have a considerable measure of success in creating a single culture. Some thirty-five million immigrants came to America in the nineteenth century and they were Americanized largely by the public schools. Still, the aim of Mann and Barnard to achieve equality and social integration was not fully realized. Many persons living in the United States today are excluded from full participation in the social and economic life of the nation. Contemporary concerns about equality for ethnic groups and Blacks are clear indications that the melting pot ideal has not been fulfilled. Mann also wanted to move away from the extreme differences between rich and poor. He believed that a strong nation must provide opportunity for all and that differences between the haves and the have-nots must be reduced. Although many Americans have achieved affluence in the modern era, there are still many who are poor or the victims of discrimination.

Black education in the South was almost nonexistent before the Civil War and very limited in northern states. About four million slaves were liberated by President Lincoln, almost all of them illiterate. The Fourteenth Amendment of 1866 specified that states should not deprive any person of life, liberty, or property without due process of law. Nevertheless, they remained second-class citizens. Jim Crow laws of the 1880s were passed to "keep the Colored in their place" and discrimination was universally practiced. The separate but equal doctrine of *Plessy v. Ferguson* in 1896 legalized racial segregation until 1954. Private Black colleges and those created by the Second Morrill Act helped to improve the quality of teachers but Black schools lacked funds and the extreme poverty of the people made progress very slow. States claimed to provide equal support for Black and White schools but many actually put more dollars into education for the majority race.

This difficulty has not been resolved in the modern era. An end to legal segregation and plans for achieving racial balance in school systems have had an impact, but problems remain. Many American cities are still segregated de facto. The situation is not improving in many areas that are becoming almost totally populated by one race or ethnic group. Affluent Blacks (and other minorities) who represent the professions or the middle class have little difficulty in assimilating with White society. Integration in schools works well when all the students come from a similar socio-economic background. However, there are major problems when Black children from urban slums are placed in classrooms with students from more affluent families. The issue is especially clear when busing is used as a means of bringing together students from different races, ethnic groups, and socio-economic backgrounds. Demographic patterns in many large cities are shifting so rapidly that efforts to integrate schools are frustrated. Atlanta, Houston, Washington, and Newark are cities that have experienced dramatic increases in the number of minority students just when they began to implement plans for desegregation.

In the years covered by this chapter, much effort was devoted to creating and expanding public schools, high schools included. Educational leaders like James Carter were doing their best to make schools available to all and to improve their quality. The goal of providing equal educational opportunity to everyone and also of having excellent programs is still a difficult one to reach.

Even before Thurgood Marshall argued that segregated schools are inherently unequal (as lawyer for the NAACP in 1954), there was general agreement that minority schools had lower standards. It could have hardly been otherwise for those schools enrolled many children who were poor and culturally deprived. Black schools had less equipment, worse buildings, and teachers with very limited training. Beyond question, minority students have gained a great deal since desegregation. It stands to reason that placing children in better schools will be of some benefit to them. Still, many schools have not been integrated and critics say that progress in those that have been is not satisfactory. Lower overall achievement sometimes occurs when children with a poor educational background are placed in the same classrooms with those who have done better. This is especially true if the school is not used as an agency of selection to weed out those who are slow. The current attacks on social promotion and soft pedagogy reflect public dissatisfaction with attempts to meet all children where they are and to allow them to learn at their own speed.

There are also many current issues over attempts to teach the same values in schools and to Americanize all the youth. Ethnic and minority groups often argue that this takes away from the unique characteristics of children who are not of the White, middle-class, dominant culture. The struggle for equality and for excellence is far from over in American education.

BIBLIOGRAPHY

Binder, Frederick. *The Age of the Common School, 1830–1865*. New York: Wiley, 1974

Brubacher, John. *Henry Barnard on Education*. New York: McGraw-Hill, 1931

Cremin, Lawrence, ed. *The Republic and the School: Horace Mann on the Education of Free Man*. New York: Teachers College Press, 1957.

Curti, Merle. *The Social Ideas of American Educators*. New York: Littlefield Adams, 1966.

Mann, Horace. *Lectures and Annual Reports on Education*, Cambridge, Mass.: Cornhill Press of Boston, 1867.

Pratte, Richard. *Ideology and Education*. New York: Wiley, 1977

Rusk, Robert, and James Scotland. *Doctrines of the Great Educators*. New York: St. Martin's Press, 1979

Veblen, Thorstein. *The Higher Learning in America*. New York: B.W. Huebsch, 1918.

Silver, Harold, ed. *Robert Owen on Education*. Cambridge, Mass.: Harvard University Press, 1969.

Woody, Thomas, *A History of Women's Education in the United States*. New York: Farrar Strauss: Octagon Books, 1966.

American Education 5
1865-1918

Wars are by no means the most significant checkpoints in educational chronology, but the period between the Civil War and the First World War was the era for the development of the modern American school system. Westward expansion and the growth of industry, agriculture, and population put vastly increased demands upon existing schools and required the building not only of new schools, but of whole new educational systems. By 1890 the frontier had almost ceased to be and with the addition of New Mexico and Arizona to the union in 1912, the continental United States was formed. Industrial growth carried with it the new problem of educating children in the urban slums and the need for Americanizing foreigners on a grand scale. Natural increase and immigration swelled the population from just over thirty million in 1860 to more than one hundred million by 1920.

Before 1860 the northern states had largely developed the outlines of their educational systems, and some had made substantial progress in bringing state education to all the people. States were not uniform in their growth, those first to be settled usually developing their systems earlier. By 1873 laws for the organization of a state school system, including the school tax and some form of state control, were to be found all over the nation. Before World War I,

Reconstruction	Herbartian Movement	Progressive Era
1865 Slavery Abolished by Thirteenth Amendment	1870 School Superintendents in 28 American Cities	1890 Second Morrill Act Provided Black A.M. and N. Colleges
1866 Fourteenth Amendment Protects Life and Property	1872 Kalamazoo Case Made Tax Support Legal for High Schools	1893 Rhode Island Begins Special Education Programs
1869 Fifteenth Amendment Guarantees Civil Rights	1890 National Herbart Society	

public school education in America typically included an eight-year elementary school and a four-year high school. State universities capped the systems, although only a small percentage of the people could take advantage of them. Public kindergartens, junior high schools, and junior colleges were found in only a few areas before 1920 and were not yet a significant part of the public school organization.

Educational theory passed through a series of stages which included sectarian dominance, *laissez faire*, slavish copying of European models, and the scientific-progressive movement. Professional training for teachers and administrators became firmly established as an ideal with the growth of normal schools and colleges or departments of education in the universities. Compulsory attendance, expanded curriculum, fully graded common schools, public high schools, and large increases in spending for buildings and equipment marked the period. However, the late nineteenth century witnessed extreme sectional differences in educational structure and quality.

INHIBITED DEVELOPMENT OF EDUCATION IN THE SOUTH

The War Between the States interfered with education all over the nation, causing schools to be closed and governmental revenues to be directed to the immediate expenses of the conflict. But northern states were able to continue their school programs in spite of the reduction in available money and the loss of many teachers. Sometimes an entire student body and faculty went off to join the army, as in the case of Illinois College at Jacksonville, Illinois, but elementary schools in the Union states continued to operate through the war-

Urban and Industrial Growth		Social and Political Reform
1909 Junior High School in Berkeley, California	1913 Thorndike Published His *Educational Psychology*	1916 Dewey Published Democracy and Education
1910 Junior College in Freson, California	1914 Smith-Lever Act Encouraged Agriculture	1917 Smith-Hughes Act Encouraged Vocational Schools
Vast Growth of High Schools		

time years. It was not so in the South where battle devastation and increased sacrifice to support the war severely crippled the embryonic school systems. Southern states spent many years recovering even the low educational level they had enjoyed before the national strife, and some of the scars are still visible in the slower school development of the rural South.

Southern Collapse.   The war left southern states in physical and economic ruin with crops destroyed, buildings burned, livestock slaughtered, and the labor force demoralized. Civil authority broke down, courts were nonexistent, and four million Black citizens were without economic resources or leadership. Presidents Lincoln and Johnson hoped to enlist the cooperation of former Confederate leaders in rebuilding the South, but the radical Republicans in Congress wanted to punish the southern states. In the struggle, Andrew Johnson was nearly impeached and a military reconstruction government dominated by northern interests was imposed. These governments, consisting of "carpetbaggers," former slaves, and fortune seekers, failed to obtain the support of the southern White majority.

By 1876, when the radical reconstruction government finally ended and the Union army of the occupation was removed, very little real progress had been made. Southerners, bitter about their treatment after the conflict and fearful of Black power, set about to undo the acts of the reconstruction era. Measures providing for public education, especially where racially mixed schools were concerned, were either ignored or removed from the books. Sectional hatred and opposition to Black schools might have paralyzed education even if money had been available, but the war and the waste of the first post-war governments left the South bankrupt.

New-found freedom did nothing to improve the living standards of the southern Blacks. Most of them were as economically dependent and as subject to exploitation as they had been in slavery. Economic expansion was slow to develop and both races remained poor, especially small farmers and sharecroppers. Industry received a boost in the 1880s with the founding of textile mills. Tobacco products, lumber, and even steel mills in Alabama contributed to a stronger economy. But agriculture continued to be the mainstay of southern economy, and very little tax money was available for school purposes until the twentieth century. Many southern statesmen deplored the low level and retarded growth of public schools, but were powerless to provide adequate support.

Black Education.   Some money for educating the newly freed citizens came from private and church associations which sent teachers to the South in considerable numbers. In 1869 there were about nine thousand such teachers, working mostly in schools for freedmen. Several societies for the aid of freed slaves were formed, the most important of which were the American Freedman's Union (secular) and the American Missionary Association (religious). Congress established the Freedmen's Bureau in 1864. Its head, O. O. Howard, considered education to be the most pressing need of Blacks in the South.

There was considerable enthusiasm for schooling among former slaves in the period immediately following the war; but adults soon learned that education was something for which they had neither the time nor the preparation. The economic support was often sporadic, and it appears that many of the schools were very ill-equipped and of poor quality. Social liberals and political propagandists among the teachers from the North were unpopular. Like all things "Yankee," the freedmen's schools became objects of attack once the power of reconstruction government was broken after 1873. While the South was still organized as a series of military provinces, new constitutions were adopted which included provisions for education. But for all practical purposes the states of the South were bankrupt, so that little more than a paper system of education existed in 1870.

Hoar Bill.   In 1870, a bill was introduced in Congress by George F. Hoar of Massachusetts which would have established a federal school system in southern states. The measure was designed to compel the establishment of a system of instruction and the appointment of a federal superintendent in all states where a minimum standard was not met. Textbooks were to be prescribed by the United States Commissioner of Education, and the schools were to be supported by a centrally collected direct tax. The bill was defeated partly because of the opposition of the National Education Association and Superintendent Wickersham of Pennsylvania. They felt that national control over part of the nation's schools could not be tolerated, although gifts of federal money with local autonomy could be. Roots of the modern day issue over federal aid to education can be seen in the arguments over the Hoar Bill.

Blair Bill.   A second effort to get national aid for states unable to maintain schools came in the form of a proposed national school fund from the sale of public land in the tradition of the Ordinance of 1785. When it appeared that this plan would not be adopted, Senator Henry Blair of New Hampshire introduced a bill to give temporary help to states with the greatest educational need. The Blair Bill (in final form) provided for seventy-seven million dollars to be divided among the states in proportion to the number of illiterates in each. The money was to be used as the states saw fit, provided that it was used only for education. This measure passed the Senate three times, but was never successful in the House of Representatives. No further bills of this nature were proposed until recent times, although the federal government continued to aid colleges through the second Morrill Act of 1892.

Philanthropy.   Private agencies made an effort to fill the educational void in the South and to stimulate greater local effort. George Peabody gave two million dollars for this purpose. The Peabody fund was administered by a board of trustees headed in turn by Barnas Sears, Horace Mann, and J. L. M. Curry. Curry was a southerner, under whose direction the money was used to develop a limited number of high quality schools as models. Part of the Peabody Fund went to normal schools for women teachers of both races and also to what became George Peabody College for Teachers in Nashville. Agents who supervised private funds also visited schools and opened lines of communication between groups interested in school improvement.

Southern Associations.   About thirty years after the Civil War, a Conference for Education in the South was organized and numerous meetings were held for the purpose of improving education. Out of this grew the Southern Education Board and the General Education Board (1903). A Southern Association of Colleges and Schools was established as well as many private boards which were connected with philanthropic societies, such as the Carnegie Foundation and the Rosenwald Fund. While stimulation and information were given, the public systems tended to make only limited progress before 1920. Only meager tax support was available in agricultural areas, and even southern cities were poor by northern standards. The educational conservatism of the pre-war period and hostility toward schools introduced in the reconstruction era dampened interest in public schools. The most negative factor of all was insistence on separation of White and Black schools. This segregation required the building and maintenance of a dual system with duplication of buildings and teachers in states that could least afford them. While schools for Black children were seldom given equal support with others, their very existence divided funds and lowered the capability of communities to give quality instruction. This was a major factor in keeping the educational level of southern states lower than that of the rest of the nation for several decades.

In the early 1900s the South was still marked by short school terms (seventy days in North Carolina), high illiteracy, ineffective administration, poorly trained teachers, and meager tax support. Salaries of southern teachers in 1900 averaged about half that of northern ones and Black teachers were paid lowest of all.

NATIONAL AFFAIRS AND PROGRESS

If progress was slow in the southern states between the Civil War and World War I, those years also marked the transition from an old agrarian to a modern, industrial America. In less than half a century, wounds of the Civil War were largely healed and America entered the era of industrial world powers. Territorial expansion had given way to a greater and faster development of northern industrial capacities. The growth and development of industry was at least as important a factor as immigration in the population growth figure. This was the period in which it was possible for the Goulds, Carnegies, and the Rockefellers to build vast industrial empires and accumulate great fortunes due to a favorable attitude by the government, untapped industrial resources, and cheap labor. Many of the industrial barons were interested in education and helped to found colleges, universities, and better public schools.

Industrial Exploitation. The other side of the Industrial Revolution had a negative effect on education. Exploitation of children and working men was widespread, and it was not uncommon for immigrants in the cities to labor sixteen hours a day. The growth of great industry swallowed up the small businessman, and there was much corruption in government at all levels. City slums also presented a different kind of educational problem. The need for reform was seen, but many of the people in power sought to make more severe laws and to develop additional penitentiaries, rather than to cure the problem through education.

The Republican Party dominated politics and held control of the presidency between the end of the Civil War and the election of Woodrow Wilson in 1913, with the single exception of the two terms of Grover Cleveland. Distinctly the party of business, industrial, and commercial interests, it did not promote mass educational reform supported by federal and state governments. What was done for the education of the masses in the cities was done largely through private enterprise and with the interests of individuals who saw most clearly the need for reform. The dissatisfaction of the laboring masses began to show itself in the latter part of the nineteenth century. Numerous labor reform parties came into being in the 1870s and the agrarian and labor groups organized the Independent or Greenback Party in 1874. Later, several independent groups organized the Populist Party, which became part of the Democratic Party in 1896 and came very close to electing William Jennings Bryan over William McKinley.

The tremendous increase in industrial growth in the United States, which was especially obvious in the northern and eastern sections, together with the growth of large corporations controlling vast amounts of wealth, changed the nature of American society considerably. There was a strong belief in a hands-off, or *laissez faire*, governmental policy. This was the period of change of the basic nature of American society from rural to urban. The great cities were beginning to take their present-day shape, and the idea of the independent farmer class as the dominant one in America was beginning to fade.

Vocational, Agricultural, Population Changes.   There was also a revolution in farming due to such inventions as McCormick's reaper and the new scientific knowledge about agriculture which had been greatly advanced by the agricultural colleges set up under the Morrill Acts. The farmer, however, did not immediately benefit from the better technology because the increase in production caused prices to fall. Hence, the period from 1865 to 1900 saw the rise of many farm organizations designed to aid the plight of the farmer with his decreasing income. This, too, was the beginning of the period of organized labor in America. The Knights of Labor gave way to the American Federation of Labor and the union movement was well underway by 1900.

The character of the population changed at this time. Immigrants coming to the United States had previously been largely from northwestern Europe, especially England, Ireland, Germany, and Scandinavia. But the people who arrived after the Civil War came from other parts of Europe such as Spain, Russia, Austria, Hungary, and Italy. There were also a few from non-European nations such as Japan and Mexico. This meant that the immigrant population became radically different during this period of time, making the educational task considerably more difficult. Tremendous growth in communication and the transportation system, together with an increased centralization in American life, also had an effect on the educational needs of the people.

THE PUBLIC SCHOOL IDEAL

A major principle of education put into practice after the Civil War was that public education should be free to all. In contrast with the European dual system, where elementary education was for the lower classes and secondary reserved for the elite, the United States established a ladder system by which one might advance from the first grade through college in a series of yearly steps. In theory at least, each child was free to begin at the lowest level and progress as fast as his or her abilities would allow. It was an American belief that the schools could be used for advancement up the social ladder, and the person of ability could qualify for a high paying job by acquiring education. This was an age of social revolution in which the industrial and financial leaders accumulated great wealth as industrial and technological expansion increased. With the commercial production of petroleum starting in 1859, the opening of the West to farmers and ranchers, and the joining of the Union Pacific with the Central Pacific to make the first transcontinental railroad line in 1869, growth of wealth and commerce accelerated. While wealthy families seldom sent their children to public schools before 1900, class distinctions were foreign to the educational ideal. Laboring and middle-class families demanded high quality public schools for their sons and daughters. Training for making a good living was important, but so too was education for citizenship, morality, and self-improvement. Common elementary schools for all citizens were established in theory before the Civil War. They became a reality between 1865 and 1900 for the majority of Americans. The theory was extended upward to include secondary education before World War I. The standard American high school became a major part of the educational program and cultural experience of the nation.

THE AMERICAN PUBLIC HIGH SCHOOL

The academy reached its zenith of popularity by the middle of the nineteenth century and declined rapidly after that time. Growth of high schools was slow at first. In 1875 there were fewer than 25,000 students enrolled in public high schools. In the 1880s more students attended high schools than academies, and by 1890 some 2,500 high schools enrolled more than 200,000 students. By 1900 there were more than 6,000 high schools operating in the United States with over 500,000 students.

Kalamazoo Case.   While the age of the common school revival clearly established the principle of free, tax-supported elementary schools, considerable controversy continued over taxation for high schools. Public secondary schools in some states were financed from common school funds while others charged tuition. Since one major function of high schools was to prepare students for college, and they were not patronized by all children, some citizens felt the states had no right to tax the public for their support. Others, led by such spokesmen as California superintendent Ezra Carr, argued that high schools were an important part of the basic public educational system.

The best known case dealing with tax support for high schools came after the town of Kalamazoo, Michigan created a public secondary school in 1858. Three taxpayers brought suit to restrain the school board from collecting and using taxes to support the high school. In 1872, the case reached the Supreme Court of Michigan, which decided in favor of the school authorities. The opinion, written by Justice Cooley, held that high schools are common schools and they constitute a vital link between elementary schools and the state university. He pointed out that the absence of public secondary schools would discriminate in favor of the rich and prevent others from entering college. While other cases were tried, the Kalamazoo decision became a precedent which established the right of the several states to levy taxes for public high schools. This precedent contributed to the vast growth of high schools in the period before World War I.

Curriculum.   High schools offered both traditional and practical programs; but the emphasis was usually placed on the college preparatory curriculum. In spite of the fact that only about one tenth of the students in high schools in 1900 expected to enter college, the "classical" course was taken by a majority of youngsters. Latin and algebra were the subjects which had the highest enrollment. Sometimes the college course was divided so that a student could elect an English or a scientific major, but there was no free choice of subjects. Many schools had whole programs or courses such as "manual training" or "commercial," for the terminal student; many studied the "English" course even if they had no plans for higher education. A few high schools had specialized vocational courses and some offered preparation for teaching. Physical education, art, music, and religion were included in the subjects offered by many high schools at the end of the nineteenth century. There was very little standardization. Some high schools offered as a four-year course what others gave in one semester or one year.

Standardizing Associations and the NEA.   The United States had developed a large number of secondary schools. Many difficulties arose concerning the subjects of the curriculum, the length of time spent on each subject, and the quality of the instruction. Associations of standardization were created to deal with these issues. They also considered the preparation of teachers, the length of the school year, libraries, physical facilities, and graduation requirements. The New England Association of Colleges and Secondary Schools was founded in 1789. It was followed by the Middle Atlantic States Association (1892), the North Central Association (1894), the Association of College and Preparatory Schools of the Southern States (1895), and the Northwest Association of Secondary and Higher Schools in 1918. All of these organizations had the purpose of improving and making standard the offerings of various secondary schools and some colleges.

In 1857, forty-three leaders from state teacher's associations organized the National Teacher's Association in Philadelphia. This organization merged with the National Association of School Superintendents and the American Normal School Association to form the NEA in 1870. The National Education Association held an annual convention and published reports dealing with all aspects of education. Later, it became involved in defining the functions and standards for schools at all levels.

Committee of Ten.   Confusion over standards in secondary schools, curriculum issues, and the argument between "modernists" and "traditionalists" caused the National Education Association to take action in 1892. In that year the NEA appointed a Committee of Ten to examine the high school curriculum and to make recommendations about methods, standards, and programs. Commissioner W. T. Harris and Harvard president Charles W. Eliot were well-known members of the Committee. There were four other college presidents, two headmasters, one professor, and one high school administrator; but no high school teachers. College interests dominated in the Committee of Ten and the report was a bastion of educational conservatism.

One of the major weaknesses of the report of the Committee was that it based its findings on the psychology of mental discipline. The assumption was made that all subjects for general education had equal value for training the powers of the mind, such as expression, memory, reasoning, and observation. At a time when faculty psychology and mental discipline were already under attack, the Committee of Ten held that all its recommended subjects were of equal value for building sound mental habits in children. There were subcommittees on Latin, Greek, English, modern languages, mathematics, physical sciences, biological sciences, history, and geography. These subjects represented vested interests and were given support by the Committee, but vocational and commercial courses were largely ignored. In every case, the purpose of studying a subject was held to be mental discipline and exercise of the powers of the mind. It was also held that any recommended subject which was studied for one period each day, five days each week for a year was equal to any other recommended subject studied for the same length of time.

The Committee of Ten influenced the Committee on College Entrance Requirements (1895) and the subsequent work of the Carnegie Foundation for the Advancement of Teaching. The result was the establishment of the standard unit of credit for high school subjects (Carnegie unit), the support of traditional subjects and faculty psychology, and the limitation of any new or innovative high school programs. The Committee of Ten recommended intensive study of a few subjects for long periods of time in the high schools. It supported an eight-year elementary school followed by a four-year high school. No special subjects or methods were recommended for students who expected to terminate their formal education with high school graduation.

Accreditation.   The NEA Committee on College Entrance Requirements not only defined units of study in secondary schools but also recommended a set of constant or core subjects to be taken by all students. In 1902 the North Central Association set up a Committee on Unit Courses which required fifteen units for high school graduation. For college entrance the Committee recommended at least three units of English and two of mathematics. Those recommendations became standard requirements in accreditation for all high schools. A College Entrance Examination Board was also established.

Cardinal Principles.   In 1918 a Commission on the Reorganization of Secondary Education was appointed by the NEA. This Commission recognized the high schools as instruments for social integration and building values. It warned against specialized schools which would divide the population of students and supported the idea of a comprehensive secondary school offering a variety of subjects and courses.

While providing some theoretical basis for the later development of a truly comprehensive secondary school, the Commission is best known for issuing its seven Cardinal Principles of Secondary Education. These became standard objectives for teachers, school boards, and administrators. They were:

1. health
2. command of fundamental processes
3. worthy home membership
4. vocation
5. citizenship
6. worthy use of leisure time
7. ethical character.

Obviously, these principles could serve as a guide for curriculum and methodology, but they did not fill the need for a carefully articulated educational philosophy. The meaning of each principle may be interpreted in a variety of ways.

Rapid growth of high schools continued even though most of those before 1920 were noncomprehensive and strictly college preparatory in curriculum. By 1900 the public high schools were almost all coeducational and more than half of the students were girls. In the early decades of the twentieth century, high schools doubled in enrollment every ten years, until they became common schools in fact as well as name.

Reorganization.   Public high schools retained the same general characteristics and organizational structure well into the twentieth century. In addition to a principal and his staff, the schools usually had departmental divisions with a chairman or "head" for each major program area or department.

Charles W. Eliot was an enthusiastic supporter of electives both in colleges and in high schools. He was one of the first to suggest a new school organization in order to provide more choice for high school students. Basically, Eliot wanted to extend the high school courses downward into elementary education. G. Stanley Hall, author of the first book on adolescents and no friend of Eliot's proposal, felt that reorganization was necessary to meet the needs of older elementary pupils who were no longer children. Others believed that the elementary and high schools did not provide a smooth transition from childhood to young adult life. It was felt that the opportunity for advanced elementary education of a general sort as well as some industrial and commercial training should be provided outside the senior high school. The Committee on College Entrance Requirements had recommended the division of elementary and secondary schools into six-year blocks, and the Committee of Ten had considered reorganization of some type.

As a result of these and other suggestions, junior high schools were created in Columbus, Ohio and Berkeley, California in 1909. Other cities soon followed, and the junior high school became a common institution in the United States after 1930. Typically, the elementary school was reduced to six years with junior and senior high schools requiring six years together. This 6-3-3 plan was not always used; some schools retained a four-year high school and used a 6-2-4 system. Reorganization is still in process today with many schools experimenting with a 4-4-4 or other "middle school" plans. The junior high school stressed socialization, guidance, individual differences, and survey or exploratory courses of a general nature.

VOCATIONAL AND INDUSTRIAL EDUCATION

The history of vocational education spans a long period of time in America. Apprenticeship was first used for vocational training when literary and religious education was the only prerogative of the school, but by 1820 a few mechanics' institutes for technical instruction were found in eastern cities. Worchester Polytechnic Institute was opened in 1868, and there were some manual labor schools built along lines suggested by the European educators Pestalozzi and Fellenberg. Manual training demonstrations were given in Philadelphia in 1876. Some cities had manual and vocational courses in high schools by 1890.

Shop work of various kinds replaced manual training in many high schools, but some secondary schools were designated as manual training high schools with no college preparatory courses. The vocational value of shop work was considered part of general education and special trade training was avoided in favor of mechanical principles. Students learned general skills on the transfer-of-training theory rather than how to make specific articles. The need for skilled workmen and the desire for high school education for those not bound for college caused the manual training movement to gain speed after 1880. Columbia University began training teachers for manual training classes and an industrial education association was organized in 1884.

Gradually the movement for training teachers of manual arts spread through the universities. Some labor leaders feared that industrial education would develop a surplus of cheap trained labor; but labor generally approved industrial and vocational education. Manufacturers were also generally in support of this movement; but the opposition from traditional educators with classical backgrounds was more difficult to overcome.

Smith-Hughes Act.   The vocational school movement continued to grow from 1907 to 1917, receiving its greatest boost in the latter year when the federal Smith-Hughes Act was passed. This law provided federal aid for the states by paying vocational teachers' salaries in the high schools and aiding teacher training institutions in the education of such teachers. The states were required to match the federal grant on a dollar-for-dollar basis. In an effort to provide aid for the child trying to make a choice between vocational subjects, the Vocation Bureau and Breadwinner's Institute was established in 1909. Vocational and manual training also received support from new experiments and theories in education. John Dewey attracted attention by insisting that children learn through activities. His book *School and Society* made this point in 1899. New interest in psychology led to the beginning of professional guidance for students in industrial and vocational schools. Guidance developed slowly, but the first counseling services were offered in the vocational high schools.

Demand for practical vocational skills and scientific information was especially great among the farmers of the nation. Farmers' institutes started in 1854 and led to an interest in agricultural education on both the high school and the college levels. Colleges which resulted from the Morrill Acts of 1862 and 1890 gave college status to agriculture and the mechanical arts. Demonstration farms, agricultural experiment stations, and training for improvement of agricultural techniques were provided by these colleges and by the Department of Agriculture which was established in 1862. The Hatch Act of 1887 provided federal funds for agricultural experiments. In 1914 Congress passed the Smith-Lever Act which created agricultural extension programs for farmers and led to vocational agriculture courses and 4-H clubs. Many high school students took advantage of vocational work offered because of federal funding, but often vocational agriculture was the only practical course offered in rural secondary schools. There was no attempt to offer general federal aid to public schools until after World War II.

PAROCHIAL AND PRIVATE EDUCATION

It is difficult to get exact figures on school enrollments before 1900 because neither schools nor reporting techniques were standardized. Public and private sectarian schools were often reported together as late as 1870. While the states of the West and South were behind those of the North and East in percentages of children enrolled in public schools, it is clear that very rapid growth took place between 1860 and 1900. In the latter year, about ninety percent of the American secondary school students attended public high schools.

Catholic doctrine has always insisted that the state should have only a secondary role in education while the parents and the Church have primary responsibility. Catholic schools existed in such areas as New Mexico, California, and Louisiana early in American history, but intolerance and discrimination prevented rapid growth on the eastern seaboard. In colonial America only Pennsylvania allowed Catholics to conduct schools. The appointment of Father John Carroll as "Superior of Missions in the United States" and guarantee of religious freedom in the Bill of Rights provided a foundation for Catholic education in America. With the large influx of Irish

Catholics during the first half of the nineteenth century, interest in parochial schools increased. By 1840 Catholics had created seventy-five elementary parochial schools, twenty-five high schools, and six colleges. Many Catholic children obviously attended public schools, but there was great controversy over Protestant creeds and the use of the King James version of the Bible in public schools. Catholic children were often punished if they objected to non-Catholic religious practices. In 1854 the Maine Supreme Court rejected a Catholic plea to exclude the Bible from the public school curriculum, although the Ohio Supreme Court upheld a similar Catholic plea in 1872.

The Third Plenary Council of Baltimore in 1884 required all parishes to provide schools for Catholic youngsters. As a result, Catholic parochial schools increased in number to about 3,000 in 1884. Secondary Catholic schools were developed through Jesuit leadership partly in an effort to train boys for the priesthood. Parish high schools were largely an extension of the parochial school. They emphasized Latin, literature, grammar, and religion. Few if any vocational courses were offered. By 1910, there were more than 300 Catholic high schools in operation in the United States.

The largest number of non-Catholic parochial schools were founded by the Lutheran Church. There were also schools created by Quakers, Jews, and other religious groups. Much smaller in numbers than the Catholic schools, these sectarian efforts nevertheless provided alternative educational opportunities for students in many parts of the nation.

Oregon Case.   Bitter public reaction against parochial schools has existed in the United States for many years. Discrimination has been expressed in many ways, but direct efforts have been made to outlaw parochial schools. The most famous case occurred in the state of Oregon in 1925 and has remained unchallenged. The Oregon legislature passed a law which required all children to attend public schools until they reached sixteen years of age. The Society of Sisters of the Holy Names of Jesus and Mary and the Hill Academy brought suit against Governor Pierce in an effort to keep their schools. While the Oregon Supreme Court upheld the state law, the Supreme Court of the United States declared the action unconstitutional. It held that the state has a right to inspect and regulate private and parochial schools, but that the state does not have a monopoly on education.

In addition to religious schools, a number of private schools and academies continued to operate. These were sometimes military schools or elite "college prep" institutions for wealthy children. Military academies declined after the second world war but other kinds of private schools grew rapidly in number.

HIGHER EDUCATION

Colleges and Universities.   Higher education had a steady growth during this period and as a result of the Morrill Act of 1862, almost every state created a land-grant college. Industry and scientific agriculture were emphasized by these institutions, but they were by no means confined to such subjects. The land-grant schools grew slowly at first because they lacked the prestige of liberal arts colleges. However, they had the support of science and they were powerful as a democratizing influence. Nine of these colleges developed into state universities and many added colleges of engineering, home economics, and education. The Second Morrill Act of 1890 made fifteen thousand dollars annually available to each of the original institutions, which caused vast expansion. By 1918, many state universities became major institutions of higher education. Efforts to develop private colleges met with limited success. A high percentage of the sectarian colleges founded before the Civil War closed by World War I, but others were created. Some degree-granting colleges were really only secondary schools, although there were high quality denominational colleges as well as good secular universities.

New University Model.   The most significant development in higher education during this period was the establishment of graduate programs based on the German example. Early supporters of this idea included Henry P. Tappan (later president of the University of Michigan) and Louis Agassiz who developed science programs at Harvard. It was not, however, until Johns Hopkins University opened in 1876 that a real scientific research university existed in America.

Johns Hopkins was a wealthy Baltimore businessman who provided a large endowment for a university which would include a medical school and hospital. Much of the credit for the success of Johns Hopkins University goes to its first president, Daniel Coit Gilman (1831-1908). Gilman was a Yale graduate who became president of the University of California before being selected for Johns Hopkins. He was a keen administrator and a careful judge of talent. Gilman selected professors who had not yet reached national status;

but who had demonstrated their potential ability. The new institution had a graduate school aimed at creating new knowledge and supporting scientific investigation rather than merely transferring information and skills. It required graduate students to do research as a regular part of their program and provided the necessary laboratory equipment and other support. Inquiry, observation, freedom to seek truth without institutional restrictions, and high quality scholarship became standard at Johns Hopkins. The idea that faculty members should do research and publish the results of their work also found favor there.

Professional Schools.   Johns Hopkins was the first American university to have a medical college with full-time professors. In the post-Civil War period professional schools rapidly replaced the private practices of "reading law," apprentice doctors, and self-education for ministers. In 1899 there were 532 reported professional schools operating in the nation, about half of which were departments in colleges and universities. The practice at Johns Hopkins of requiring college graduation for admission to the medical school was rare, and numerous professional programs were offered for short periods of time. Low standards due to a lack of state supervision were common until after 1900 when regulations began to increase. The growth of graduate schools had a major effect on professional schools because of the training they offered to college and professional school teachers. Graduate departments and professional schools began to differentiate between universities and liberal arts colleges, even when such colleges referred to themselves as universities.

Curriculum Changes.   Traditions in education are very strong so that change normally meets with great resistance. College faculties have always been very conservative with regard to altering the curriculum. Nevertheless, colleges did begin to expand their offerings in the period under consideration, in spite of great faculty reluctance. Science and research made the addition of many courses necessary, although most colleges merely added the new programs without altering or eliminating the old. Agriculture, mechanical arts, and military science gained a foothold in higher education because of the Morrill Acts. The sixty-five colleges and universities established under these acts by 1900 obviously had a profound effect on the curriculum. Massachusetts Institute of Technology began instruction in 1865 with theoretical support for scientific and practical subjects provided by Herbert Spencer and T.H. Huxley. Darwin's

Origin of Species (1859) caused a great deal of interest in the intellectual world, and evolution was soon discussed by such scholars as John Fiske at Harvard. The tycoons of the "gilded age" gave substantial gifts to higher education and in return their influence was felt on the programs. Practical, utilitarian, and business courses often had the support of philanthropists, together with conservative views of social change and classical economics.

Before the Civil War it was unusual to allow students free selection of courses or programs in colleges. Although Ticknor had experimented with electives, the real development of the college elective system came when Charles W. Eliot was president of Harvard. By 1894, Harvard required only French or German, English composition, and some work in physics and chemistry; all other courses could be selected by the students. Educational conservatives bitterly opposed the elective system, but leading universities soon adopted it to some degree, although a core of "disciplinary" courses was often required. The major effect of the elective system was to break the hold classics had on higher education and to allow the introduction of popular modern subjects such as history, sociology, psychology, economics, and the sciences. Breadth of the curriculum and the freedom to examine various theories or ideas became part of the university ideal.

While coeducational colleges existed before the Civil War (Oberlin 1833, Antioch 1852, and Iowa 1856) the major development came between 1860 and 1920. By 1880 about half of the colleges and universities admitted women. Vassar, Smith, Wellesley, and Bryn Mawr were women's colleges which offered programs equivalent to colleges for men. Affiliated or "coordinate" colleges for women also were established, such as Radcliffe at Harvard. A wide curriculum was offered for women, but teaching was still the only career generally open to females in 1918.

SCHOOLS AND COLLEGES FOR MINORITY GROUPS

The adoption of the Fourteenth Amendment in 1868 gave Black Americans citizenship, but few opportunities for higher education existed then. In 1826 the first college degree granted to a Black went to John Russwurm; only twenty-eight Black college graduates were recorded before the Civil War. Northern colleges open to Blacks after 1860 found many ill prepared for college work because of the inadequate segregated public schools from which they came. Progress is shown, however, in the increase in literacy from ten percent in 1866 to over ninety percent in 1936. According to Edward Knight, 132 Blacks received Ph.D. degrees in this same time period.

Black schools and colleges in the South developed through the efforts of educators like Booker T. Washington. Hampton Institute for Negro higher education had been established in Virginia in 1870 under the sponsorship of the American Missionary Association. Washington became a student there arriving on foot and with only fifty cents to his name. When Washington graduated in 1875, he was recommended by principal Samuel C. Armstrong as a teacher for a proposed Black normal school at Tuskegee, Alabama. Under Washington, Tuskegee Normal and Industrial Institute became a model of Black education and its director a national figure. Washington received an honorary degree from Harvard University and became the recognized leader of Black education. Realizing the attitudes of White Americans in the South, Washington agreed to a subservient role for Blacks in return for practical and vocational education. His Atlanta compromise speech is a classic political concession. At Tuskegee, Washington stressed hard work, vocational skills, and economic advancement. He won wide support among Whites in the South and although his Institute became a model for Black colleges, his willingness to accept social discrimination may have retarded the advancement of his race. Washington always avoided the demand for social and political equality made by W.E.B. DuBois and his followers.

Minority education outside the South grew slowly but steadily during the period between the Civil War and the First World War. A few liberal colleges like Antioch admitted Blacks early; but discrimination was practiced in most areas of the nation. Numerous Black A. and M. colleges were established with funds from the Second Morrill Act, and these colleges often included programs for teachers. Federal money was badly needed and the Black Agricultural, Military, and Normal schools soon became as important as Tuskegee and various church–related Black colleges. These colleges admitted Indians, Orientals, and other minority students. Numerous northern state universities were open to minorities, but the number actually admitted was small, due in part to entrance requirements which screened out graduates from the poor public schools. Public school segregation was maintained either legally or *de facto* almost everywhere.

Indian Schools.   Most of the formal education provided for native Americans was through philanthropy or missionary efforts, until the Office of Indian Affairs was opened in 1819. Thereafter, schools of various kinds were supported by government grants, although religious organizations continued to operate the majority of mission schools for Indians. A number of Indian scholars attended Hampton Institute, and in 1879 an Indian training school was authorized for Carlisle, Pennsylvania. Except for boarding schools on Indian reservations and a few specific programs aimed at training for vocations, very little was done by federal or local government to meet the needs of education for Indians.

TEACHER EDUCATION

While colonial teachers were sometimes college graduates, there was nothing available to them which might be called professional training. Academies and female seminaries in the early national period often advertised pedagogical programs which consisted of a review of basic elementary subjects and some lectures on keeping school. It was long considered adequate for secondary teachers to have a sound knowledge of their subject field without also receiving training in psychology or methods of teaching.

The first normal schools were academically low level institutions — a problem that continued to exist until they were made into four-year colleges in the twentieth century. Early normal schools usually had some sort of practice teaching and a course in mental philosophy, but there was no sound theoretical foundation. Some private normal schools and academies for teachers offered programs with higher academic standards, but they also lacked a professional basis. Nevertheless, the growth of teacher education was rapid in the latter part of the nineteenth century. One hundred fourteen schools for teachers replied to an inquiry about programs and enrollments made by the United States Bureau of Education in 1871. At least 70 normal schools were receiving some state support in 1875. By 1900 there were 345 normal schools reported in the United States. Women outnumbered men in the state normal schools, while the sexes were about evenly divided in private schools for teachers. A great many students in normal schools already held teaching certificates and most had some teaching experience before entering the program. Large numbers of teachers attended normal schools for short periods, but only about one third of the public school teachers were normal school graduates. Many normal school programs were offered for two years or less and usually were on the secondary school level. Most had meager equipment, insufficient support, poor facilities, and an underpaid staff.

Before World War I, however, these institutions began enlarging their curricula and requiring high school graduation for admission. Some, like Illinois State Normal, were able to erect expensive modern buildings and to develop college level courses. Both the numbers of and quality of normal schools improved very rapidly in the last decades of the nineteenth century and the first decades of the twentieth. Nevertheless, fewer than half of the trained teachers needed to staff public schools at all levels were provided by normal schools, high school normal departments, academies, or college departments. District schools continued to be taught by underpaid young women with little or no education beyond elementary school and perhaps a summer institute.

Sheldon and the Oswego Movement.   A much better conceptual framework for the professional training of teachers was provided by Edward Austin Sheldon. Sheldon became secretary of the Board of Education of Oswego, New York in 1853. He visited a number of cities in order to find ways of improving the schools, and in 1859 in Toronto, Sheldon came across a Pestalozzian program produced by the Home and Colonial Training Institution of London. Instruction there was based on charts, pictures, manuals, and objects developed by Charles and Elizabeth Mayo, who had been teachers in schools conducted by Pestalozzi.

Having purchased three hundred dollars' worth of materials and secured the services of Margaret E. M. Jones to demonstrate them, Sheldon proceeded to reform the Oswego schools along lines developed by Pestalozzi. The success was impressive and in 1866 the New York legislature made Oswego a state normal school. Teachers flocked to the new program and Oswego soon became the most famous teacher-training institution in the United States. Graduates of the school found positions in various parts of the nation, so that the Oswego movement had influence far beyond New York.

Some of the improvement attributed to the Oswego movement came from the enthusiasm of Sheldon himself; but new techniques of learning and respect for the unique personality of the child were also important. Object teaching began with something familiar to the environment of the child and moved to an abstract description of the object. Geography was taught from the local community outward, until the whole nation and the world could be understood. Child study and discipline through mutual understanding and respect were also stressed. Unfortunately, the term "object lesson" was also used by textbook companies who merely wanted to sell books, and some other normal schools made highly formalized lesson plans out of what the Oswego movement had intended to be flexible. Nevertheless, Oswego provided a new model of teacher education which included new principles, better psychology, creative methods, and an effort to understand how children learn.

University Departments of Education.   For many years pedagogy and teacher training were excluded from universities. Faculty members in the academic disciplines held all professional education in low esteem and many had only contempt for teacher training programs. For example, President Barnard of Columbia was turned down by the trustees when he proposed a department of education in 1882. Instead, he assigned Nicholas Murray Butler to offer Saturday lectures for teachers. The interest was so great that over 2,000 teachers applied for Butler's lectures; but the trustees again refused to authorize a department of education or even a senior elective in pedagogy. Finally, Butler organized the New York College for the Training of Teachers. In 1892, that college was accepted as an affiliate of Columbia University under strong opposition.

Teacher education at the college level began at Washington College in Pennsylvania in 1831 and at New York University in 1832. The University of Iowa had a chair for didactics (education) in 1873. By 1900 professors of pedagogy were to be found in many universities; although sometimes only one man constituted the whole department. Graduate work in education was offered by New York University in 1887. Starting about 1890 teacher training institutions tended to become degree-granting colleges which required secondary school graduation for admission. The scientific study of education and psychology came to be linked with certification. A body of educational theory slowly developed out of work done in education at universities and graduate schools.

DEVELOPMENT OF EDUCATIONAL PHILOSOPHY

American educational theory had been dominated by theology and philosophical idealism before 1900. Contributions to pragmatism were made by William James, Charles Peirce, and John Dewey before World War I but their influence was much greater during the progressive era of the 1930s than in the first decades of the twentieth century. It was so difficult even to provide the rudiments of education to the whole population that little effort was made to define educational goals, to equate theory with psychological principles, or to work out the logical consistency of educational positions. Once schools were established, a host of new educational demands were made, and many began to debate the proper role of education. The early influence of Rousseau, Pestalozzi, Froebel, and other European philosophers continued to be felt, but American educational theory also began to develop.

Harris.   William T. Harris, who developed a public kindergarten in 1873 as part of the school system in St. Louis, Missouri, was superintendent of schools there from 1867 to 1880 and United States Commissioner of Education from 1889 to 1906. He was one of the best known school administrators in America and his ideas had wide influence throughout the nation. Harris was philosophically an idealist, a follower of the German philosopher Hegel, and a traditionalist in education. He believed education should emphasize the cultural subjects and prepare children for harmony with the absolute order of the universe as well as for life in an industrial nation. He accepted some of the methods of Pestalozzi, but was basically opposed to the manual training movement, science, and materialism. As commissioner, a member of the major committees of the NEA, and a leader in the National Herbart Society, his influence was very great. Harris was the great spokesman for the idealistic-traditional theory of education.

Parker.   Quite a different educational position was taken by Francis W. Parker, who was principal of schools in Carrollton, Illinois, before the Civil War. His school career was interrupted by the conflict, in which he served as a colonel in the Union forces. Parker studied in Germany where he became familiar with the practices of Pestalozzi and Froebel. He returned to America to become superintendent of schools in Quincy, Massachusetts, and later was head of the Cook County Normal School in Chicago. Parker was a democratic individualist with a practical outlook. He followed Pestalozzi closely with regard to respect for the creative activity of the child. Parker experimented with many kinds of school programs, including the core curriculum which attempted to relate subjects of the curriculum through such interrelated studies as history and geography. Parker provided the background for the work of John Dewey and the progressives.

The total impact of Pestalozzi and Froebel was relatively light although kindergartens did develop and university scholars began to study the child as an individual. Public education changed very little before the American Herbartian movement started around 1890.

Herbart.   Johann F. Herbart was responsible for a much greater revolution in American education than any previous European thinker had been. Herbart held that the aim of education was attainment of good moral character; which could be acquired only through the process of analyzing the social interests of man to discover ideals appropriate for education. The first step in character realization was the "many sidedness of interest." Although he used the word interest, Herbart was really referring to a stimulus to learning. He once said that the person who lays hold of information, and because of that information reaches out for more, takes "interest" in it. In the study of history and literature, Herbart saw a core for the curriculum which could encompass or could be co-related with all other subjects. His principles of co-relation and concentration, by which he meant relation with emphasis at the core, became central to his doctrine. Despite Herbart's insistence on the social and moral aims of education, he took an intellectual approach to the learning process. He also developed a psychology which is still of some value today.

Herbart was an associationist; that is, he believed that we have to account for every new idea on the basis of ideas already in the mind, and hence we must consciously relate or associate new ideas with previous experiences. For Herbart there could never be a totally new idea. He believed that we receive impressions to the conscious mind (presentation). These presentations are then associated with other ideas which lie together in masses in the subconscious part of the mind. When a new idea in the mind is related, it is transferred from the conscious to the subconscious mind and becomes part of an "apperceptive mass." The idea will not appear in the conscious mind again until it is needed to clarify some new presentation. Herbart's own psychology was not rigid, and his insistence upon the mind as a unity tended to break down the older faculty psychology, which understood the mind to be divided into separate faculties or powers.

American Herbartianism.   Herbart's followers in America used his insistence upon association and interests to develop a very rigid educational program. This program came to be known as the Five Formal Steps of Teaching and Learning. They were: (1) preparation, in which old ideas useful in learning new materials are called to the learner's mind; (2) presentation, or the actual giving of the new material; (3) association, in which new material is compared with and related to the old; (4) generalization, in which rules, definitions, or general principles are drawn from specific cases; and (5) application, in which general principles are given meaning by reference to specific examples and practical situations.

These Herbartian steps were made popular by Charles De Garmo, Charles McMurry, and Frank McMurry, who were among the early leaders of the American Herbartian Association. It must be remembered that during the late 1800s most teachers were largely without training and there was no rational philosophy of education. The formal steps of the American Herbartianists filled a void in educational theory and hence the influence of Herbart through his American followers became dominant in this country in the 1890s. Unfortunately, the set methods of the followers of Herbart led to a "lock-step" in American education; the same subjects were taught in the same way using the same methods and the same textbooks in every public school from Boston to Berkeley. The beneficial part of this uniformity was that it became possible for children to transfer from one school to another without a change in curriculum or loss of time; but the respect for individuality, new ideas, and creativity, which had been so much in the theories of Froebel and Pestalozzi, were largely lost.

Protest against Rigid Systems.   One of the first to raise a cry against the rigid *lock-step school* was John Dewey. His influence was first felt in the closing years of the nineteenth century and his importance increased considerably during the first three decades of the twentieth century. Dewey continued to write until the 1950s but his greatest amount of influence on education came in the 1930s when the Progressive Education Association was at the height of its popularity. Dewey felt that Herbart and his followers had emphasized formal methods to the extreme, and that they failed to account for natural growth and individual differences. He attacked schools for being antidemocratic and the curriculum for being subject-centered. For Dewey, education must be part of life itself.

Other developments also contributed to the changing climate of opinion out of which new educational theories were developed. In 1859, Charles Darwin published his *Origin of Species,* a book which set off the explosive theory of evolution. Scientific evolution and social Darwinism were theories that challenged the conceptions of man and the universe held by conservative educators. Evolutionary principles contributed to the formation of the philosophy of pragmatism by Charles Peirce and William James. Pragmatism emphasized the practical questions of how we can understand and control the world instead of the metaphysical question of how we can know reality. John Dewey popularized pragmatism and made it the philosophy of his educational reform. Herbert Spencer and others applied the theory of evolution to society in order to explain the existence of social classes and social institutions. Resulting studies in sociology altered traditional conceptions of humanity and opened new windows through which to view education. Evolutionary science became part of the curriculum in universities, but it created an issue in public schools where it was often banned. The conflict of religion and science culminated in the Scopes trial over the teaching of evolution in Dayton, Tennessee, in 1925.

Schools continued to grow in number before World War I. Children tended to remain in school longer, teachers received more training, and education became a subject for university study. New scientific subjects were added to the high schools, and public high schools became the standard American secondary schools. Child study and psychology led to new concepts of method and new interest in the individual child.

THEN TO NOW

Events leading up to the American Civil War and the conflict itself bear a strong relationship to numerous conditions in the modern era. Extremely bitter sectional and ideological arguments not only caused the Civil War but also altered the attitudes of people for generations. Although the union survived, negative feelings about Civil War issues continued to dominate political life well into the twentieth century. Social and educational problems created by the freeing of slaves plagued the nation while the burden carried by the impoverished South caused a very low level of public schooling for both races. No struggle divided and alienated the American people like the Civil War until the outbreak of the conflict in Viet Nam.

American involvement in Southeast Asia during the 1960s and 1970s caused caustic criticism of national policy, especially on university campuses. Like the Civil War, Viet Nam raised ugly moral issues, created an erosion of patriotism, and shook the very foundations of the national culture. Just as the Civil War closed schools, promoted illiteracy in most of the South, and led to a system of schools segregated by race, Viet Nam also created a major educational crisis. It caused violence in colleges, alienation of students from the values of their parents, and the withdrawal of financial support to educational institutions. While the two world wars and the Korea action had significant educational influences, only the Civil War and the conflict in Viet Nam caused fundamental rifts in the very core of American culture. It is easy to trace the modern issues over desegregation of schools to the Civil War period but the whole impact of the Viet Nam era on education and the American culture may not be known for generations to come.

Intellectual and cultural historians argue that life conditions have major effects on the attitudes, values and beliefs of all people. We need to identify the most significant forces that shape values and concepts about the good life for each generation.

Those who grew up in the 1920s held establishment values. They were influenced by World War I, prohibition, and the Model T Ford. Young people were interested in gin and jazz but close family ties and patriotism dominated the nation. Education remained conservative although the Scopes trial, over the teaching of evolution in high schools, created a major issue. By the 1930s the economic crash had taken place and the nation was in the Great Depression. There was mass unemployment, soup lines, and social unrest. Radical economic solutions including socialism were suggested and Franklin Roosevelt became popular with his New Deal. Great emphasis was placed on the value of the dollar and those who grew up in the 1930s are still very security minded. This was the age of progressive education and radical school reform.

At the beginning of the 1940s, the dominant interest was keeping America safe from the Germans and the Japanese. World War II touched every family while patriotism permeated the culture. This was an age of working women, geographic mobility, rationing, and support for the armed forces. People became used to the idea of scarcity and waited for better times when peace would be restored. Education turned back to the basics and the G.I. Bill increased enrollment in colleges. When the war ended, Americans bought all of the things they could not have in a wartime economy. Fifty million TV sets were sold in America and children began growing up with Big Bird. Crew cuts gave way to longer hair, children were materialistically indulged, and the rock and roll age was personified by Elvis Presley. School desegregation began in the 1950s and Martin Luther King gained a great following. The Korean conflict was considered a great tragedy but it did not draw the patriotic support common in the second world war. People growing up at this time were influenced by hedonism, materialism, affluence, and the mass media.

The 1960s saw rapid economic growth, the space program, computers, and Viet Nam. Alternative life styles were manifest in the hippie sub-culture while campus rebellion shocked conservative Americans. Those who grew up in this period recall the bitterness over the Viet Nam war and the conflict between generations. It was an age of assassination but also of continued financial growth and affluence. Education focused on school integration, equal opportunity, and the needs of the culturally different child. By the end of the decede, deep-rooted value conflicts had divided Americans to a degree quite similar to the era of the Civil War.

By 1970, inflation and a weaker economy were evident. Many people began to fear a return of the conditions of the Great Depression of the 1930s. Some twenty million mothers entered the work force in order to improve family income. The energy crisis was taken seriously and there were concerns about environmental deterioration. Richard Nixon and Watergate caused the erosion of respect for government, while the people began to distrust motives of oil companies and other industrial corporations. Music, the mass media, fast foods, and automobiles were major interests of the young. Drug abuse and alcoholism became widespread among students. Educators concentrated on computer-assisted instruction, a relevant curriculum, and compensatory education for the culturally deprived.

History shows that following wars and periods of social conflict there is often a conservative reaction. The beginning of the 1980s indicated such a movement in all aspects of American society. There was a demand for an end to social reconstruction through legislation, relaxation of regulations on industry, and opposition to spending for welfare. Education moved back to basics with major interest focused on tests of accountability and training for jobs. Declining economic strength, continued inflation, competition for jobs, scarcity of energy and natural resources, and concern about world peace were major interests. Meanwhile, rapid advances in technological invention and especially in communications continue to alter the environment and to create new life conditions.

There is a strong tendency in America for each new generation to reject the ideas and the values of the generation just past. John Dewey and the progressives rebelled against the lock-step schools and the rigid systems of the followers of Herbart. The counter culture did not accept the materialism and the need of security so characteristic of the depression era and the period of affluence following World War II.

Such beliefs were scorned in turn by the youth of the 1970s and early 1980s. It is also probably true that change in basic value orientation takes place more rapidly in an age of accelerating economic and technological invention than in a more stable environment. If this is the case, present conservative trends in American culture cannot be expected to continue for very many years.

The Civil War was a time of social and ethical conflict. When it ended, not only had the old South disappeared but the whole of American society was altered. The Black revolution and the demand for civil rights evolved slowly from the Civil War to the 1950s but certainly they began in the aftermath of that conflict. Likewise, the whole of American society was changed by the turmoil of the Viet Nam era. Changes of this magnitude necessarily have an impact on education and the socialization of the next generation. Periods of revolutionary conflict and social change may be followed by conservative reactions but the culture is never restored to what it was before the conflict. Rapid, though uneven transformation of American society has been evident since the 1860s. American values and the culture of the people can never again be what they were in the ante bellum South or the period before the Viet Nam conflict.

BIBLIOGRAPHY

Beale, Howard. *A History of Freedom of Teaching in American Schools.* New York: Farrar, Straus; Octagon Books, 1974.

Butts, Freeman. *The Education of the West: A Formative Chapter in the History of Civilization.* New York: McGraw-Hill, 1973.

Cubberley, Ellwood. *Readings in Public Education in the United States.* Boston: Houghton Mifflin, 1934.

Kandel, Isaac. *History of Secondary Education.* Boston: Houghton Mifflin, 1930.

Mayer, Frederick. *A History of Educational Thought.* 3rd ed. Columbus, Ohio: Charles Merrill, 1974.

Nassaw, David. *Schooled to Order.* New York: Oxford University Press, 1979.

Sheldon, Edward. *Autobiography.* New York: Ives-Butler, 1911.

Silver, Harold, ed. *Robert Owen on Education.* Cambridge, Mass: Harvard University Press, 1969.

Washington, Booker T. *Up From Slavery: An Autobiography.* New York: Doubleday, 1938.

Vaughn, Preston. *Schools for All: The Blacks and Public Education in the South, 1865–1877.* Lexington. Ky.: University of Kentucky Press, 1974.

Warren, Donald. *To Enforce Education: A History of the Founding Years of the United States Office of Education.* Detroit: Wayne State University Press, 1974.

Westerhoff, John. *McGuffey and His Readers: Piety, Morality, and Education in Nineteenth Century America.* Nashville: Abingdon Press, 1978.

Developments in Modern American Education 1918—Present

6

Several volumes could be written on the subject of educational expansion, change, and controversy since the First World War. The most obvious feature has been the tremendous growth in the numbers of students, teachers, and facilities at all levels. Secondary education grew during this period until it became standard for almost all children, just as the elementary school had done in the previous century. Higher education expanded, especially in the years following the Second World War, so that some kind of college or university experience was enjoyed by more than two-thirds of all American high school graduates. Many modern cities in the United States now contain more individuals engaged in formal schooling than could have been found in the entire colonial area at any one time. Sophisticated training offered by industry, early childhood education (both public and private), the federal government, and the mass media are illustrative of agencies and techniques now active in education which were not so significant in earlier times. Education is now big business in terms of money spent, teachers trained, physical plants utilized, materials developed, and students served.

This magnification of the educational enterprise raised new issues concerning the relationship of the school and the society. Advances in technology, the fluid social order, economic depressions, recessions

(World War I	Great Depression	World War II)
1919 Progressive Education Association	1932 New Deal Educational Programs	1941 Military Training for National Defense
1925 Oregon Case Guaranteed Right of Private Schools	1930–38 Eight Year Study Confirmed Value of Progressive Schools	1944 G.I. Bill for College Tuition 1945 UNESCO
1930 School Year Became 172 Days and All States Had Compulsory Attendance		

and recovery, wars both hot and cold, and conflict over the meaning of democracy led to demands for a re-evaluation of educational aims.

MAJOR EDUCATIONAL CHANGES

Integration of all Americans into a national community was a goal of such early leaders as Mann and Barnard. Schools were viewed as social ladders for individual and group improvement and as the means for Americanizing immigrants. Since World War II, the civil rights movement, and the Black revolution, much more attention has been given to the educational problems of children from various social, economic, religious, ethnic, and racial backgrounds. Desegregation, helping the culturally disadvantaged, and meeting social needs in urban centers have become major goals of American education. Schools have made great strides, but large numbers of children are still excluded from equal educational opportunity, and national unity through social integration has not been realized. Much current educational theory centers upon the role of the school in solving major problems of the culture and upon the kind of education which will be required to prepare the young for meeting the challenges of an uncertain future.

Among the more significant changes in education during the last half century were the following: (a) a broader educational philosophy with social as well as individual objectives, illustrated by progressive education and the social reconstruction movements; (b) a new psychology and more sophisticated learning theories,

1954	1964	1975
Brown v. Board of	Economic Opportunity	Public Law 94–142
Education in Topeka	Act	Provided Education for
		the Handicapped
1957	**1965**	
Sputnik	Elementary and Secondary	**1976**
	Education Act	Education Appropriations
1958		Act
NDEA	Higher Education Act	
	Rebellion on College	**1980**
	Campuses	Establishment of a
		Separate U.S. Office
	1967	of Education
	Bilingual Education Act	

which led to new teaching methods and curricula based on the needs of children and society; (c) new areas of educational concern such as vocational guidance, scientific testing, and special education for the handicapped and the gifted; (d) reorganization of schools to include junior high schools, junior colleges, night schools, correspondence courses and the like, as well as an explosion of graduate education; (e) new emphasis on health, welfare, improved buildings and equipment, and the relationship between schools and the culture; (f) enormous increase in attendance at all levels and an extension of the years of formal schooling for the average student; (g) an extension and improvement of teacher training and the scientific study of education; and (h) the impact of cultural changes such as the mass media of communications, research conducted by private organizations, and the increased role of the federal government in educational affairs. Perhaps the most difficult problem for educators in the United States today is now to provide varied, realistic, general, and individual education for all children and produce the experts necessary for an industrial democracy at the same time. Can we really be equal and excellent too?

Social, Political, Economic Influence. Many of these changes, and others less dramatic, began in the nineteenth century and were developed in recent decades; but there were also innovations which came about as a result of economic and social changes during the two world wars. Older concerns with physical expansion gave way to new problems of technological discovery and scientific development. Reforms in government pursued legal measures to prevent the waste and exploitation of dwindling natural resources. Contact with the sophisticated culture of Europe during World War I and the economic crisis which followed the conflict altered many of America's basic conceptions. Woodrow Wilson's failure to persuade America to join the League of Nations, and the isolationism, fatalism, and inflation of the post-war era did not destroy European influences.

However, the decade-long depression which started in 1929 shook American optimism and altered the role of government in economic affairs. When Franklin Roosevelt became president in 1932, the immense task of economic rebuilding began. The New Deal program attempted to place eleven million unemployed persons in various types of meaningful jobs and to establish emergency measures to solve the economic crisis. It was not, however, until the beginning of World War II that the United States found its way out of the depression and into a new era of war boom and post-war prosperity.

The Second World War caused a rapid increase in the rate of technological revolution and stimulated American interest in the international situation, thus leading to an ideological struggle against communism which culminated in the cold war of the 1950s. The impact of space achievements resulted not only in federal support for the advancement of science, mathematics, and foreign languages in the schools; but also in efforts to locate and train the exceptional pupil who could be a leader in scientific and military development. Under Truman and Eisenhower, programs were developed which provided a greater amount of social security and a higher rate of employment; but the nation was faced again with a need for protection against external aggression. America became involved in the United Nations (chartered in 1945), and American foreign policy was dominated by a need to develop peaceful coexistence with communistic countries. American efforts to limit communist expansion led to commitments in Korea, Berlin, and Viet Nam.

The leadership of John F. Kennedy brought new reforms and policies to the internal social development of the country, including economic stimulation and programs of health and medical care for the aged. Vast increases in federal aid to education, the war on poverty, and greater federal expenditure for education marked the presidency of Lyndon Johnson. It is important to remember that the United States contained a population of about one hundred million in 1918, while it is over two hundred million today. Social mobility and new industry gave rise to teeming cities with very different educational problems from those of agrarian communities. Americans became the most affluent people in history, and an increase of wealth produced demands for amenities, more education, and solutions to new kinds of problems. Today, more than fifty percent of our high school students express interest in attending a college or university. While education is still the road to economic advancement, the role of the schools in social change, education for leisure, and the evaluation of major institutions now take on new significance. The trend to begin school earlier and to stay in school longer has by no means reached its zenith. A major educational problem of the twentieth century centers on the need for both general education (common school experiences for all children) and for increased specialization. While cultural changes since World War I are of primary and major importance in the progress of education, we must now turn to specific educational developments.

EVOLUTION OF THE MODERN INSTITUTIONAL STRUCTURE

A serious argument rages among educators over the adequacy of the current educational system in meeting the needs of our young people. Many studies show that children are capable of learning such skills as reading at a younger age than we had previously supposed. Children mature at different rates so that starting all six-year-olds in the first grade is psychologically unsatisfactory. Many students seem to benefit from early childhood education, such as a structured nursery school or a Montessori school. Most American communities now offer some kind of preschool educational experience of a formal kind. While some people became interested in the educational ideas of Maria Montessori as early as 1911, the rapid growth of Montessori programs for young children has taken place only in the last decade. A major problem for Montessori and other preschool programs is that most must be supported by private tuition. A notable exception is the federally funded Head Start program. Often children who could benefit from formal educational experience prior to entering kindergarten are from families unable to pay the fees and Head Start is not available to all. Since 1970, kindergartens have been publicly supported as part of the public school system in almost all American communities. Before that date, some kindergartens were private and some cities had none at all. Some schools now offer developmental programs for kindergarten age children who are found to be immature by testing. By 1980, a large number of American pre-kindergarten children were in day care centers. Day care centers often have educational programs and most of them teach social skills.

Elementary Programs.   Before the beginning of the twentieth century, the modern school system had emerged as a single track from the elementary grades through college. American schools are still divided into fifty different state systems with a great deal of control vested in local boards and state departments of education. However, the past fifty years have clearly demonstrated a trend to build larger units, standardize programs, and to put more schools under the jurisdiction of centralized administrative units.

In 1893, the NEA appointed a Committee of Fifteen on the organization and program of primary and grammar schools. The Committee stressed good English usage including literature, United States history, geography, writing, arithmetic, physical science, and music. Manual training for boys and cooking or sewing for girls were suggested along with Latin for children in the eighth grade. The effect of the recommendations was to standardize the curriculum of elementary schools throughout the nation.

Most modern elementary schools do not extend beyond grade six. Curriculum changes have taken place; but most elementary students still devote the majority of their time to skill subjects such as reading, writing, grammar, and mathematics. History and geography have been combined into "social studies," biological sciences have been added, "new math" has replaced arithmetic, while art and music have somewhat increased in status. Certainly social studies now receive more attention than spelling. Physical education may be organized sports, calisthenics, or merely free play at recess or noon. Many minor subjects such as sex education have been added to the curriculum. Sometimes state legislatures have taken it upon themselves to pass laws requiring additional subjects such as drug education to be taught. Educators have experimented with the curriculum and much new information has been added; but there have been more changes in attitudes and methods than in basic subjects.

Innovations now found in many elementary schools include team teaching, nongraded schools, individualized instruction, open classrooms, and programmed learning. While traditional methods are still dominant, a great many districts are experimenting with innovative plans and programs.

In contrast with the self-contained classroom, team teaching provides for the cooperation of a group of teachers working with children at the same time. A team of teachers with a leader may be responsible for all the instruction of children in a school who normally would be assigned to the primary grades (grades one through three). Teams normally use some large group, some small group, and some individual instruction. Advantages include more time for planning, better evaluation of the progress of pupils, the opportunity for teachers to help one another improve practice, and flexibility in meeting the needs of students. It is difficult to have team teaching in a building designed for self-contained rooms. Success also depends upon the degree to which teachers are able to work together effectively.

Nongraded schools allow the child to progress at his own rate without being locked into the content of a given grade. A student in a graded school who is unable to satisfy the requirements of a given area (say third grade reading) must either be retained or promoted at the end of the year. In nongraded schools, a student who needs a year and a half to master third grade reading is neither punished by failing the grade nor promoted beyond his ability to cope.

It has long been known that children mature at different rates, have different interests, and are not motivated in the same way. Experiments in individualized instruction are designed to meet needs by a flexible program which allows each student to participate in planning his own program of instruction. Some individual instruction plans operate by providing a large number of groups at different levels for various subjects. A low teacher-pupil ratio and adequate support (including a high quality instructional materials center) is needed for successful individualized instruction.

Herbert Kohl and others who advocate the open classroom say that the standard curriculum prevents creativity and good communication. By his standards, not many American elementary schools are "open." However, many schools now offer the pupil a wide choice of activities and provide numerous opportunities for self-expression, the development of interests, and creative activities.

Various kinds of programmed learning, including teaching machines and computer assisted instruction, are used in connection with other innovative programs. They are often found in the media centers of schools with open or individualized plans for instruction. Machines, including closed-circuit television, microfilm, tape recorders, and projectors for slides and films are also used in the traditional schools. In the early 1980s, computerized information systems and electronic data systems began to appear in schools. The minicomputer is now found in classrooms as well as in many homes. It seems safe to predict that the media will find increased utilization as

America moves into a life-long learning society and the information age.

The School Survey.   Educational leaders as early as the period of James Carter and Horace Mann had taken a hard look at the adequacy of schools in various states; but it was not until 1910 that a formal survey of schools took place. In that year, superintendent Kendall of Indianapolis was invited to visit and make a report on the schools of Boise, Idaho. His survey covered teachers, the curriculum, the organization of schools, buildings, and the attitude of citizens toward their educational system. By 1914 the school survey was an established practice, but not many were as detailed as that conducted in New York City which cost almost one hundred thousand dollars and required three years.

Early surveys utilized the services of well-known educators and ranked the subject system against others that were regarded as comparable. Nothing more sophisticated than observation was used as a tool for measurement. Criticism of the large numbers of changes recommended and failure to consider the limitations of resources caused surveys by teams of experts to be unpopular. The *Thirteenth Yearbook* of the National Society for the Study of Education offered suggestions about how surveys might be conducted by local educators with only slight assistance from experts.

Detailed surveys are still conducted in the United States. They serve a variety of purposes such as planning for consolidation, desegregation, new building, curriculum change, and administrative reorganization. Surveys are also used by organizations for accrediting schools and evaluating programs.

Consolidation.   One of the earlier shifts in design resulted from the consolidation of one-room district schools in rural areas. Local elementary schools were first built just far enough apart to permit scholars to walk from their homes. Concentrations of population, the wide use of automobiles, and a reduction of the number of farm families made it possible to build united schools which were larger and more efficient. Just after the First World War, about seventy percent of the public school buildings in the United States were of the one-room variety. Such schools were expensive to maintain, lacking in equipment, poorly supervised, and without specialization. Consolidation has reduced the number of one-room schools to less than five percent of the total. Today, even sparsely populated communities often have modern multiroom physical plants, complete with gymnasium, cafeteria, and modern equipment. Bus service is normally provided by consolidated school districts.

The modern elementary school has changed both in consolidated and urban school districts. Elementary schools are not as directly linked to colleges as high schools. This has allowed more flexibility in the curriculum and in scheduling. Team teaching, programmed instruction, and the use of instructional technology are more common on the elementary level than at any other in American education. The organization, administration, structure, and curriculum of schools in America is not fixed or final. Further evolution of schools and programs may be expected in the future. Many schools have specially trained teachers for art, speech correction, guidance counseling, and the like. Extracurricular activities such as team sports, and a federally subsidized lunch program are commonly found in elementary schools.

Junior High Schools.   Eight-year elementary schools and four-year high schools are still found in the United States but other organizational plans are more common. Junior high schools increased slowly in number during the first half of the twentieth century but their number increased markedly in the past thirty years. Middle schools or mid-high schools are now found in many communities. Since the middle of this century, the 6-3-3 or 6-6 plan of organization has become more common than the traditional eight-year elementary school followed by a four-year high school. Some cities have experimented with a 6-2-4 or a 4-4-4 organizational plan, while the two-year junior college has sometimes been added as an extension of the common school system. The typical junior high school consists of grades seven, eight, and nine. Part of the theory behind junior high schools relates to a need for vocational or terminal secondary education. Their success may also be attributed to an exploratory curriculum with general courses in science and introductory work in various fields. The student receives guidance concerning his or her abilities and limitations. Fewer subjects are studied; but greater detail is given than for elementary subjects, and the pupil normally has a different teacher for each course. It is assumed that junior high school students no longer need the security of belonging to one classroom with one teacher. They are expected to have a longer attention span than younger children. Perhaps the most important reason for the popularity of the three-year junior high school is that it separates youngsters just starting the adolescent period of life from both older and younger students. This contributes to the development of social skills and avoids cramming children of all ages into a matrix of social and intellectual competition. Junior high schools may be attached to an elementary or high school or may be completely separated.

High Schools.   The most important thing about the American high school in the past fifty years is its phenomenal growth. In the sense that it caters to a range of abilities, interests, and goals, the secondary school has become a school of all the people, just as the elementary school was in an earlier period. In 1920 there were about two and one-half million secondary school students in the United States, or approximately one-third of the population between the ages of fourteen and seventeen was in school. In 1965 there were more than fifteen million secondary school students or approximately 85 percent of the high school age group. There are a number of vocational or technical high schools, especially in large cities, but the typical American secondary school has become the "comprehensive" public high school.

Comprehensive is a term used by scholars such as James B. Conant who have studied the program of the high schools in detail. Basically, it refers to a secondary school that has a program designed to meet the various needs and interests of students, regardless of whether or not they expect to attend college. Vocational courses have long been offered by high schools, but the major emphasis is still on college preparation. With the increasing affluence of the American people and the growing scarcity of jobs for which little training is required, college preparation is not likely to lose ground as the major purpose of the high school. It is predicted that college enrollment will triple in the period from 1970 to 1990. Nevertheless, the purpose of secondary education and the program of the high schools continues to be one of the most hotly debated issues in American education.

Shortly after the Kalamazoo decision insured tax support, the public high school took on qualities of both the academy and the classical school. It offered courses that were practical and cultural on the one hand, and college preparatory on the other. Training of the mind came to be equated with preparation for life and the best mental training was considered to be the college preparatory course. Electives were offered in high schools but the curriculum was shaped by what colleges would accept for entrance. The report of the Committee of Ten of the NEA in 1892 emphasized that high schools were for the elite. The twentieth century gave rise to an increase in national wealth, an improved living standard, and a need for a better trained labor force. High schools were forced to cater to the needs of the entire population in a growing industrial democracy. An NEA Commission on the Reorganization of Secondary Education, meeting in 1911, developed the Cardinal Principles of Secondary Education. In contrast with the college-centered and mental-discipline-oriented Committee of Ten, these principles stressed guidance, a wide range of subjects, adaptation of content and methods to the abilities and interest of students, and flexibility of organization and administration. High schools began to stress health, citizenship, vocational preparation, ethical development, and the worthy use of leisure time, in addition to fundamental processes and the academic subjects. In short, they became comprehensive.

A demand for experts to improve industry and to help win the cold war resulted in more science courses, while new subjects such as driver training, mental hygiene, and personal relations reflect the needs of individuals in a complex society. The American comprehensive high school has received harsh criticism, especially from those who emphasize traditional subject matter and academic excellence. There is still a question of whether or not the high school should be specialized, and if so, how specialized and how early in the student's career. In 1946 a Harvard committee published *General Education in a Free Society* in which specialization on the secondary level was attacked as being unsound. Others have joined the battle to extend general education through the high school on the grounds that modern society demands generalized knowledge of many areas for true human fulfillment and good citizenship. Whatever the criticisms, no other institution has ever provided education beyond the elementary level to all the people of a large nation. This the American high school has done.

Higher Education.   High schools in the United States have never entirely lost their function of college preparation due to the phenomenal growth of colleges and universities. With the exception of the period of the great depression, college enrollments have had a steady increase throughout this century, but the great explosion in size and number of colleges has taken place since World War II. Colleges have become more utilitarian and scientific in nature, although the liberal arts college is still a major American institution. With the addition of colleges of a professional nature (education, agriculture, engineering, commerce, dentistry, and veterinary medicine) to universities, and the organization of separate departments within colleges, higher education has become highly specialized. Practical and scientific courses were in demand before World War I; but the expansion of industry and the explosion of knowledge have made college training indispensable to many occupations which previously needed little formal schooling.

Furthermore, hundreds of new special occupations resulted from the changes brought about by scientific research in the universities. Veterans returning from the Second World War demanded and got practical courses from colleges and universities that had previously offered only liberal education. Governmental ·support of veterans education through the G.I. Bill stimulated a trend toward considerable federal interest in higher education. Large numbers of students attended colleges and graduate schools through grants made by the National Defense Education Act of 1958 or other scholarships. The 500,000 students enrolled in college in 1918 seem a mere drop in the bucket compared with today's figure which exceeds twelve million students. It seems fair to predict that college enrollments in America will follow the same general growth trend as did high school enrollments fifty years ago. Already, graduate schools are growing more rapidly than did colleges in the nineteenth century.

Junior Colleges.   A direct result of the expansion in higher education which could not be accommodated by existing colleges was the junior college movement. Two-year terminal colleges, often staffed by senior high school teachers, began to appear before World War I. There have been both private and public junior colleges; but those with public control and tax support have increased most rapidly in recent years. The government established some junior colleges during the depression years; but the greatest number have been developed by city or state junior college boards. Municipal junior colleges have often provided the first two years of standard college education, thus taking some of the pressure off colleges and universities. Public junior colleges are either free or their tuition charges are very low, and students usually live at home while attending them. The junior college therefore offers an extension of educational opportunity to students who could not otherwise afford higher education. There is a vastly increased demand for more junior colleges of both the terminal and the nonterminal type. One serious problem is financing in communities where all available taxes are required for lower public schools. In 1971, there were 1,120 junior colleges operating with a total enrollment of about 2.7 million students.

The average length of time spent in school has expanded at both ends of the continuum. Many students now have the opportunity to attend kindergarten before starting public school at the age of six. Quite a large number of school systems have public kindergartens, with the K-6-3-3 or K-4-4-4 plans being most common. Public kindergartens are found in all but the smaller rural schools. Day care centers and Montessori schools for pre-kindergarten youngsters are available in most cities but they usually require tuition. Head Start programs make an effort to give underprivileged children some of the preschool experiences enjoyed by middle-class youngsters.

SCHOOL FINANCE AND CONTROL

An issue which is developing into a major educational argument in America concerns the location of authority and the source of support for public schools. As the federal government becomes more active in providing money through such measures as the Elementary and Secondary Education Act of 1965, the role of the central government in education becomes larger. Many leaders feel that the schools ought to remain in local hands, and they fear that federal aid to education will eventually lead to complete federal control of schools. On the other hand, national authorities have allowed a good deal of local administration of federal funds when local governments have been unable to raise sufficient money for high quality schools. We can predict that the argument over federal control of schools will continue; although it also seems likely that a larger share of future school finance will be handled by the national government.

Local and State Control.   Educational support and control in the United States has been a curious composite of local, state, and national functions. Because education was not considered a federal responsibility by the founding fathers, each state set up its own unique educational system. Many of the states have similar laws, but each is autonomous with regard to public schools and educational requirements within its own borders. While the states have guarded their authority over schools and generally opposed federal financial aid, local school boards have been granted a considerable degree of freedom in managing the schools. State boards of education have served largely for making policy while state superintendents or commissioners have been responsible for administration and general supervision. States differ widely in their method of selecting boards and executive school officers. Sometimes they are elected, sometimes appointed by the governor, and sometimes appointed by the state legislature.

Most states have well-organized educational offices with specialists for inspecting schools, certifying teachers, and allocating funds that are distributed by the state. There are normally smaller administrative units presided over by township, county, or district superintendents. Cities often have independent school districts with superintendents who work directly for the locally elected board of education, and who perform the functions otherwise delegated to county superintendents. There is no uniformity with regard to the size and type of school districts in the United States. One superintendent and board of education in a metropolitan area may be responsible for hundreds of schools at all levels. At the other end of the extreme is the school board and executive officer governing only one small school building. Although teachers' salaries are uniform in some states, it is still common to find adjacent school districts which differ in money paid to teachers and otherwise expended for the education of children. The inequality of educational opportunity in various districts has encouraged state and federal participation in education.

School Finance.   In the twentieth century, states began to play a much more important role in school finance. State funds originated as early as 1795, when Connecticut sold her vast Western Reserve lands and put the money in permanent school funds. Most states have such funds, drawing money from public land sale, taxes, special appropriations, and the like. Historically the states have used their meager allotments for encouraging local effort and for equalizing educational opportunities, for giving state aid to local districts that agreed to tax themselves for schools, and payments to districts unable to obtain sufficient local revenues for a minimum standard. By and large, the concentrated wealth and population of cities has made it possible for urban areas to levy taxes and support schools more easily than rural communities. Local taxes have paid the lion's share of public school costs and the states have confined their administration to a minimum. However, state funds have encouraged the keeping of accurate records of attendance, school inspection, and the establishment of accepted minimum standards. Between 1930 and 1970, the percentage of locally raised public school funds dropped from about 83 to 51 percent. As the proportion of local support has fallen, state and federal support has increased. Quite naturally, the larger governmental units have begun to place more restrictions on the money which they have collected and distributed. Such restrictions have usually been confined to general rules for the use of money; but there is no question that centralized control is increasing. Historically, the federal government has been interested in the improvement of higher education and specialized training in such subjects as agriculture. Local property taxes are still widely used for school finance; but they are neither sufficiently flexible nor adequate to care for the changing population distribution. Knowledge of the emergence of the federal government as a major educational agency is vital to an understanding of the current issue over support and control of the schools.

FEDERAL PARTICIPATION IN EDUCATION

The amount of involvement of the United States government has increased so much in the past few years that a listing of all the laws is not possible here. Only major areas of activity will be considered. The United States Office of Education has grown rapidly in size and influence, due largely to the need for administering federal funds and advising participants in federal projects. The Office has had a varied history, having been moved from the Department of the Interior and given separate status in 1930, moved again to the Federal Security Agency in 1939 and made part of the Department of Health, Education and Welfare in 1953. Large grants made through H.E.W. to schools and universities contributed to the importance of the Office of Education and it was made a separate cabinet level position under the Carter Administration. Cutbacks in federal spending in the Reagan Administration created some loss of prestige and some members of Congress suggested that it should be abolished. The future of the office of Secretary of Education will depend upon politics and federal policy concerning finance.

Support for Industrial and Vocational Education.   Among the earlier efforts of the Congress to aid education were acts designed to fill a need for industrial and vocational education. Through the Smith-Hughes Act (1917), the George-Reed Act (1929), and the George-Deen Act (1937), Congress attempted to promote vocational education in public schools. A Federal Board of Vocational Education was created in 1917 and after 1919 was given the additional task of supervising training of the handicapped. Ten years later, the Capper-Ketcham Act extended the previous Smith-Lever Act to cover education in home economics and agriculture. During the First World War, the government found it necessary to train many technicians, but industrial inactivity during the depression resulted in a great shortage of trained technicians and engineers. The National Defense Training Program of 1940 provided courses for more than seven million workers during World War II. The Rural War Production Training Program trained farm youth for industry and for jobs in food production. Vocational training also benefited from the National Defense Education Act (1958), but the Vocational Education Act extended previous legislation to cover any skilled, technical, or semiskilled occupation and included provisions for keeping potential dropouts in schools.

The original purpose of federal efforts to promote vocational and industrial education was to provide the nation with skilled workers and technicians when other agencies had failed to do so. Clearly, this was the same rationale that fostered the agricultural and mechanical colleges developed from the Morrill Acts. However, Congress has increasingly turned its attention to vocational education which may serve social needs by improving the economy, keeping children in school longer, fighting poverty, and creating new jobs for the unemployed. Further legislation to strengthen vocational education in order to fight against unemployment seems almost certain.

New Deal Acts.   Attempts to improve the national welfare and increase equality of opportunity were made through the so-called New Deal legislation passed during the administration of Franklin D. Roosevelt. The Civilian Conservation Corps employed young men and gave them vocational training, especially in conservation, while small grants were given to needy students through the National Youth Administration. The Works Progress Administration subsidized teachers' salaries for programs in the training of adults and aliens, and for nursery schools. The Public Works Administration provided loans for communities to use in building schools and libraries. In 1935 the Secretary of Agriculture was authorized to distribute surplus foods to schools and this led directly to the National School Lunch Act of 1946, which has made both food and money available to school lunch programs. Loss of tax funds for schools during the depression led to loans to school boards through the Reconstruction Finance Corporation. This trend has been continued in legislation such as the Economic Opportunity Act (EOA) of 1964. Title I of this law set up the Job Corps to train youth between the ages of sixteen and twenty-one for useful employment and citizenship.

Job Corps training centers were built around the nation under this plan. Students were given training in basic skills as well as in vocational subjects. There has also been a work-study program for students still in high school who needed to earn money and a college work-study program for students with financial need. Title II of the EOA authorized aid to adult education and gave cultural enrichment for children from disadvantaged families. The Head Start program was aimed at children from three to five years of age who would not normally have had the advantage of nursery schools or kindergartens.

Wartime Measures.   Wartime activity has also contributed to the involvement of the federal government in education. During the First World War, the government trained technicians and troops drilled on college campuses. In World War II, loans were made to students majoring in subjects like medicine, for which there was a critical need. Congress began giving assistance to those school districts which absorbed large numbers of children of military or defense personnel. Laws aiding such affected areas were extended in 1950 and 1966. In addition, equipment purchased by the government for special war training was later turned over to schools and surplus property was made available to all nonprofit educational institutions.

In an effort to meet the needs of veterans whose schooling had been interrupted by military duty, the Servicemen's Readjustment Act of 1944 (G.I. Bill) was passed. This measure has provided subsistence and school cost allowances for veterans who have continued their education and it has resulted in the expansion of colleges to accommodate them. The G.I. Bill was revived for veterans of the Korean War and the benefits were increased for Vietnam veterans in 1972.

NDEA.   A new period of federal activity in education started with the cold war and the Soviet success in launching the first space satellite. The National Defense Education Act of 1958 was designed for the purpose of giving aid to education as a means of strengthening the nation. NDEA loans have been made to prospective teachers in amounts up to five thousand dollars, and half of the loan has been cancellable through service as a public school teacher after graduation. Funds have been made available for laboratory equipment and other materials to improve instruction in science, while fellowships have been offered to persons training to be college professors. State testing and guidance to find and encourage able students, an extension of vocational education, and research on new educational media have also been financed by NDEA funds. Out of the administrations of John F. Kennedy and Lyndon B. Johnson came a host of federal measures designed to promote equality of educational opportunity, to fight poverty, and to strengthen defense. The Higher Education Facilities Act of 1963 made funds available for the construction of college buildings with matching sums provided by the college or state.

Elementary and Secondary Education Act.   Federal aid to education took another big step with the Elementary and Secondary Education Act of 1965. This measure provided funds for textbooks and other instructional materials and services in public and private elementary and secondary schools. The primary purpose was to insure that children from low-income families had access to adequate materials. Control of the funds was in state and local hands rather than those of federal agencies. The act also included one hundred million dollars for research in the field of education to be administered by the United States Office of Education. This act was extended for four more years in 1966, at a cost of about twelve billion dollars.

Since 1965 the Higher Education Act, which includes the Education Professions Development Act of 1967, has provided large sums of money for the acquisition of books and other library materials in colleges, for improving and extending teacher education programs, for strengthening programs related to community problems like housing and poverty, for supporting developing institutions of higher education, for giving financial assistance to students through grants and loans, and for developing the National Teachers Corps.

Teacher Corps employed specially trained teachers and college students to supplement instruction in schools with numerous low-income students. The education given Teacher Core trainees included living in the neighborhoods near the schools and studying ethnic and minority culture. In 1980, Teacher Core shifted from teacher training to in-service education. Congress has not always appropriated funds for Teacher Corps and many of the training centers were closed during the Reagan Administration. The Higher Education Act provided about twenty-five thousand graduate fellowships for teacher trainees yearly, supported research and development in colleges of education, and established a National Advisory Council on Quality Teacher Education.

Although the federal government entered the educational arena in a big way in the 1960s, new legislation dropped off after the Johnson Administration. One reason is that the shortage of teachers at the time of the National Defense Education Act changed into an oversupply of teachers by 1970. Another reason is the fear of federal control over local schools. In the early 1980s the mood of the nation favored reduced federal spending and a cut in bureaucracy. Nevertheless, educators now predict a shortage of teachers in the future because of low pay and the impact of inflation. Equality of educational opportunity can hardly be guaranteed with only local taxes. Central Tax collection and distribution by the national government appears to be the only way of insuring equal education for the mobile American population. A number of educators have suggested some sort of federal equalization fund to make up for differences in economic support between states. Of course, fear of federal control has also caused many of the states to take steps for the reformation of their own tax laws. Inequality within school districts or cities, such as that demonstrated in the Rodriguez case of San Antonio, Texas, put pressure on state legislatures to make their taxation more equitable.

Congressional efforts to aid education have not been uniform over the past several years. Funding of bills passed during the Kennedy and Johnson administrations was not always continued during the presidency of Richard Nixon. Few new federal education measures were proposed during the Nixon administration; but President Ford signed a new elementary and secondary education act into law as one of his first official acts. In spite of the economic recession of the 1970s, efforts to provide federal help for schools and local educational programs have not ended. Less money was provided in the 1970s than in the 1960s, but the impact of federal aid continued. The Department of Health, Education and Welfare used the withholding of funds (or the threat of such withholding) as an instrument for enforcing plans for racial integration. This was continued under Carter but President Reagen voiced strong opposition to using the power of the federal government to control local action. The courts have also taken a less vigorous stand as in the Los Angeles case of 1981 where busing to achieve racial balance in schools was not supported.

One of the burning issues in American education is the control and support of schools. Public opposition to national educational policy is illustrated by the controversy surrounding the integration of South High School in Boston in 1974. Many laymen fear that local school boards may be vanishing and that an increasing role for the federal government in educational affairs is undesirable. On the other hand, federal funds and programs are felt to be necessary for the success of many schools.

PSYCHOLOGY AND EDUCATION

Assumptions about the nature of the mind and the learning process have always been present in education. Plato wrote about the three divisions of the soul and the need to make reason paramount. Locke examined the human understanding and held that ideas enter the mind through the senses. Rousseau saw learning as an extension of natural interests through a series of developmental stages. Puritan schools were predicated upon the belief that the child had an evil nature and that his mind must be "formed" through discipline and effort. Horace Mann supported the phrenology of Franz Joseph Gall, which held that intelligence and aptitudes can be determined by the configuration of the skull.

New respect for the personality of the child came out of the work of Pestalozzi. Froebel, Sheldon, and Parker contributed to an understanding of the psychology of learning. Nevertheless, words like intelligence, consciousness, and mind were still vague and mystical at the end of the nineteenth century. While Herbart had insisted that the mind is a unity, faculty psychology, with its concept of separate mental powers and transfer of training, still ruled educational theory. Mental discipline was the basis of the report of the Committee of Ten and the foundation for almost the entire public school curriculum.

Psychology as a science developed in Europe and to some degree in America before the beginning of the twentieth century. Herbart sought clues to mental development in the facts of physiology. Darwin's work on evolution stimulated others to study the nature of the child from a biological standpoint. Pavlov's conditioned reflex experiments on animals in Russia created a new wave of interest in psychology. Of even more significance was the founding of the first experimental psychology laboratory by Wilhelm Max Wundt at Leipzig in 1878. A great many American psychologists were trained by Wundt, and he is often regarded as the father of structural psychology. Other European leaders included Ebbinghaus, who worked with nonsense syllables to measure memory, and Freud, who developed psychoanalysis from the dynamics of motivation in personality formation.

Although not strictly an experimental psychologist, William James (1842-1910) did much to create a link between education and psychology. His Principles of Psychology (1890) was an outstanding contribution which made him internationally known and helped to develop psychology as an independent area of study. James extracted some of the more practical ideas from his major work in psychology and published them under the title *Talks to Teachers.* This was the first attempt to provide psychological guidance for practical educators. Although his work was partly philosophical and introspection was his method, James helped to make psychology a valid field of educational inquiry.

American psychologists, heavily influenced by Europeans, attacked formal discipline and formulated new concepts of mind. Among the first were Edward Titchener, G. Stanley Hall, James M. Cattell, John Dewey, and Edward L. Thorndike. The history of educational psychology is best approached through the various types or schools of psychology.

Structuralism.   Titchener was a student of Wundt and a leading psychologist at Cornell University for thirty years. Concerned with the study of consciousness, Titchener treated psychology as an impersonal science and approached it atomistically. That is, Titchener and the structuralists attempted to isolate and analyze the basic elements of mental processes. He believed that a microscopic examination of the basic blocks of the nervous system and psychic elements would lead to a complete science of the mind. Since structuralism did not concern itself with the living organism, its relationship with education was indirect. Members of this psychological school dominated many college departments of psychology for years.

Functionalism.   William James and John Dewey were the first to identify functionalism as a division of psychology. For them, a study of consciousness could not be isolated from feelings, sensations, thoughts, and activities of the living organism. In 1900, as president of the newly formed American Psychological Association, Dewey called for the application of psychology to social and educational practice. For Dewey the complete act of thought is the same for a child in school and a scientist working on a problem in a laboratory. Both go through the same process which may be described in five steps: (1) activity, (2) problem, (3) data gathering, (4) formation of a hypothesis, and (5) testing. Learning can only occur when students are engaged in genuine activities rather than in artificial ones imposed by the teacher. Problems occur when activity is blocked. Children learn how to gather data from simple sources like their own memories or from more complicated sources like libraries. Hypothesis formation is merely the posing of a possible solution to a problem, and the learner must examine what consequences may occur if the hypothesis is accepted. Only by testing the proposed solution against empirical evidence can learning be completed. Dewey's books *Psychology* and *How We Think* described his functional theories. His *Human Nature and Conduct* (1922) is a statement of the interaction between the individual and his environment.

Other functional psychologists include Harvey Carr and James R. Angell who established laboratories for studying the adjustment of animals to various environments. Functionalism contributed both to education and to other schools such as associationism, connectionism and behaviorism.

Connectionist Psychology or Associationism.   Edward Lee Thorndike (1874-1949) was a student of William James and James McKeen Cattell. Building on Herman Ebbinghaus's curves of learning and forgetting and studies of animal learning made by Lloyd Morgan in England, Thorndike began a series of learning experiments with animals using puzzle boxes or a maze. After a series of trial and error activities, the animal would chance upon the "solution" which released food. Further trials in the same puzzle box resulted in the animal's making the proper response more rapidly than at first. This led Thorndike to his "law of effect" which he also extended to human activity. He found a very strong effect from rewards, but also discovered that punishment was a less effective means for the control of behavior. Following Pavlov's lead, Thorndike assumed a connection between stimuli and responses. He developed this into S — R bond psychology, using the equation: Learning = Stimulus — Response. If stimulus *A* is known to be associated with response *B*, repeat *A* until *B* is produced without hesitation whenever *A* occurs. Teachers rapidly accepted Thorndike's laws of learning which they found to be highly useful devices for classroom instruction.

Since Thorndike had an impeccable reputation as a scientist, his pioneering experiments opened new fields of psychological research at the time modern conceptions of pedagogy were being born. He was one of the first to understand that education and psychology were closely linked. Psychology forms the foundation for the science of education; while schools furnish subjects and data sources for psychological research. At Teachers College, Columbia University, Thorndike stimulated hundreds of students to esteem scientific research. Although his psychology was highly statistical and mechanical, connectionism became the leading educational psychology of the 1920s.

Behaviorism.   The logical extreme of associationism or connectionism gave rise to the psychological school known as behaviorism. John B. Watson (1878-1958) is generally regarded as the founder; but his student Karl Lashley also contributed to this strictly objective division of psychology. Today the best known scholar in the field of behaviorism is B. F. Skinner of Harvard.

Although he had studied with Dewey, Watson believed that psychology should be confined to those activities which could be varified by an outside observer. Behaviorism discarded consciousness as a subject of investigation and refused to use the method of introspection. It limited its findings to laboratory experiments which could be controlled and dealt only with those factors capable of analysis. Behaviorists believe that we have no right to project our feelings or ideas into the subjects we investigate. For example, if a person gives a piece of meat to a dog, it is legitimate to describe the dog's behavior; i.e., the animal jumps up, drools, opens its mouth, and eats the meat. It is not legitimate to say that the dog "likes" the meat since that projects the attitudes or feelings of the human into the dog and there is no evidence to support the statement.

Watson held that environment is far more important than heredity in the determination of human behavior. He rejected innate ideas and most instincts. His experiments with infants caused him to conclude that almost all emotional responses are learned. Watson held that any normal child could be raised to be a mechanic, athlete, professional man, or thief if the environment could be strictly controlled. Lashley was able to demonstrate that even human glands could be conditioned.

The early work of the behaviorists helped to discredit many theories about learning that were held by other psychologists. They did a great deal to foster objective evaluations of experiments. Sometimes their claims were extravagant and certainly many educators objected to what they described as "rat in a box" psychology and the restriction of investigation to a fractional part of human behavior. Nevertheless, behaviorism won the respect of scientists in other fields and its rigorous techniques helped to support objective educational research.

B. F. Skinner's work spans the period from early behaviorism to the present. In the late 1930s he began a series of animal learning experiments in which he taught animals to perform complex tasks. He accomplished this by giving the subject a reward after each step of the task was successfully accomplished. Out of this grew the idea of programmed instruction and teaching machines. During the Second World War, new programs for using electronic devices in teaching were developed by Skinner and his students. Computer assisted instruction, now used in numerous aspects of education, was adapted from the work of behaviorists. Skinner's books, *Science and Human Behavior, Walden II,* and *Beyond Freedom and Dignity,* have had a profound effect upon educators in modern America. Few of the findings of Skinner and other behaviorists have been scientifically rejected. The criticism of behaviorism normally comes from those who say it is too narrow, mechanical, and nonhumanistic.

Gestalt.   At about the same time that behaviorism began to influence education in America, German gestalt psychology also became important. Gestalt is a German word meaning "form" or "pattern," and it refers to the whole configuration or sum of integrated experiences present at any one time. The apparent motion created by flashing a series of photographs in the cinema is not explained by examining individual still pictures; nor can music be understood merely through the study of notes. Gestalt psychology was started in Germany by Max Wertheimer, Kurt Koffka, and Wolfgang Kohler. Beginning in 1914, Kohler began a series of experiments on the island of Tenerife using apes as subjects. He concluded that learning takes place as sudden insight, rather than by simple trial-and-error. This led to the examination of the pattern perceived by the learner in his total environment, rather than to an atomistic consideration of essential elements in the learning process.

American gestalt psychologists such as R. M. Ogden and Raymond Wheeler made important contributions to learning theory. Their stress on total understanding of the problem to be solved and the consequences of acting were acceptable to Dewey and the functionalists. Gestalt psychology was adopted by most members of the progressive movement because it dealt with the whole child in context.

Kurt Lewin (1890-1947) was a German gestalt psychologist who migrated to the United States when Hitler came to power. He believed that behavior is the result of energy derived from the needs or wants of the individual and the organism's efforts to meet those needs. Lewin's psychology is called "field theory" because of the emphasis of the "life space" or field of the individual as he perceives it. Lewin used the term "vector" to describe the attractive or repulsive forces which motivate the organism to act.

Learning theories and psychological ideas associated with field theory are still popular in the United States. Most studies of motivation, needs, personality, feelings, and attitudes have been carried on in the light of field theory. Another group of psychologists with similar views of the child and his environment are called "holistic." Holistic psychology emphasizes the child as a "whole" and insists that the individual can never be studied and understood except as he relates to the forces present in his entire environment. Modern humanistic psychologists such as Abraham Maslow and Carl Rogers have been highly influenced by gestalt, field, and holistic psychological theory. Members of these schools have had at least as much impact on American education as behaviorists.

Psychoanalysis.   While not strictly an educational or learning psychology, psychoanalysis has contributed to an understanding of childhood experiences and to programs for those with learning disabilities or who need therapy. Sigmund Freud, Carl Jung, Alfred Adler, and Karen Horney were major leaders in this movement. Freud's stress on the sexual attraction of infants and children to the parent of the opposite sex (Oedipus/Electra Complex) and his discussion of the animal nature of human beings (id) which must be governed by social norms (superego) has had great educational influence. Modern concerns for the impact of conflict and stress on the development of personality as found in the work of Erik Erikson are linked to Freudian concepts. A body of educational literature supporting freedom of choice for students and attacking barriers to personality development is based upon psychoanalytic theory.

Modern Developmental Psychology and Stage Theory.   A major thrust of educational psychology in recent years has been directed toward the relationship of curriculum and methods to stages of development in children. Conflict exists between various theories of development but there is agreement that poor pedagogy results from attempting to teach information or concepts before the learner has reached the stage at which such information and concepts can be understood.

David Ausubel distinguishes between learning by reception and learning by discovery. Reception learning requires the student to internalize material in order to recall it at a later date (as on a test). Discovery learning does not present material in finished form but sets up an environment in which something has to be discovered or invented by the student before it can be assimilated. In discovery learning, it is the process that is emphasized while reception learning concentrates on the product. While Ausubel contends that discovery learning enables the student to understand how new knowledge is generated and stimulates the learner, it is an inefficient method for delivering large amounts of information. Ausubel therefore believes that there must be a balance between process and product but that schools which have no discovery learning inhibit the progress of children and make education uninteresting.

Jerome Bruner is recognized for his efforts to apply scientific methods to teaching and for his research on the formation of concepts in children. Bruner is interested in the structure of subject matter. He believes that the teaching of particular subjects can be integrated into the way the students see the world so as to permit learners to discover the basic principles of the discipline under study. Motivation therefore should be stimulated by the subject matter itself and not from external appeals to interest or the arrangement of consequent events. Obviously, this differs from Skinner's operant conditioning. Bruner believes that it is possible to teach any subject in some intellectually honest way to any child at any developmental stage.

Child psychologist Robert Gange is well known for his contributions to programmed instruction. He believes that children pass through developmental stages of learning which are determined by what is to be learned. Gange identifies eight conditions for learning. Signal learning occurs when infants learn responses to a general cue, stimulus-response learning is more precise and voluntary, chaining is the result of putting together previous responses, while verbal discrimination is the association of names with objects. More advanced learning includes multiple discrimination to identify and classify groups of stimuli, concept learning or the ability to identify important differences and similarities between sets of stimuli, relating one complete concept to others or "principle" learning, and problem solving in which several principles are used for dealing with a new situation. Gange urges educators to give more attention to the way in which instruction is sequenced because he holds that no learning stage can be skipped. Because Gange believes that it is the nature of the skills to be learned that determines the sequence of stages, the curriculum must be ordered accordingly. Ausubel, Bruner, and Gange all see the subject matter or the learning tasks as central to learning stages. On the other hand, Piaget holds that stages are related to the maturation and development of children.

Jean Piaget was born in Neuchatel, Switzerland, in 1896. He began his career as a zoology assistant at the age of eleven and published papers on mollusks at the age of fifteen. Piaget worked with Alfred Binet in Paris on standardizing tests of intelligence and became interested in the levels of logic used by children taking such tests. Building on Rousseau and Pestalozzi, Piaget attempted to establish a body of psychology to give support for educational techniques truly adapted to the laws of mental development. For many years he carried out experiments on learning tasks with children in the J. J. Rousseau Institute. He was active in the field until he died in 1980.

Piaget believed that the two fundamental characteristics of a child's learning and cognitive development are organization and adaptation. Organization is described as the systematizing of information into meaningful patterns. These patterns are used to structure new information so that it does not seem random or chaotic to the learner. Adaptation is the process of coping, or integrating new information into existing perceptions and patterns. Intelligence for Piaget must follow from our ability to organize and adapt. Like Dewey, Piaget saw human beings as born active, curious, interested in communication, and with a need to assimilate information. His principles of organization and adaptation are in basic agreement with the theories of Bruner and Gange. Piaget parted company with other developmental psychologists on the matter of specific stages of growth and development. His stages are determined by genetic development in connection with experience. The stages or levels are age related but they are determined by a combination of age and experience.

The *sensorimotor* stage covers the period from birth to about the age of two. This stage consists mostly of reflexes, but during this time, foundations are laid for later mental growth and development. Trial and error is used for mastering the environment and oral language develops. At about the age of two the *preoperational* stage begins. From two to four the child is preconceptual and in an intuitive stage of development but experiences vast growth in language use. Judgments are incomplete and modeling is a basis for learning. From three to seven children reach a symbolic stage where drawing, role-playing, size, number, and distance begin to follow some semblance of order. From seven to twelve the child begins to think logically and not in the impressionistic way associated with the *preoperational* stage. The span of attention expands and a clear sense of time emerges. Children at this level can count, weigh, test solutions, and conserve. They are not, however, able to think abstractly nor are they motivated by delayed rewards. At the stage of *formal operations*, learners can think hypothetically. They do not require visible concrete cues for each stage of the thinking process. Abstract or ideal concepts are used and the child has a clear concept of time.

Piaget and his followers urge educators to be realistic about what children can accomplish at each stage. Tests have shown that many freshmen entering universities still think on a concrete level. Even after a person has reached the formal level of operations, it is common to revert back to earlier stages under stress. Teachers, in the view of Piaget, must avoid abstract and theoretical tasks if any of the learners in their classrooms are still operating in a nonformal way.

The belief that early experiences are crucial to later development is challenged by Jerome Kagan. For Kagan and his associates, the most recent experiences are more important than the earliest ones. His research shows dramatic improvement when children from deprived backgrounds are exposed to an enriched environment. Rather than dealing with stages of development, Kagan urges teachers to create a stable and positive learning situation. Past experiences of the teacher and of the student are less significant to Kagan than a sense of involvement and experiences that are supportive of intellectual growth. Kagan believes that the environment is all-important and he is optimistic about programs like Head Start. His cognitive interpretation of child development is a theory which states that learners do best in an environment characterized by moderate discrepancy from their existing world view. Uncertainty and challenge are emotionally satisfying, but the shock of something totally new may create resistance in the learner.

Other Contributions to Educational Psychology.   The Mastery Learning concept of Benjamin Bloom has had considerable influence on the theory and practice of teaching in twentieth-century America. Mastery Learning calls for individualized instruction with each student going at his or her own pace. Students must demonstrate that each level and condition of learning has been mastered before going on to the next level. Bloom is also known for his two taxonomies, the cognitive and the affective. Values and attitudes in the affective domain must be understood as being different from the intellectual tasks of cognition. This distinction has been supported by split-brain research and its implications for educators. Neurologists like J.E. Bogen and Michael Gazzaniga claim education has stressed verbal skills to a fault and that both language and nonlanguage techniques are needed.

B.F. Skinner's major contribution to educational psychology was discussed in the section on behaviorism but not all behaviorists agree with his orthodox position. Albert Bandura and Richard Walters concern themselves with the way people acquire behavior appropriate to social circumstances. Loud expressions and slang language may be appreciated in an informal meeting of peers but is not appropriate in a classroom setting. These psychologists build on the principles of Skinner to form a theory of social learning.

Noam Chomsky of M.I.T. has criticized Skinner on quite different grounds. He sees Skinner's learner as a robot responding to external stimuli only. Chomsky believes that all human beings have an inborn inclination to master language, regardless of the environment. His theory of Transformational Grammar states that learners respond not only to the environment but also to internal events.

Another area of psychology that has created considerable educational interest in recent years is described as humanistic and phenomenological. Carl Rogers is known for client-centered or non-directive therapy. He feels that psychology has focused on the experimental laboratory and Freudian theory instead of human growth and the potential of mankind. In books like *On Becoming a Person*, Rogers concerns himself with the infinite possibilities of human development, creativity, and how people can help each other to become more fully human.

Abraham Maslow is one of the best known humanistic psychologists. He has focused on counseling and identified the needs which are basic to the educational environment. Maslow's hierarchy of needs is included in the basic preparation of many American teachers. Basic needs like food and shelter always take priority over others. This is not different from the position of the progressives who believed that before a student can be taught the school must see that he is properly fed and physically well. Needs for safety and security come next in Maslow's scheme. Beyond security, we all have needs for affection and love. A desire for self-esteem and the respect of others takes the next place on the hierarchy. The final need is for self-actualization.

For Maslow, the best education is one that deals with the real and serious problems of life. In order to understand the wider world, it is necessary to have self-knowledge and to become an authentic individual. Teachers should have deep concerns for children but teachers cannot be effective unless their own needs are met and they have healthy mental attitudes. Teachers must understand that growth has two components. The learner needs to venture out, to stretch and to be challenged but the learner also wants to remain safe and in familiar territory. Optimum learning occurs somewhere between absolute safety (with no risk at all) and maximum risk which causes the learner to feel threatened and under stress. Compassionate and caring persons are good teachers. To help a child become a better person requires an atmosphere of acceptance in the classroom and a balance between objective and subjective learning experiences.

CHILD STUDY AND MEASUREMENT

Education as a science or discipline is grounded in psychology; but child study and the measurement movement also provide instruments for research and development. Most of the efforts to measure ability or study children prior to 1900 were not objective. Demands for understanding the nature of the child were made as early as the first century by the Roman educator Quintilian and were repeated by Rousseau, Pestalozzi, and Froebel. However, nothing more sophisticated than the common diary existed as a tool for measuring the ability or characteristics of the child until Francis Galton (1822-1911) developed the mathematics of Karl Pearson into a means of using quantative units of the measurement of deviation from the mean differences between and within groups of children. Galton was a cousin of Charles Darwin, and it was Darwin's research that caused him to become interested in measuring the deviation of characteristics within and between groups of people. Both Galton and Darwin invented tests to measure the abilities or capacities of individuals. Methods for measuring and analyzing quantitative data was the subject of James Cattell's *Mental Tests and Measurement* (1890). Galton was the first to use curves to express the distribution of individuals in terms of characteristics such as age, height, and intelligence.

While Cattell and Charles Judd were pioneering the measurement movement in America, French psychologists Alfred Binet and Theophile Simon were creating an instrument to measure intelligence. The Simon-Binet test was published in 1906, and ten years later Lewis Terman produced the Stanford revision of that test. Millions of soldiers were given the Stanford test of intelligence during World War I, which resulted in the first massive data on the subject and created a model for later intelligence tests for use in public schools. The significance of both group and individual testing of intelligence can hardly be overemphasized in the modern history of American education. They became the basis for new programs, curriculum changes, ability grouping, and a host of other educational alternatives which are still hotly debated in professional circles.

Another contribution to the statistical measurement of learning began with the work of Dr. Joseph Rice. As editor of the *Forum*, Rice undertook a study of the achievement of students studying spelling in elementary schools. Having tested 30,000 pupils, he concluded that those who spent only fifteen minutes a day on the study of the subject learned to spell just as well as those who devoted an hour or more to the task. Naturally, there was a negative reaction from those who still supported mental discipline, but in 1912 the NEA went on record as favoring candid investigation of schools and methods. The "Measurement of Educational Products" was part of the *Seventeenth Yearbook* of the National Society for the Study of Education published in 1918. It contained eighty-four standard tests for use in elementary schools and twenty-five for high schools and covered virtually every subject of the curriculum. Thus, Thorndike's scales for measuring academic achievement and Cliff Stone's objective test of arithmetic reasoning (1908) had developed into a set of standardized achievement tests which were published and adopted by schools throughout the United States.

A firm foundation for the quantitative approach to measuring academic achievement had been laid. William McCall, one of Thorndike's students, is credited with the statement, "Whatever exists at all, exists in some amount and can be measured." While educational investigation continued to revise and refine both tests of achievement and of intelligence, mere comparison between students soon gave way to the study of groups. Homogeneous grouping, the effects of social class, studies of educational age, and attempts to diagnose defects of underachieving students became areas of investigation between the world wars. A great many modern issues in education are related to measuring intelligence and achievement. Such measures seldom account for the cultural background of the child. Students with low scores may be discriminated against with regard to future activities such as entering college. Insofar as test scores reflect social or cultural differences, they are unfair measures of comparison between individuals, and this has been the subject of a major debate in recent years. The abuse of individual intelligence testing has also been widespread. If IQ scores are made available to teachers, there is often a tendency to classify the student as "bright" or "slow," on the basis of that evidence alone. Cultural bias in intelligence testing has become a major target of educational research. There is considerable concern today that achievement scores used for meeting accountability requirements (now a legal obligation in most states) may create excessive emphasis on basic skills and information to the detriment of personality development or "affective" learning. Tests for general intelligence had other problems in addition to cultural bias. The Stanford-Binet scales were devised for children fifteen and under. In 1944, David Wechsler, a clinical psychologist at New York's Bellevue Hospital designed tests of specific mental abilities in adults. These tests measured both verbal ability and performance at tasks. Later the Wechsler Scales were adapted for children and the Stanford-Binet was extended for adults.

Child Study.   Quite a different approach to the study of children and learning came out of the work of G. Stanley Hall (1844-1924). Hall established a center for applied psychology at Johns Hopkins in 1884 and founded the American Journal of Psychology. He asked trained kindergarten teachers to test children for their understanding of about one hundred words ranging from common objects to general concepts. From this study he published The Contents of Children's Minds on Entering School. In reporting the results of tests on children, Hall included information on social background and sex, and remarked on the high degree of emotion and superstition shown by the young. Later, as president of Clark University, Hall brought together the first group of scholars interested in scientific child study. Among his students were Arnold Gesell and Lewis Terman.

Making a formal study of the adolescent child, Hall concluded that emotional development and personality growth were just as important as cognitive learning. As an evolutionist, he sought to combine the culture epoch theory of the Herbartians with the recapitulation theory of biology. He saw childhood play as the recapitulation of man's primitive stage and believed that inhibition of play might result in the expression of violent tendencies.

Child study through the observation of youngsters at play or school, efforts to measure the interests of preschool children, and the stage theory of modern learning theorists like Jean Piaget follow logically from the pioneering work of G. Stanley Hall. The specialties of child and adolescent psychology as well as developmental psychology and the study of exceptional children owe their beginning to his work.

Arnold Gesell's Clinic for Child Development at Yale, A. B. Hollingshead's Elmtown's Youth (1949), and James S. Coleman's famous The Adolescent Society (1961) represent efforts to understand youth in a cultural setting. Dealing with the personality of the whole child, the efficiency of the school and teacher, or the sociology of education requires methods of evaluation different from those used in the measurement of intelligence or achievement. Interest in human relations and the clarification of values grew out of the realization that the needs of youth are different from those of adults, and that existing educational programs sometimes fail to meet these needs. In 1935 the American Council on Education formed the American Youth Commission which studied problems of youngsters. It found that economic factors, shattered homes, discrimination, and social stratification played major roles in the attitudes of young people and their school achievement. Similar commissions founded by the Progressive Education Association in the 1930s called attention to the fact that schools were subject oriented and not interested in the personal lives of students. Caroline Zachery, chairperson for one of the commissions, insisted that the personality of the individual is formed only through positive functioning relationships with others. She went on to found the mental hygiene movement in American schools. A considerable interest also developed in the area of research on the dynamics of instructional groups and the interactions between students and teachers in a classroom situation.

By 1950 the scientific measurement of groups had developed into a major interest of educational research. European sociologists such as Durkheim and Weber joined psychology and sociology in an effort to understand the psychodynamics of group interaction. Since World War II, there has been a vast increase in the research and literature dealing with the effects of teacher behavior on the student. Some of this has centered on T-groups, group encounter, and sensitivity training. Some has been concerned with the dynamics of instructional groups and is represented by the work of Ned Flanders and Henry Nelson. Sociologists interested in bureaucracies and systems functioning have also contributed to this field of study.

Tests for measuring personality, such as the Rorschach, are also commonly used in education. It is now understood that the temperament, aptitudes, and attitudes of students have a profound effect upon what they are able to learn and what program best fits their needs. Guidance especially has depended upon aptitudes and job analysis in an effort to fit students into a meaningful curriculum.

Educational testing and measurement now occupies a large share of the time and effort of professionals at all levels in education. Research skills are regarded as important for college and public school teachers alike, and almost all educational programs depend upon research for their support. The literature relating to measurement and testing is now so vast that considerable skill is needed just to find material that relates directly to a given problem or issue. A neglected area of measurement has been creativity and means for identifying the gifted. High IQ scores as used by Terman are not adequate for finding all students who might benefit from programs for the gifted and talented. Julian Stanley of M.I.T. has worked out a way to find and help mathematically talented college students but many gifted youngsters go undetected.

EXPERIMENTS AND INNOVATIONS IN THE
TWENTIETH CENTURY

Colonel Francis W. Parker tried out many new ideas in school organization and curricula in the late nineteenth century and built the foundations for an experimental program in the Cook County Normal School. John Dewey expanded Parker's beginning into his experimental school at the University of Chicago, which was truly a laboratory for testing educational innovations. The laboratory school lasted only seven years but it was a child-centered school which experimented with democratic organization, nontraditional methods and equipment, and a curriculum based on the natural needs and interests of children (activity curriculum). Many of the ideas which appeared in Dewey's 1916 educational classic, *Democracy and Education,* were tried in the laboratory school, and the Dewey school gave rise to new educational experiments by the progressive educators.

Progressive Education.   Even before the organization of the Progressive Education Association in 1919, schools were being organized according to the liberal ideas of Rousseau, Pestalozzi, Froebel, Parker, and Dewey. In 1907 Marietta Johnson pioneered a "School of Organic Education" at Fairhope, Alabama. Tasks in her school were not assigned by teachers so that students were free to follow their own interests. Natural growth and development according to nature replaced early emphasis on reading and accumulating knowledge. Johnson's program followed Rousseau's *Emile.* The curriculum included nature study, physical education, music, handicrafts, field geography, drama, storytelling, games, and number concepts.

A similar school was established under the supervision of the University of Missouri by Professor Junius L. Meriam. Meriam's school had a flexible time schedule with no rigid periods for drills, exercises, or formal lessons. Others soon followed the lead of Meriam and Johnson. The Cottage School of Riverside, Illinois, and the Little School in the Woods at Greenwich, Connecticut, were activity-centered institutions. John and Evelyn Dewey reported on a number of these efforts in *Schools of Tomorrow* in 1915.

Within a few years of the beginning of progressive education as a movement, the number of private experimental schools increased rapidly. Few sound statistical studies of their programs were made, but they were highly publicized by their founders and others who were critical of "traditional schools."

PEA.   Although the Progressive Education Association existed as an organization only from 1919 until 1955, its influence on American education was profound. Marietta Johnson joined with Eugene R. Smith of the Park School in Baltimore and Stanwood Cobb (a Naval Academy instructor) to organize the society. Aimed at the coordination of educational reform among private school leaders, the group was highly influenced by the theories of John Dewey. At an organizational meeting of the Association held in Washington D.C. on March 15, 1919, the eighty-five charter members adopted the following principles:

I. Freedom to Develop Naturally.
    The conduct of the pupil should be governed by himself according to the social needs of his community, rather than by arbitrary laws. Full opportunity for initiative and self-expression should be provided, together with an environment rich in interesting material that is available for the use of every pupil.

II. Interest as the Motive for All Work.
    Interest should be satisfied and developed through: (1) Direct and indirect contact with the world and its activities and use of the experience thus gained. (2) Application of knowledge gained, and correlation between different subjects. (3) Consciousness of achievement.

III. The Teacher a Guide, Not a Taskmaster.
    It is essential that teachers should believe in the aims and general principles of Progressive Education and that they should have latitude for the development of initiative and originality.
    Progressive teachers will encourage the use of all the senses, training the pupils in both observation and judgment; and instead of hearing recitations only, will spend most of the time

teaching how to use various sources of information, including life activities as well as books; how to reason about the information thus acquired; and how to express forcefully and logically the conclusion reached.

Ideal teaching conditions demand that classes be small, especially in the elementary school years.

IV. Scientific Study of Pupil Development.

School records should not be confined to the marks given by teachers to show the advancement of the pupils in their study of subjects, but should also include both objective and subjective reports on those physical, mental, moral and social characteristics which can be influenced by the school and the home. Such records should be used as a guide for the treatment of each pupil, and should also serve to focus the attention of the teacher on the all-important work of development rather than on simply teaching subject-matter.

V. Greater Attention to All That Affects the Child's Physical Development.

One of the first considerations of Progressive Education is the health of the pupils. Much more room in which to move about, better light and air, clean and well ventilated buildings, easier access to the out-of-doors and greater use of it, are all necessary. There should be frequent use of adequate playgrounds. The teachers should observe closely the physical conditions of each pupil and in co-operation with the home, make abounding health the first objective of childhood.

VI. Co-operation Between School and Home to Meet the Needs of Child Life.

The school should provide, with the home, as much as is possible of all that the natural interests and activities of the child demand, especially during the elementary school years. These conditions can come about only through intelligent co-operation between parents and teachers.

VII. The Progressive School a Leader in Educational Movements.

The Progressive School should be a leader in educational movements. It should be a laboratory where new ideas, if worthy, meet encouragement; where tradition alone does not rule, but the best of the past is leavened with the discoveries of today, and the result is freely added to the sum of educational knowledge. (Progressive Education 1 [April 1924]: 2)

Charles W. Eliot agreed to become the first honorary president of the Progressive Education Association, lending his prestige to the organization. The journal *Progressive Education* appeared in 1924 and continued to be a major publication until 1957.

In the early twenties the membership of PEA consisted largely of teachers and parents in private schools; but by the late thirties there were more than 10,000 members. Most of the professional educators in colleges and universities joined, as did the superintendents and administrators of many public school systems. In addition to the experimental schools supported by the organization, there were annual public conferences devoted to educational reform. Scientific study of pupil development and strong cooperation between schools and the society were major beliefs of PEA. William H. Kilpatrick, developer of the project method, was a major spokesman for progressive education and made the views of John Dewey popular among many educators at all levels. With Ellsworth Collings, Kilpatrick recommended that the school organize its work through a series of activities which would develop the student's purposeful effort. His projects included drills, problems, appreciation activities, and creative or construction projects.

The Progressive Education Association soon broke into camps with quite different interests. The "Social Frontier" group led by George S. Counts wanted to use education as a means for social revolution and reform. Dewey and his followers were interested in a sophisticated educational theory and careful research. Other progressive educators merely developed new methods or supported freedom for children.

Extended School Use.   Not all the early innovations were aimed at the individual development of the child. Intensive use of the school facilities to relieve social problems caused by unexpected urban growth was tried by William Wirt in Gary, Indiana. In an effort to meet the failure of the culture to provide for the needs of city children, the school offered a longer day with workshops, gymnasiums, laboratories, auditoriums, and playgrounds constantly open and supervised. To give all children the opportunity for extended school participation, schools were kept open on Saturday and during vacation periods. Adult night classes were offered, and pupils did their own repair and maintenance work. Costs were kept low by the "platoon system" by which work in classrooms, laboratories, and workshops alternated with activities scheduled in auditoriums, playgrounds, and gymnasiums so as to keep all facilities continuously occupied. This plan for maximum school use spread widely in the United States and by 1929 more than a

thousand schools were using a platoon organization. Today, crowd-
ing in some schools is relieved by scheduling one school day early
in the morning and another beginning in the afternoon.

Other important efforts to relate the schools to the needs of the
society were made by Carleton Washburne in Winnetka, Illinois, and
by Helen Parkhurst in Dalton, Massachusetts. The Winnetka plan
divided school offerings into "creative and group activities" and
"common essentials" like science and basic skills. Work in the
essentials was by units and given at the student's own rate of learning, a practice now common in schools using programmed instruction. The Dalton laboratory plan incorporated Dewey's educational
principles and many of the methods suggested by the Italian
educator Maria Montessori. Both the Dalton and the Winnetka plans
sought to develop the "whole child" and were concerned with
physical and social as well as intellectual education.

Influence of Experimental Programs.   While the early experimental schools did not become standard in America, they served as
models for a different approach to basic educational questions. Ideas
put into practice in laboratory or innovated schools were often
adopted, with modifications, into the programs of the more traditional institutions. Sometimes new schools were created in response
to criticisms of existing conditions and were intended to serve as
contrasts with older plans.

Charles W. Eliot prepared a report for the General Education Board
in 1916 in which he called for changes in American high schools.
Partly at the urging of Eliot, the Lincoln School was established as
an experimental arm of Teachers College, Columbia University, and
it continued to operate until 1948. Today, many of the leading
teachers' colleges and universities which have departments of education maintain laboratory schools. Research and development centers for testing all sorts of educational innovations are appearing in
teacher-training institutions. Sophisticated statistical processes and
refined methods of testing have given a new dimension to educational testing and the growth of graduate programs has created an
explosion in research. Doctoral dissertations in the area of educational psychology alone now provide us with a vast body of knowledge concerning the effectiveness of various pedagogical
techniques.

PROGRESSIVE EDUCATORS AND THEIR CRITICS

By 1928 Dewey had become critical of the Progressive Education
Association for its lack of sound social philosophy. In the 1930s the

interest of the progressives shifted from a reaction against formal subject matter and harsh discipline to the social and economic problems of the whole culture. Many of the members continued with their experiments in natural development, the activity curriculum, and the child-centered school; but the possibility of the schools as leaders in improving or reconstructing society became the theme of progressives like George Counts.

Social Reconstructionism.   Counts wrote a book entitled *Dare the Schools Build a New Social Order?* His position was considered radical by some progressives and many outsiders, and the reconstruction movement finally split the Progressive Education Society. Counts did raise the question of whether or not the school can play an active role in changing society, and modern reconstructionists like Theodore Brameld still address their efforts to this issue. Counts was joined by such liberal educators as W. H. Kilpatrick, John Childs, Bruce Raup, and Harold Rugg in founding the John Dewey Society for the Study of Education and Culture (1935), and they began publishing *Social Frontier*. This journal openly attacked the evils of capitalism and was responsible for some of the conservative attacks on the Progressive Education Association.

While the progressives continued to meet until 1955, their organization was divided into factions with different points of view and their efforts provoked a growing amount of controversy. Meanwhile, significant projects were being carried on that were to alter major educational concepts. The Eight Year Study of the Progressive Education Association involved thirty high schools interested in experimentation and exploration. They altered the secondary curriculum and made it conform to known laws of learning and the various social environments. The report, published in 1942, showed that students in the progressive high schools did at least as well in college as their counterparts in traditional secondary schools had done, and that they were better oriented to adult life.

Essentialism.   While the progressive movement was still popular and educators were popularizing Dewey's philosophy of education and such innovations as the community school and the project method, others were taking issue with the child-centered ideal. Protests against wasting time with "frills" and the lack of emphasis on fundamentals gained momentum with William Bagley and the Essentialists. Bagley and his followers believed that the progressives had gone too far in catering to children's interests and that they were ignoring basic skills required for successful living. The Essentialists were concerned about children who could not spell ordinary English words, or who were ignorant of the basic facts of American history. In 1938 at a convention of the NEA, the Essentialists provoked a fight with the Progressives that continued for several years. Bagley was not interested in forwarding the position of any particular philosophy, but he was soon joined by idealists like Herman Horne in his rejection of Dewey and progressivism. Nor was Bagley the only professional educator who criticized the progressive movement. Boyd Bode of Ohio State University, himself the philosophical kinsman of Dewey, found progressive theory to be full of contradictions.

Life Adjustment Education. In 1947 a group of educators launched the Life Adjustment Movement. This group was theoretically related to the progressive education movement and its concern was mostly with those students who were not preparing for college. The Life Adjustment Movement was aimed at a greater equalization of educational opportunity and was critical of any program which was not suitable for the majority of young Americans. The movement was short-lived because of the bitter attacks from many segments of the American people. Life Adjustment had the support of several educational organizations and the United States Office of Education; but was bitterly condemned by many college professors and by those interested in the subject-matter curriculum.

Dr. Charles Prosser pointed out that high schools failed to meet the needs of the sixty percent of the students who were not being trained for a vocational skill. In 1947 Commissioner of Education John Studebaker called attention to the twenty percent of the children who did not enter secondary schools and to the forty percent who dropped out before graduation. Attention was also given to the wide range of individual differences among secondary school students and the effect of family or cultural background on achievement. Twenty-nine states developed some kind of curriculum revision associated with Life Adjustment by 1954. Many school systems became interested in how to meet the needs of those who seemed not to benefit from standard courses. Studies were made of the holding power of secondary schools (dropout rate) and of the relevance of programs in the view of students.

Because of the heavy criticism by those interested only in intellectual development and a great public fear that academic standards were being lowered by Life Adjustment, the program was terminated in the late 1950s. Nevertheless, Life Adjustment gave attention to the concern for equal educational opportunity and the problems of cultural deprivation which later brought about such programs as Head

Start and the Job Corps. A basic issue remains in American education over whether we should concentrate on educating the whole
child or whether intellectual excellence has priority. Many believe
that meeting the psychological needs of the child is not enough, nor
is developing the mind enough. Few would argue that mastery of the
essential subjects — particularly those that can be called tool subjects — is not important; but the great challenge is one of relating the
experiences of the child to the cultural environment. American
schools continue to have large numbers of students who leave
school because they are unable to compete, bored, poorly adjusted,
or merely uninterested in the programs offered. Today, numerous
school systems are attempting to offer alternative high schools,
work-study programs, store-front schools, or "schools without
walls" in an effort to meet the needs of students for whom the
regular educational program is unsatisfactory. This is exactly what
the Life Adjustment plan intended to accomplish.

Another progressive innovation which seemed to offer a possible
solution to some of the social problems in modern America was the
Community School. Based on such books as John Dewey's *Schools
of Tomorrow*, the concept centered upon organizing the curriculum
around the lives of students and involving members of the community as resources. The school was to be used for all sorts of community projects such as recreation activities and as a local center for
communications. It was also expected that students and adults
would work together on problems that involved the whole community. Experimental community schools were founded by several
universities with a grant from the Sloan Foundation in the 1940s,
but only a few remain in operation. George Leonard's book
Education and Ecstasy describes a future school of this kind.

Critics of Progressive Influence.   Idealists, realists, essentialists,
and others with a philosophy opposed to pragmatism were critical of
progressive education from the beginning. Dewey himself believed
that many of the members of the progressive movement had been too
quick to adopt new programs or methods without a proper theoretical base. Boyd Bode, one of the outstanding leaders of progressive
education, criticized the determination of educational needs by
searching the individual child, rather than the society and the child
together. Bode insisted that the meaning of liberty and democracy
are linked and that the whole people must make a moral commitment to the kind of society they want before content and authority in
education can be established.

In addition to philosophic criticisms, a number of studies of academic achievement pointed up certain weaknesses in the students who had attended progressive schools. These studies were not conclusive and most were less impressive than the Eight Year Study which was favorable to progressive schools; but they provided support for those who disagreed with progressive theory. It should be remembered that while the progressive movement had great influence on public elementary schools and colleges of education, the effect on secondary schools was slight and practically nonexistent on the academic disciplines in the universities. Some of those who blame Dewey and the progressives for the ills of education and society attribute more influence to the progressive movement than the historical evidence supports.

In the 1950s equality of educational opportunity took on a new aspect. Life Adjustment had been concerned with the terminal student but during the cold war years the great cry was for the academically talented student to receive adequate training. Arthur Bestor, James Conant, John Gardner, and Hyman Rickover were among prominent critics making new demands on education. They claimed that equality of opportunity did not mean the same education for everyone, and that the national welfare demanded special provisions for the gifted. The success of the Soviet Union in launching Sputnik in 1957 shifted emphasis from life adjustment to excellence and led to the National Defense Education Act. This law greatly increased technical and scientific offerings in American high schools and colleges. Not all educators were enthusiastic about the narrow emphasis on quality for the elite or the stress placed on mathematics, science, and foreign languages.

The 1960s were dominated by concerns for equality of opportunity. In the wake of the Black revolution following the Brown case and a new concern for civil rights, efforts were made to meet the needs of all children. Ethnic and multi-cultural studies became popular and bilingual programs were started in schools with many non-English speaking students. Efforts at reorganizing schools to bring about desegregation and the use of busing to create integrated schools dominated the 1960s and 1970s. Efforts were made to help the lower class youngster compete in middle class schools through programs like project Head Start. Critics felt that integration and equality efforts took away from the drive toward excellence and public support for education was in decline by 1980. Others expressed concern about the lack of literary and humanistic emphasis in school programs. These issues will be discussed in detail in the chapter on controversial issues.

ACADEMIC FREEDOM AND THE EDUCATIONAL PROFESSION

Early in this century, American schoolteachers were forbidden to smoke, to drink alcoholic beverages, or to express political preferences, on pain of losing their jobs. While this situation has improved, public school staff members are still attacked for what they teach and for their personal activities. Thus, a teacher who asks children to read Huxley's *Brave New World*, or advocates adding fluoride to water, or supports racial integration, may be branded a "communist" by those who fear such ideas. Nor are the schools themselves free from attack. Frequently, a school board, a superintendent, or even an entire school system will find itself under violent fire from organized groups or powerful individuals. During the Joseph McCarthy era, mere accusation of "red influence" was sufficient to frighten many school officials into firing teachers or removing books from the school libraries. In some cases, however, school boards have been willing to stand up to criticism and to make their assailants prove their case, if they have one. Teachers have often been unable to fight due to the lack of support from a strong professional organization, a scarcity of financial backing, or the reluctance of some school administrators to take a stand. Thus, a teacher who has a controversial point of view, or who refuses to sign a loyalty oath, may be asked to resign quietly in return for "keeping his record clean." Significant increases in the quantity and quality of teacher training have been made in the last few years, but teachers still lack autonomy to control the admission requirements to their own profession, a professional code of ethics, or an organization which represents them all. American public school teachers still lack the academic freedom enjoyed by university professors.

TEACHER EDUCATION

Divergent educational practices in the United States have been reflected in teacher education; today this diversity is becoming less pronounced but it still exists. Many normal schools early in the twentieth century were more like secondary schools than colleges. For years a shortage of teachers created a reluctance to enforce general standards of certification. Large numbers of rural teachers were given certificates on the basis of passing examinations or on the strength of a year or two of college work. While temporary or emergency certificates are no longer issued except under most unusual circumstances, state requirements differ with regard to the number and type of professional courses demanded.

Without exception, normal schools did become four-year colleges and most universities developed colleges of education. The forty-five colleges for teachers in 1920 had grown to four times that number by 1940. Depression years caused the first oversupply of teachers, a condition which gave rise to higher minimum standards. After World War II most teachers were prepared with a general or liberal college education, specialized knowledge of the field to be taught, professional courses including methods and psychology, and practice teaching. Beyond question, American teachers are better qualified to practice their profession than ever before in history. Nevertheless, there is considerable criticism of teacher education.

The education of American teachers is a persistent national problem. Parents complain about the performance of teachers, university professors question their subject matter competence, administrators feel the universities certify people who cannot cope with school problems, and teachers themselves often feel ill prepared to work with children. Numerous studies of teacher education have been published in recent years, most of which give a negative evaluation. Scholars report that teacher training appears to make little difference in the ability of teachers to affect student achievement. Radical critics like Ivan Illich and Everett Reimer question having teachers trained and certified at all.

In spite of the dissatisfaction and criticism, it appears that there is still a need for people specially trained to work with children. Public education employs well over two and one-half million people. So long as an institutionalized system of schools is in operation in America, the development and improvement of instructional skills will be required.

Formal and informal surveys and studies reveal that seasoned teachers rate field experience as the most relevant and beneficial part of their training. In 1972, the Commission of Public School Personnel Policies in Ohio reported that 78 percent of the teachers who had graduated from the 53 teacher education institutions in the state thought student teaching was the most valuable part of their preparation. This study also indicated that educational practice or student teaching is insufficient, poorly supervised and comes too late in the course sequence. Inservice training for teachers already certified and working is also criticized for being of little use to the teacher in actually improving methods, classroom management, communication skills, and techniques for motivation of students.

Alternative programs are being developed each year by colleges and other institutions in an effort to build more relevance and skill into teacher education. Teacher Corps required interns to live and work in school communities (often lower economic areas with large numbers of minority students) while receiving instruction in theory. Colleges of education now offer programs to help middle-class teacher candidates understand the problems of lower-class students.

The major problem of teacher education is providing sufficient field experiences and practice teaching. Institutions of teacher education now usually require many hours of observation and work in schools or with children in other settings prior to practice teaching. There is general agreement that at least one year of internship would be a vast improvement over a semester of practice teaching with one cooperating teacher. By 1980, Florida and Oklahoma had passed laws requiring teacher candidates to spend a fifth year in schools as teacher interns before granting full certification. One problem is that teachers are not paid well enough to justify the extra year of entry level training.

CBTE, commonly referred to as competency based or performance based teacher education, is now used in many university-based colleges of education. CBTE is directed toward the development of specific skills or categories of behavior which have a direct connection to meaningful and observable learning on the part of the student. Instead of merely having students accumulate credits in various courses, CBTE attempts to offer methods and content selected for their ability to accomplish the goals of professional training effectively and expediently.

Some colleges are now cooperating with urban school districts to provide experiences for teacher interns designed to prepare them for work with the special educational problems of children in the ghettos of large cities. Others have developed "teaching centers" where professional teachers, practice teachers, college professors, and students can have more interaction.

As Silberman has pointed out, new teachers are often thrust into a situation fraught with anxiety and fear, and these fears and anxieties do not necessarily evaporate with experience. The techniques most frequently used to help teachers overcome their problems are inservice training and graduate courses given in colleges and universities. Inservice programs often include workshops, guest speakers, and seminars, but vary from one district or system to another. Some schools have no inservice education for teachers and the programs in others are inadequate for real professional growth. Graduate courses in education for teachers are popular because many schools require teachers to obtain a master's degree within a few years from the time of employment, and salary increases are often tied to the acquisition of graduate credit hours or advanced degrees. Graduate work in psychology, administration, statistics, educational philosophy is certainly of value; but there is a minimum of clinical experience or training designed to aid teachers in procedures of instruction and curriculum development. Of course, many teachers use graduate schools of education as a means of preparing themselves for positions as administrators, college teachers, or research workers.

The fact that large numbers of teachers feel that they are poorly prepared and the learning problems of so many students illustrated by failure in achievement is helping to support the development of new programs. With more certified teachers than jobs available, administrators can be more selective if they know what kinds of skills and what type of teacher training is most effective. Many persons now entering the field of education are serious about becoming as skilled and professional as they can. They are demanding clinical training of the sort provided in professional fields such as medicine. Pressures are building for college faculty members to become more directly involved with students and teachers in actual learning situations.

Illich has suggested that teachers should have easy access to "learning webs," centers in which teaching, learning, and communication skills can be developed. Centers where teachers can voluntarily meet to exchange experiences, thoughts, feelings, and suggestions for improving practice are now being suggested nationwide. Such a center was created in Bay Shore, New York in 1972, and pilot programs have been established for teacher centers in Vermont and Florida.

New Methods.   An effort is made to introduce students to methods such as the use of programmed learning, team teaching, individualized instruction, laboratory techniques, and methods of research. Many states now require student teachers to have some competency in the use of instructional technology before they can be certified. A better understanding of remedial reading and learning disabilities is sometimes demanded. The knowledge explosion, the way learning is affected by mass media, social problems of students, and the development of new techniques require that teachers continue their training as long as they work. An example is the "new mathematics" which required arithmetic teachers to relearn teaching concepts through graduate courses or workshops.

Teacher education has become a topic for debate among educators with different points of view. Most professors of education, leaders of teachers' organizations, and professional teachers and administrators favor present training practices. They agree that teacher training needs to be improved; but they maintain that professional courses must form the core of teacher education. Several critics who have never had work in professional education nor made a study of teacher-training institutions argue that good teachers are made through mastering subject matter. Admiral Hyman Rickover, American history professor Arthur Bestor, Jr., business tycoon Albert Lynd, and columnist Dorothy Thompson are among the enemies of professional education. They argue that a knowledge of subject matter and a good liberal education can replace a knowledge of child psychology in the training of teachers. This same point of view was expressed earlier by perennialists, the Great Books advocates, and the Council for Basic Education. The Carnegie Corporation provided funds for a study of teacher education conducted by James B. Conant, former president of Harvard University. Conant published his conclusions in 1963, making the colleges primarily responsible for selecting courses for teachers. This study negates the role of the states in certification of teachers.

Recent Growth.   In recent years, there has been an unprecedented growth in schools at all levels from the elementary school through the college. This growth has been accompanied by vast numbers of new developments which affect education. Technological advances have given rise to educational television, filmstrips, motion pictures, overhead projectors, computers for assisting instruction, and the like. Boys and girls who enter the first grade after years of exposure to television and other mass media bring new vocabularies and new experiences into the classroom. Closed-circuit and airborne television programs are received in schools, while new sources of information are found in modern instructional-materials centers. The teaching machine, in both its simple and complicated forms, is now a subject of conversation in schools and homes. While these "new-fangled gadgets" have been viewed warily by school boards and administrators, few informed educators doubt that they will have a part in the educational future of America. Self-instructing machines, team teaching projects, individual assignments, and non-graded organization are now being tested in schools and by research and development centers in colleges of education. Language laboratories, developed by the Army specialized training program, have made a considerable impact on the teaching of foreign languages.

The knowledge explosion has encouraged thinking about a year-round school and the lengthening of the school week through longer hours or Saturday classes. If this is not done, we may still expect the average school year to lengthen from 185 days to more than 200 days within a decade. The proliferation of subjects seems only to have begun as the scientific explosion continues to gain momentum. There is still the task of providing adequate challenge for the gifted child, appropriate work for the retarded, and adequate guidance for all. Even with the work of modern psychologists Jean Piaget and Jerome Bruner, we still have much to find out about the learning process.

The history of American education can never be finished. As this book goes to press, new innovations in education and cultural changes in the society are making new demands. We can only expect that past traditions and trends of development will provide some indication of the future path of our schools.

TWENTIETH-CENTURY PHILOSOPHY OF EDUCATION

Webster defines philosophy as the "love of wisdom," which is a literal rendering of the Greek word. It deals with ultimate questions such as the nature of truth, what is real, and what is of value? Educational philosophy has a more narrow focus. It is concerned with the questions of who should be responsible for education, who should be taught, and what should be in the curriculum. The goals and purposes of schooling are also subjects for philosophy of education. Classical philosophies determined an entire system of education while modern ones may merely evaluate, analyze and critize. Linguistic analysis and existentialism usually perform this role rather than creating new educational programs. Some philosophic positions are very old, realism and idealism being examples. Pragmatism, social reconstructionism, and behaviorism also have historical roots but their actual development has been in the twentieth century.

Many of the issues and conflicts in modern American education stem from basic differences in philosophic belief.

Idealism.   Idealism is a term which applies to any theory which views the world as being made up of mind, spirit, or reason. Plato recognized the existence of both mind and matter but considered mind superior. Hegel believed that consciousness if the basis of reality, including the common-sense world. George Berkeley took the extreme position that nothing is real except in the ideas or impressions of some mind. Immanuel Kant accepted the view that the mind can never know an object "in itself" but he held that phenomena, or impressions about the object can still be used as a guide to action. All of the world's major religions have some kind of idealistic philosophy. The notion that the materialistic universe depends upon God is highly idealistic.

Since idealism emphasizes moral and spiritual reality, truth and values must be universal. Froebel, Thoreau, and W.T. Harris stressed the importance of values in moral development. History, literature and models of the good person should be part of the curriculum according to idealists. The method of Socrates is encouraged as a way of bringing students to a knowledge of the basic principles of reality. Modern idealists like J. Donald Butler believe that the curriculum should be regular and orderly. They believe that reality and truth exist in the mind of the child and the function of the school is to allow this truth to be realized.

Realism.   The realist sees the world in material terms, independent of any mind or spirit. Realism is also a classical philosophy, tracing its roots to Aristotle. The work of British empiricists such as Bacon and Locke contributed to realism, as did the naturalistic theories of Rousseau. Science and natural laws are important. Through science, the universal laws of nature can be discovered. Physical, mental, and moral life all can be governed by the laws of the natural world. Although Thomism is often treated as a separate philosophy, Thomas Aquinas accepted the realistic view that while values are absolute and eternal, they are based on the laws of nature.

Pestalozzi was a realist in his educational theory. Modern realists like Harry Broudy believe that knowledge involves sensation and abstraction. The curriculum should be organized into separate subject matters or disciplines. Objective knowledge comes from the study of courses in history, botany, zoology, and physics. Rules of logic and abstract thinking will allow the student to gain eternal and universal values from organized subject matter. Realist theory holds that a universe exists that human beings did not create but which can be known by the human mind. Perennialistic theories (such as the neo-Thomism of Jacques Maritain are also grounded in realism.

Pragmatism.   Pragmatism is often considered the logic that lies behind the scientific method. John Dewey, William James, and Charles Sanders Peirce were the founders of this theory. Pragmatists hold that we cannot judge an idea as true or false just by looking at it or performing logical operations on it. The truth of a proposition depends upon its use in linking the past and the future. Judging an idea by how it works means that it may be true under some circumstances and false under others. It is not the case that any idea that works is true. We must postpone judgment until all the results of a plan of action are known and the final judgment must be public and open. Pragmatists deny the existence of absolutes. Values to them are situational or relative. Knowing results from the application of scientific thinking to experience. It is necessary to constantly reconstruct our experience in the light of new data and feedback from new experiences. Reality is the interaction of an individual with the environment, and not the environment alone.

John Dewey's pragmatism is also known as experimentalism. The theories of social reconstruction and progressive education are based on pragmatism. Skills in problem solving, personal experience, and viewing the child as an organism interacting with his or her environment are stressed by pragmatism. The basic theory of progressive education was a mixture of Dewey's early ideas with the naturalism of Rousseau and quite a few other ingredients including some social philosophies. But Dewey's experimentalist theory had not fully developed in 1919 and, indeed, there is still considerable argument about Dewey's position. Nevertheless, modern educational philosophy in America may be best understood in terms of Deweyan pragmatism and conflicting ideologies.

Dewey.   For Dewey, the proper concerns of philosophy are social conflicts, especially those found in a scientific industrial democracy. All things are experimental and nothing is fixed or sacred. The metaphysical question of how can we know ultimate reality is of little concern for Dewey as compared to the question of how we can control the world. Such control depends on utilization of the scientific experimental procedure for solving social as well as individual problems. Creative intelligence becomes the instrument for realizing the possibilities for collective human experience. The five-step problem-solving process as a model for the operation of the mind was discussed in the section on psychology, and this complete act of thought was Dewey's instrument for man's adjustment to practical situations of life.

There are no innate ideas already in the mind at birth and action must precede knowledge. Further, the world is constantly changing so that adequate solutions today may be inappropriate in the future. For the experimentalist, every tradition, problem, and belief must be constantly subjected to testing against experience. There is no absolute truth or absolute reality. Truth today is relative; it depends upon the information we have and the environmental conditions which make our conceptions of truth practical in the sense that they are working solutions to problems. We may find what we have considered to be true at one particular time in history will be cast out as error or falsehood at some future time.

Education for Dewey is the continuous reconstruction of experience which goes on throughout life. The school should be part of life itself, not merely preparation for adult living. Education is a social process which attempts to promote values clarified by philosophy. The psychological and the social aspects of education cannot be separated and the offerings of the curriculum should capitalize upon the interests of the child. Creative activity should be guided and every experience should lead to further learning or growth. Freedom is a major principle because the child should develop naturally and should be confronted with situations in which he has a genuine interest. But freedom must be achieved through intelligence, for the child who is free to become a thief engages in activity which is likely to block his further growth.

The pragmatic educational philosophy has had a tremendous impact upon professional educators in the United States. As a theory which uses science as a measuring stick and judges the value of an idea by its practical use in solving real problems, it appeals to many segments of the modern American society. While pragmatic or experimental philosophers differ widely with one another and are often critical of Dewey, the influence of this philosophy on education in the United States can hardly be overestimated.

Reactions to Dewey.   But the outcries against Dewey and his followers represent the major alternatives in twentieth century education in America. Idealist philosophers like Herman H. Horne insist that God is the center of the universe and that truth is absolute rather than relative. Religious and spiritual experience is central for the idealist and not all educational experience should be practical. It is not experience which is reconstructed, but the pattern of life which must ultimately conform to a fixed and pre-existing absolute. The goal of education is harmony with the Infinite. The theocentric philosophy which undergirds Catholic education and is based on the scholastic theory of Thomas Aquinas (1225-74) is much closer to idealism than to pragmatism. Many Catholic educators have been sympathetic to Dewey's concern for social improvement and the interests of children, but they are fundamentally opposed to pragmatism as a philosophy.

Perennialists.   Another group of like-minded educational critics are the perennialists. They accuse American education of falling under the evil influence of Deweyan pragmatism. This group would include Robert M. Hutchins, Mortimer Alder, and Stringfellow Barr, whose criticisms have been less concerned with progressive education than with a restatement of the importance of Western culture. These men hold that education ought to cultivate intellectual powers and virtues. Only the disciplined mind can come to grips with the major issues of the time. A great many pragmatists have argued that change is the essence of reality and that the school program needs to constantly be reappraised and restated in terms of changing circumstances.

But the perennialists maintain that there is really very little change either in life or the universe and that fundamental values like truth and goodness have not really changed at all. They believe that the literature in Western civilization, from the days of Plato on, contains the best statement of unchanging human nature and society. Modern perennialists hold that the Great Books of the Western World provide an excellent curriculum for school children at all ages.

While perennialism has not been supported by many professional educators, it has had a wide appeal to Catholic educators and to many professors in liberal arts colleges. Critics argue that perennialism is unscientific, bookish, past-centered, and too much concerned with subject matter for its own sake. Psychologists have said that the assumptions of perennialism about transfer of training and mental discipline will not hold up. Nevertheless, there are many influential perennialists among modern educational thinkers.

Neoscholastics like Jacques Maritain object to the dominance of science, technology, corporate industrialism, and institutionalized political units in the United States. Maritain dislikes the secular nature of modern schools and holds that neither social change nor cultural evolution are necessarily good. Like Hutchins, Maritain accuses Dewey of fostering cultural chaos through anti-intellectualism, vocationalism, and cultural isolation. Modern realists in education such as Frederick Breed, Harry Broudy, and Henry Morrison differ with both idealists and pragmatists on basic issues like theory of value (axiology), but their educational beliefs are similar to those of Hutchins and Maritain. For them the experience of the human race is invaluable and the cultural heritage must be mastered before any person can be called educated. Giving free choice to ignorant children is to destroy the sophisticated and refined knowledge which is a major aspect of civilization. Mastery of the cultural heritage requires effort and the teacher must always hold the reins of discipline.

Another critic of Dewey who fits within the category of perennialism was Herman H. Horne (1874-1946). In his books *Idealism and Education* and *The Democratic Philosophy of Education*, Horne identified intelligence as a super-human gift which links man with the absolute. Dewey's philosophy is naturalistic while Horne's is theistic. Truth for Horne is absolute and spelled with a capital "T," while for Dewey truth is merely a term for ideas which work in a given situation. Rejecting the view that education is the reconstruction of experience, the idealist sees education as an understanding of the individual and social life patterns antecedent to present experience. Dewey tells us that education is growth or evolution. Horne says that education is growth toward Truth and God.

The influence of perennialist philosophy on recent American education has been considerable but varied. Robert Hutchins's argument that higher education is dominated by materialism, the love of money, over-specialization, and a confused conception of democracy finds wide support; but not many colleges have adopted his Great Books curriculum. William Bagley's philosophy was basically realistic; but as leader of the Essentialist Committee for the Advancement of Education he supported the heritage of "tried and tested" skills, facts, and knowledge inherited through modern civilization. Agreement that absorbing the essential facts is education leaves open the question of what facts are most essential. Perhaps this is one reason that so many professors in academic fields have given their support to essentialism and perennialism. Maritain and other Catholic educators are anxious to see religion studied as a major school subject, while Max Rafferty wants to return to "solid fundamentals" and patriotic ideals. Some perennialists favor literary skills and modern foreign languages, while others think science and mathematics are more important. All are agreed in opposing the progressives and calling for a high degree of intellectual excellence in the mastery of subjects.

Other Philosophic Alternatives.   The debate between contemporary and traditional forces in educational philosophy is certainly the most significant argument over goals and purposes in American education today. Progressivism or experimentalism is widely supported by the faculties of colleges of education and by the educational profession in general. Perennialism has the backing of intellectual forces in many universities and the conservative religious institutions. The educational ideas of essentialism seem to emerge whenever a descriptive analysis of the educational offerings of public schools is made and when the masses of parents are consulted. In recent years, however, new philosophic alternatives have claimed attention.

Social reconstructionism is usually associated with progressivism, and Theodore Brameld is its most prolific contemporary spokesman. In his books *Education as Power* and *Education for the Emerging Age*, Brameld insists that schools can become the means of social change and improvement. To accomplish this, there must be a firm and binding commitment to ends (a concept John Dewey could not accept) and social consensus. While Brameld does not have a large body of followers, social reconstruction is important in educational philosophy. It has forced the careful examination of the role of education in a dynamic and changing society. Many educational sociologists have addressed themselves to the question of whether or not schools can alter the values of society or foster genuine change. This subject is also treated by educational theorist W. O. Stanley in *Education and Social Integration*.

Philosophic or linguistic analysis has become a major interest of philosophical scholars in American universities. Analytical philosophy has had some influence on educational theory, especially through the clarification of issues and detailed attention to meaning stressed by those interested in analysis. Certainly an attempt to carefully define what is meant by various educational concepts, arguments, statements, and slogans is vital to building a philosophy of education or to understanding the differences between the theories of Whitehead and Maritain. It is not yet clear that the contribution of philosophic analysis to educational thought is worth the amount of scholarly activity it has generated. The need to provide empirical verification of beliefs and to logically examine arguments led Bertrand Russell and G.E. Moore to start the movement. A.J. Ayer, Gilbert Ryle, and R.S. Peters have contributed to the field of philosophic analysis.

Behaviorism has been treated in this book as a division of psychology, which it properly is. Some recent treatments of educational philosophy have also given behaviorism a place as a division of educational theory. Certainly it is the case that B.F. Skinner has gone beyond the field of psychology in his books *Walden II*, and *Beyond Freedom and Dignity*. Any effort to use behavior modification as means of designing a new culture or bringing about a good society involves philosophy. The behaviorists also have very definite ideas about human nature (that it is totally determined by the environment) and about the freedom of choice. There are many American educators who appear to have followed a behavioristic philosophy of education.

Existentialism is not a functional philosophic system in the sense that educational goals or a statement of school theory can be derived from it. Existentialistic thought is highly individualistic and directs its attention to the self-fulfillment of each person. Stress on the unique experience of each individual and sensitivity to the problems of building personal values are found in the writings of the existentialist philosophers. The works of Buber, Jaspers, Kierkegaard, Heidegger, Marcel, Sartre, and Tillich are used by teachers interested in fostering spontaneity and authenticity. Educators who think of themselves as humanistic are often attracted by existentialism or its psychological counterpart, phenomenology. Existentialists raise questions about the assumption that education is primarily an agency of society for perpetuating cultural values or adjusting the child to a life-style accepted by the adult community.

Futurism is an emerging philosophy of education. So many educators and others concerned with rapid rates of change and the needs of students in tomorrow's world are giving attention to the future that it is becoming a new theory. While futurism has not yet developed a systematic philosophy of education, contributions have been made by Alvin Toffler, Robert Theobald, Christopher Dede, and Jim R. Bowman.

THEN TO NOW

One of the great tragedies of American education is that we keep inventing the wheel. Often, ideas that hold great promise for improving teaching and learning are discarded with the movement that brought them about. For example, the psychological concepts of Herbart were rejected by the progressives and by John Dewey himself. This happened because of Dewey's reaction against lock-step programs and rigid systems that developed from the followers of Herbart in America such as Charles DeGarmo. Actually, the ideas of Herbart were well ahead of their time and might have been retained by those who sought to reform teacher-centered methods and formal steps of instruction. Herbart taught that the mind is a unitary organism and therefore he could not support mental discipline or faculty psychology. He understood the need for relating one subject to another and so developed a core curriculum. Long before psychoanalysis, Herbart studied the relationship of the conscious to the subconscious mind and suggested a logical means by which new ideas from experience may be assimilated and stored by the learner. These ideas were not in conflict with the basic theories of the progressives. Indeed, they might have proved very helpful to the same progressive educators who scorned them because they were identified with the American Herbartian movement. Progressives turned to Gestalt psychology but many current notions about educational psychology were anticipated by Herbart and might have been used to improve the educational environment for generations.

Exactly the same thing happened with progressive education in its period of decline. As we have seen, progressives ruled education in the 1930s but there was much criticism of their child-centered programs and permissive practices by 1940. The movement ceased to exert much influence after the conservative reaction in education triggered by World War II. Beyond question, many progressives were extreme in their views and their schools were by no means perfect. Nevertheless, progressive education brought about numerous experiments that are of great pedagogical value today. The fact that most American teachers are not well-versed in their own professional history means that they must begin from scratch in order to create new methods and programs. Progressives anticipated and worked with numerous plans and ideas which today are called educational innovations. This point is well made by Judith Ford in an unpublished doctoral dissertation (University of Oklahoma, 1977) called: *Innovative Methods in Elementary Education: A Description and Analysis of Individualized Instruction in the Progressive Movement in Comparison with the Innovative Modern Elementary School.*

Most of the current practices designed to improve instruction were tried in some form by the progressive educators. An exception is computer-assisted instruction since computers and teaching machines were not available in the 1930s. Some of the most obvious parallels are:

1. Inquiry based instruction. This method is often associated with Piaget and science teaching. John Dewey was a strong advocate of laboratory instruction and discovery learning. Almost all of the progressive schools used inquiry as a major method and records exist of their success.

2. Mastery learning. Modern mastery learning is usually associated with Benjamin Bloom. Recall and application of learning to a problem solving situation was a mainstay of progressive schools. It was best demonstrated by Ellsworth Collings in the McDonald County Rural School in 1905.

3. Individual contracting. Using individual contracts with students to stimulate specific learning is now a practice in many schools. The formal writing of contracts with specific behavioral goals may be current, but the idea of students participating in choosing what they would learn and when goes back to Helen Parkhurst and the Dalton Contract Plan of 1919.

4. Differentiated staffing. Many professional educators now support differentiated staffing. Having all teachers trained in the same way seems inefficient and wasteful. Master teachers, general teachers, learning specialists, teaching assistants, instructional materials specialists, clerks, and nonprofessional staff members might make up a better team for instruction. The progressives used community resource people in their schools. They did not hesitate to bring in people with different training for various school-related tasks. J. Lloyd Trump, who first urged differentiated staffing in schools, was influenced by the progressive experiments.

5. Flexible scheduling. The Gary Platoon Plan organized by William Wirt in 1915 used flexible scheduling. Most of the progressive schools were not tied to the clock or the calendar. They pioneered programs which used whatever time was necessary to accomplish learning without regard to filling days with even blocks of time or earning units of credit. Numerous modern schools use computers to program flexible individualized schedules.

6. Individualized instruction. Today, a body of literature supports the idea that individualized instruction may be superior for many students. Carleton Washburne experimented with such a plan at Winnetka in 1919. Most progressives let students progress at their own speed which required special individual assignments and evaluation. The history of progressive education shows that individual

instruction worked better than group instruction for some learning, but that it required more time of teachers. Progressives supported the social interaction of groups for certain kinds of learning (such as social studies) but used individualized projects as well. They understood that each child is unique and that there are many styles of learning. In some ways, the progressive schools were similar to modern alternative schools, almost all of which use individualized instruction.

7. Open classrooms. In spite of all the modern literature on the subject, open classrooms were pioneered by the progressives. Marietta Johnson's School of Organic Education at Fairhope, Alabama, was an early example. Freedom for students to move about, small group activities, an informal atmosphere, inquiry, and freedom of expression were characteristics of progressive education. The best of open classroom instruction is described in progressive literature.

8. Team teaching and nongraded schools. John Dewey himself created teams of teachers to work with students at the laboratory school in the University of Chicago. Like the progressives who followed him, Dewey was aware that several teachers working together can provide a richer educational environment and better evaluation. Although the progressives did not establish nongraded schools in name, they did allow students to learn at their own rate of speed and they were not bound by any external standards. Progressives wrote about the perils of self-contained classrooms and rigid programs which require all children to achieve the same goals within a given span of time.

If American education is to meet the great challenges of the future, it must be efficient, flexible, professional, and stimulating. Schools cannot afford to re-invent and test programs or methods which were tried and tested in the past. Educators need to learn about both the success and the failure of earlier educational experiments and to use those experiments as guides in making a better quality learning environment.

BIBLIOGRAPHY

Brown, Ellsworth. *The Making of Our Middle Schools.* New York: Littlefield, 1970.

Burton, Warren. *The District School as It Was.* Boston: Lee & Shepard, 1897

Butts, Freeman. *Public Education in the United States: From Revolution to Reform.* New York: Holt Rinehart and Winston, 1978.

Cremin, Lawrence. *The Transformation of the School.* New York: Alfred A. Knopf, 1961.

Digest of Educational Statistics 1980. Washington: U.S. Government Printing Office, 1980.

Gutek, Gerald. *An Historical Introduction to American Education:* New York: Thomas Crowell, 1970.

Karier, Clarence. *Shaping the American Educational State: 1900 to the Present.* New York: Free Press, 1975.

Katz, Michael. *Class, Bureaucracy, and Schools.* New York: Praeger, 1971.

McLaughlin, Milbery. *Evaluation and Reform: The Elementary and Secondary Education Act of 1965.* Cambridge, Mass: Harvard University Press, 1975.

Ozmon, Howard, and Samuel Carver. *Philosophical Foundations of Education.* 2nd. ed. Columbus, Ohio: Charles E. Merrill, 1981.

Rippa, Alexander. *Education in a Free Society.* 2nd. ed. New York: David McKay, 1971.

Tyack, David. *The One Best System: A History of American Urban Education.* Cambridge, Mass: Harvard University Press, 1974.

Controversial Issues in Modern   7
American Education

Anything which has already happened is history even if it happened only a moment ago. It is often more difficult to make a good historical analysis of events just past than those which occurred in an earlier period. Recent occurrences in educational history are often surrounded by controversy, especially if there are issues or arguments involved. Very few modern events are free from criticism and even the educational community often ends up by taking sides. Political groups get involved quite often in current educational concerns and public opinion plays a vital role in numerous decisions. While it was once rare for problems over the schools to result in litigation, it is now very common for educational issues to reach the courts. Books that are critical of many aspects of education now become best sellers while past critics wrote for much smaller audiences. Since education touches all of the American people and since the means of communication is expanding so rapidly, the current history of education is very much the history of controversial issues. While judgments about current events are hard to make, an understanding of history may provide us with the best foundation we can get for placing such events in perspective.

In the last chapter, various positions in the philosophy of education were discussed. Philosophy is seldom universally accepted so that

School Desegregation	Civil Rights Movement	Campus Rebellion
1954 Brown Case Issue	Martin Luther King	1966 Coleman Report
1957 Sputnik Issue Criticisms of Bestor, Conant and Rickover	1961 John Gardner Published *Can We Be Equal and* *Excellent Too?*	1961–1968 Kennedy-Johnson Legislation
	1963 Michael Harrington's *The Other America*	

conflicting ideas and contradictory views are usual. Pragmatists and idealists did not agree in the early twentieth century and they do not agree today. The same can be said for schools of psychology like Gestalt and behaviorism. The fight over the legal status of private schools that led to the Oregon case of 1925 provides background for the issue of tax support to parochial schools and the legality of tuition tax credits for nonpublic education.

In the past few decades, critical issues have appeared in the schools which pose serious questions for the future of education. There are also controversies in the general society which translate into problems for education. Some of these issues must be solved by members of the educational profession, basing their action on sound scientific research. Others can be solved only by cooperation between the general public and the profession. Still others continue to be issues for the reason that no solution is obvious or certain, even if the best possible interaction between school people and the public takes place. Altering the curriculum of the public schools to prepare children to cope successfully with future conditions is always uncertain precisely because techniques for future prediction are inexact.

Issues involving the purposes or goals of education concern both the layman and the professional educator in a society which is, to some degree, democratic. This kind of problem is the subject of philosophy of education; but it also involves values, norms, and attitudes which may be understood through sociology, social psychology, and political science. While various groups such as realists and pragmatists have clear-cut educational goals, the educational philosophy of the whole American people is not fixed and certain. In a fluid culture, the aims of education in one period of time are often altered considerably by the next generation. Specific aims, goals, and purposes are hotly debated not only among educators, but by the

Equal Opportunity	Accountability	Return to Basics
1968 Issues Over Bilingual and Multicultural Education.	1969 Arther Jensen Studied IQ and Race	1973 Only 2,500 Black Doctorates in All Fields
Accountability Tests	1969 Theodore Roszak *The Making of a Counterculture*	1979 John Goodlad's *What Are Schools For?*
Compensatory Education for the Disadvantaged	1970 Charles Reich *The Greening of America*	
	Ivan Illich *Deschooling Society*	

whole of the body politic. Educational purposes are certainly going to be the object of much disagreement and discussion in the future as in the past.

It often happens that the role of the teacher and that of the profession in a problem or issue concerning schools consists of communication and clarification. The public may be unaware of the existence of problems, or there may be a misunderstanding of the exact nature of those problems. Difficulties concerning poverty, crime, taxation, employment, equal rights, academic freedom, racial integration, discipline, and the like often have educational significance not clear to the casual observer. Explaining what the issues really mean and outlining possible consequences of various plans of action must often fall to educators. Analysis and clarification of hidden issues or underlying problems must often be undertaken before a solution can be reached. Obviously, past experience including a knowledge of history may provide clues to the probable success or failure of alternatives.

A number of approaches may be taken to the history and understanding of current issues and challenges in American education. In this chapter, we will discuss a number of well-known educational conflicts that have reached the courts. Litigation has always been important for educational policy as in the Dartmouth College case and the Kalamazoo high school decision. In contemporary society, many cases handled by the state and federal courts are vital to understanding recent educational history. Earlier chapters examined the ideas of well-known philosophers, psychologists, and public officials who influenced education. This chapter will deal with important modern educational critics and spokespersons for major organizations. Critics

·often serve as guides to significant educational problems. Finally, we will treat a number of current educational issues for which educational institutions and teachers are accountable.

LITIGATION: THE COURTS AND PROBLEMS OF EDUCATION

Religion and Public Schools.   Religion was the major subject in colonial schools, but with the separation of church and state, public schools could teach only interdenominational or nonsectarian religious principles. Still, the curriculum remained heavily influenced by religious writings, prayer, and Christian morality. Bible reading was considered nonsectarian in most communities. The fact that a Protestant Bible was not acceptable to Catholics carried little weight, and Jews were also discriminated against in school programs. Minority groups often chose not to make an issue of religion in the public schools before the twentieth century. If Catholic, Jewish, or other minority religious groups were unable to support their own schools, they normally accepted the rules of the public schools even when the requirements went counter to their own beliefs. In the past few years, however, there have been a great number of court cases over the religious requirements or practices in public schools. While the majority of the cases have decided against the inclusion of religious practices, a large number of Americans have felt that the schools were responsible for moral training which could hardly be given without reference to religion. Beginning the school day with prayer has been attacked by religious liberals and nonbelievers, while Jehovah's Witnesses have claimed that saluting the flag constitutes worship of a "graven image." There is no clear-cut division between patriotic and religious exercises; even the Pledge of Allegiance has contained the words "under God" since 1954. Furthermore, chaplains have been assigned to military units and "in God we trust" has been stamped on coins. The major educational problem, however, concerns Christian Christmas programs, religious exercises, and the reading of Scripture as part of the public school program.

The issue of the role of religion in education is centered on two quite controversial issues: the promotion of religious instruction in public schools, and the use of public tax money to aid nonpublic schools. In 1919 Nebraska passed a law prohibiting private or parochial schools from teaching any subject in any language other than English. The Supreme Court in 1923 ruled the law unconstitutional in *Meyer v. Nebraska.* While holding that the state may require attendance at some school, the Court stated that parents may send their children to private schools where some subjects need not be taught in English. This was a landmark case concerning both religion and the language of instruction.

Two years later the Supreme Court reinforced the right of parents to choose nonpublic schools in *Pierce v. Society of Sisters*. This case made unconstitutional a 1922 Oregon law which required all children between the ages of 8 and 16 to attend *public* schools. There has been no effort to outlaw private or parochial schools since 1925 and the Pierce doctrine remains in force.

The right of the student to be protected from rules that violate his or her religious freedom was at issue in the Gobits case of 1940. Parents named Gobits were members of Jehovah's Witnesses who objected to the school requirement that all students must say the pledge of allegiance to the American flag. The Court upheld the school board in this case but three years later it reversed its position in *West Virginia v. Barnett*. Religious freedom thereafter became a valid reason for children to be excused from school activities which violate their religious beliefs.

In 1947, approximately two-million public school students were released to attend religious classes during some part of the school week. In *McCollum v. the Board of Education of Champaign, Illinois*, in 1948, the Supreme Court held that releasing students to attend religious classes held in public school buildings was illegal. A later case in New York ended with a ruling that released time does not violate separation of church and state if religious classes are held outside the schools.

Law suits have sometimes resulted in changing educational practices as in the New York Regents' Prayer Case of 1962. Using the coercive power of the school to make children participate in religious activities has been held to violate the First Amendment. Although a 1976 Gallup poll found that 70 percent of parents favored compulsory attendance, the Court has held that Amish parents may use the First Amendment as a basis for keeping their children out of high school. In *Wisconsin v. Yoder* the compulsory attendance law of the state was set aside to protect the free exercise of the religious views of parents.

Cases involving public aid to parochial schools have created major concerns in educational circles. In the 1950s the NEA and the American Association of School Administrators adopted resolutions opposing all efforts to use public funds for nonpublic education. Federal legislation provided school lunches for parochial schools in 1948 and the government allowed G. I. Bill and NDEA funds to be used for scholarships to nonpublic schools. The National Science Foundation made grants to private universities while the Higher Education Act of 1965 gave money to church-related colleges for nonreligious purposes. Private schools also got libraries and instructional materials under the Elementary and Secondary Education Act of 1965.

In the Cochran Case of 1930, the Supreme Court held that while direct aid to private and parochial schools was illegal, the state could use public funds to pay for transportation, lunches, textbooks and health services which were of benefit to all children. This "child benefit" theory was also the basis for the use of taxes to pay for the transportation of students to Catholic schools in the Everson case. Everson upheld Cochran but the Court was split and the issue has not cooled. Many advocates of the public schools fear that any aid to private and parochial schools will weaken public education. They point out that equality of educational opportunity and integration suffer in nonpublic programs. For them, any aid to private education is a violation of the separation of church and state. They illustrate the difficulty Americans had in obtaining tax support for public schools in the era of Horace Mann and quote Thomas Jefferson on the necessity of keeping religion segregated from government. Several states now prohibit the use of tax money for any kind of aid to parochial schools, whether for child benefit or not. This whole issue is also tied to the question of tuition tax credits for parents who choose to send their children to private schools and to federal aid to nonpublic education. The arguments were especially heated in the early 1980s. Criticism of public schools caused many parents to demand tuition tax credits while spokespersons for public education held that such credits would weaken the very foundation of public schools.

Although released time for religious instruction, Bible reading, and nonsectarian prayers are illegal in public schools, the issue is not resolved. There is considerable pressure to "restore religion" to the public classroom.

Involuntary Segregation.   Involuntary segregation refers to excluding certain children from schools, usually on the basis of race. The problem of segregation is clearly linked to the period following the American Civil War and to the freeing of the slaves. Public schools for Blacks and Whites established during the period of reconstruction in the South were quickly eliminated in the 1880s. Thereafter, southern states made laws which required that schools could not admit children from both races to the same classes and segregation began.

As we have seen, federal attempts to provide support to the South for education (as with the Hoar Bill and the Blair Bill) failed. This left a large part of the nation in a condition of poverty and without the resources to provide adequate schooling for its children. The problem was made even more acute by the requirement of a dual school system which was expensive and inefficient. All the schools in the South lacked resources from the 1880s to the 1950s, but the Black schools were a cut below all the others.

Northern states did not usually have laws prohibiting racially integrated schools, but many northern schools were segregated because of population patterns. White students did not attend schools with a majority of Black pupils until after the Brown Case. Many schools in northern cities were all Black or all White according to their location and the demography of the area.

So dubious was the prospect for social equality in the South at the time that Booker T. Washington thought Blacks should accept segregation in return for some access to education. The *Plessey v. Ferguson* case of 1896 affirmed the principle that separate but equal facilities were legal. In 1906, the Niagara movement was started by W.E.B. Du Bois. It led to the National Association for the Advancement of Colored People, which was organized in 1909. The NAACP began to challenge segregation laws in the 1930s, on the grounds that facilities provided Blacks were not even remotely equal.

While not attacking the segregation laws on principle, the Supreme Court began to require admission of Black students to southern professional schools unless the states could prove that they had equal facilities for Blacks within their borders.

Finally in 1950, a direct challenge to segregated education was presented to the Court in *Sweatt v. Painter* where an applicant who had been denied admission to the University of Texas Law School solely on the basis of color claimed that the instruction available in the newly established state law school for Blacks was markedly inferior to the instruction at the university; therefore, equal protection of the law was denied. In a unanimous decision the Supreme Court ordered his admission to the White school, indicating that it was virtually impossible in practice, at least in professional education, for a state to comply with the "separate-but-equal" formula.

Following the decision in the Sweatt case, the National Association for the Advancement of Colored People and other organizations pressed the fight against segregation in public schools which resulted in several public school segregation cases. The Court proceeded with a great deal of circumspection and required an unusual amount of investigation by the counsels. Their deliberation was understandable because if segregation in public schools was determined to be a denial of equal protection of laws, it would in all likelihood be impossible to defend segregation in other sectors of public life. The legal foundation of the social structure of a great part of the nation was under attack. By 1954 it had become obvious to the public that Black children in segregated states received a much poorer schooling than White students. In 1952, for example, Arkansas spent $102 for the education of each White child as against $67 for each Black. Black colleges were often substandard, and few jobs were open to Black students who had graduated from northern universities. Integration in the armed forces in World War II and the success of Blacks who sued for entry into southern universities led to the Supreme Court Decision of 1954, *Brown v. Board of Education.*

In this famous case, the NAACP lawyer Thurgood Marshall argued that equality of educational facilities was not the question. Marshall claimed that prestige, teaching standards, the academic surroundings, and the inference of inferiority were important in educational equality. The Court agreed, saying that segregation was construed to deprive minority group children of equal educational opportunity. By its decision, the Supreme Court held that all laws concerning or permitting school segregation were in conflict with the Fourteenth Amendment and ordered involuntary segregation to cease within a "reasonable time." Several major cities like Baltimore, Washington, and St. Louis made a complete transition to integrated schools on the basis of the 1954 decision.

This decision, as with most decisions, met much opposition. One of the frequent arguments against it is illustrated by an article reprinted from the *American Bar Association Journal.* Eugene Cook, Attorney General of Georgia, and William J. Potter criticized the Brown decision severely. The opinion of the Court, said these critics, "did not hold that the old 'separate but equal' doctrine, laid down in *Plessy v. Ferguson,* was a bad law. It held that it was bad sociology."

Considerable progress toward desegregation was made in border states, but in the deep South various measures designed to frustrate desegregation were tried. Boycotting or nonsupport of integrated schools, student assignment plans to minimize integration, and the temporary abolition of public schools, as in Prince Edward County, Virginia, took place. Integration of the teaching staff and token integration through bringing in a few minority group students to all White schools were common attempts to meet legal requirements without basic change. Private academies were established in parts of the South in an effort to escape court-ordered integration, especially in areas where Black people were in the majority.

A serious problem in many areas has been de facto segregation: segregation based upon school district boundaries which encompass children from only one race. The problem of de facto segregation is by no means confined to the South since Blacks, Mexican-Americans, and other minority groups have been forced to live (often for economic reasons) in a single part or section of most cities. Racial boundaries tend to move rapidly so that schools which are planned to serve students from different races or ethnic backgrounds often end up being built in areas where only one race is present. Often some sort of educational park, cluster of school buildings, or central administration assignment of students has been used as an instrument for integration.

Heavy opposition to such efforts is often encountered. Many parents object to having their elementary age children attend schools other than those in their own neighborhoods or within walking distance of their homes. Some fear that integration will have a negative effect on children, such as introducing them to foul language, crime, and drugs. Many school districts have experienced a loss of enrollment as a result of court-ordered desegregation plans. Parents move their families into suburban areas in order to avoid what they believe to be unfortunate aspects of school integration. Perhaps the greatest opposition has occurred when cities have attempted to solve the integration problem by busing students from one school to another in order to achieve some degree of racial balance. A major problem for education has been the mandate given to schools to foster integration while the general public in many communities was unwilling to cooperate. Nevertheless, research indicates that whenever Black and White students can be placed together in positive and meaningful educational experiences at an early age, racial tension is reduced and human relations improved.

Delays and circumventions in desegregation have not been confined to public schools. The attempt of Authurine Lucy to enter the University of Alabama in 1956 and the violence created by James Meredith's admission to the University of Mississippi in 1962 are illustrative of the problems of integration in higher education. Nevertheless, colleges and universities have been racially integrated with much less conflict than in public schools.

As the Black movement for freedom and integration reached revolutionary levels, plans for school integration were set into motion throughout the United States. Some plans found general acceptance;

but most efforts to move large numbers of children from one area of a city to another for integration of schools were bitterly opposed. With the assassination of Martin Luther King, Jr., in 1968 and the passage of the Civil Rights Act in 1964, desegregation entered a new phase. The Civil Rights Act specified that no person could be discriminated against on the basis of race, color, sex, or national origin in any program which received federal assistance. This meant that federal funding could be withheld from school districts or states that failed to adopt reasonable and acceptable plans for integration.

Some of the southern school districts with the greatest need for financial help have been the least willing to integrate. Plans involving the mass busing of children have drawn fire from parents, politicians, and the public. Federal courts and the Department of Health, Education and Welfare have insisted upon prompt compliance with the law; but the struggle goes on in many communities. School buses were attacked and burned in Michigan. Riots over busing Black students to South Boston High School in 1974 caused the closing of the school. Many state legislatures have issued laws against busing for racial balance, and Congress has come close to considering such a law. Meanwhile, schools attempt to follow legal guidelines and carry on the task of public education as best they can.

Although the Supreme Court has continued to uphold the Brown Decision, militant resistance to busing has not died out and many school districts still reflect segregation. Sometimes this occurs when the population of a city changes dramatically as in the case of Newark, New Jersey. The Court has held that school boards may not intentionally gerrymander attendance districts to encourage segregation (Keyes v. Denver) but some American cities are entirely White or Black. In Milliken v. Bradley the Supreme Court reversed the ruling of lower federal courts which said Detroit should adopt a metropolitan desegregation plan to include its suburbs. On the other hand, the Court in 1977 refused to review the decision of Judge Garrity in Morgan v. Hennigan. The Court let stand the placing of the school system in federal receivership because the Boston Board had intentionally increased segregation. Numerous other cases are still pending and the mood of the nation seems to be swinging away from support for court-ordered busing plans. Los Angeles was allowed to discontinue busing for racial integration in 1981. Nevertheless, desegregation has worked in many areas and America will not go back to conditions that existed before 1954.

Litigation and Equality of Opportunity.   Although some part of the educational budget for most school districts is federally collected and distributed, American school support is largely a state and local matter. Traditionally, the federal government has had no role in school finance except where federal funds were involved. This changed dramatically in 1971 with a case brought on behalf of Mexican-American children in Los Angeles. Using the equal protection guarantee of the Fourteenth Amendment, the California Supreme Court ruled that state's system of financing public schools discriminatory in *Serrano v. Priest*. The basis of the argument was that the quality of education provided was a function of the wealth of each district and therefore discriminated against poor children. Following *Serrano*, more than 50 suits in 30 states were filed against the local property tax systems. Minnesota, Texas, New Jersey, and Connecticut had their property taxes struck down by the courts.

The impact of *Serrano v. Priest* might have been even more dramatic if the Supreme Court had not taken a different stand in *San Antonio Independent School District v. Rodriguez*. A Texas federal district court had ruled the Texas system of local property taxation illegal as in the Serrano case. In 1973, however, the Supreme Court in a 5 to 4 decision reversed the district court and held that the system in Texas did not absolutely deprive poor people of education nor discriminate against any definable category of the "poor." In spite of this support for the property tax, attention was brought to the inequality of educational opportunity in various districts within states. Many state legislatures have taken a hard look at their system of school funding since *Serrano* and *Rodriguez*. New laws have been proposed and others probably will be because it is hard to justify unequal financial support for education in a democratic society.

Other Significant Court Cases.   While the most important influence of the courts has been directed toward desegregation, religion, and equality, there have been several other areas of educational importance. A common practice in many American cities was to test children and then to place them in a fixed curriculum according to the ability group into which they fall. This practice was found unconstitutional in 1967 in *Hobson v. Hansen*. This form of grouping called the "tracking system" tended to promote segregation within schools and make it impossible for students to get out of the track once they had been placed in it.

The right of privacy and to due process under the law has been extended to children in the United States. In 1971 students in Columbus, Ohio, who were suspended for ten days from school without a hearing brought suit. In this case, *Goss v. Lopez*, the Court held that high school students must be granted due process including notice of the charges against them and an opportunity must be provided for them to present their side of the story. Similar cases have protected children suspended for wearing long hair or violating school codes of dress. The Family Educational Rights and Privacy Act of 1974 (also called the Buckley Amendment) requires schools to provide access to records to students over the age of eighteen and to parents of younger students. Another landmark case on children's rights was *Tinker v. Des Moines* in 1969. Quaker students in the Des Moines public schools were suspended for wearing black armbands to protest the war in Viet Nam. The Supreme Court found that wearing armbands was a symbolic case of expression and therefore it was protected under the First Amendment, like freedom of speech. Modern courts have also been active in matters concerning loyalty oaths, violations of civil liberties, and academic freedom. As a general rule, schools are prohibited from making any rule or regulation that impinges upon rights that students would enjoy if they were adults.

MODERN EDUCATIONAL CRITICS

Clashing views on controversial educational issues have characte-rized writing in the field for many years. Historically, institutional-ized education has been characteristically rigid and that led to critic-ism by progressives and other liberal writers. On the other hand, business leaders and political conservatives have often attacked the schools for promoting socialistic ideas or for teaching about social issues. Liberal-conservative arguments over the curriculum, moral training, and the rights of children have been present in the educa-tional literature for generations.

Curriculum matters often tie in with methods and with psychology. When Charles Eliot chaired the Committee of Ten in 1892, specific subjects were prescribed for the high schools. Latin, Greek, English, German, French, Spanish, algebra, geometry, trigonometry, astron-omy, meterology, botany, zoology, physiology, geology, physics, che-mistry, history, and physical geography were the subjects that got support. Critics soon pointed out that the high school curriculum lacked vocational subjects, sociology, psychology, and the humani-ties. The Committee was also highly influenced by the popular educa-tional psychology of the time which stressed mental discipline. Later psychologists were quick to take issue with subjects chosen because of their alleged ability to train the mind. Others argued that the subjects chosen were all intended for college preparatory students while the majority of the high school's population was not college bound.

Critics of education in modern America provide a means by which issues in contemporary schooling may be studied. Some critics find philosophical fault with the aims and purposes of education. Others attack teacher education, the curriculum, or the methods used in schools. Many are concerned about the quality of programs and the products produced by schools. Not only are the critics now numerous and verbal, but also many have established themselves in staunch positions with considerable public support. Some people think that modern critics perform a service by isolating problems and illumination inadequate aspects of the educational system. Others say that responsible criticism requires offering attainable solutions and working within the system to achieve them. Clearly there are many more people ready to focus on the shortcomings than there are critics with reasonable answers or alternatives. Several critics do have a talent for providing poignant insight into the teaching-learning process and the total school environment. Many critics reach professionals within the educational system who take them seriously enough to attempt change. Colleges of education have been especially sensitive to the charges of critics. Of course, critics also create anger, frustration, disgust, and other negative reactions both inside and outside the system.

During the 1950s, the nation enjoyed a period of relative prosperity and tranquility. The hysterical fear of communism which had caused attacks on academic freedom began to subside. Various social and legal movements toward the achievement of racial equality began to alter the educational system.

This tranquil period came to an end in the reaction against the successful launching of Sputnik. In the wake of fear and criticisms of American educational failures, European schools were compared favorably with those in the United States. James B. Conant, former president of Harvard, called for the reorganization of high schools with more emphasis on excellence. Admiral Hyman Rickover insisted that the major purpose of education is to produce the experts who create the technology and science upon which a modern nation depends for winning wars, hot or cold. These views carried the day, and through such programs as the National Defense Education Act, emphasis was placed upon science, technology, mathematics, foreign languages, and high standards.

In the 1960s a new wave of criticism arose following the politically, socially, and emotionally turbulent decade marked by civil rights activity at home and war in Viet Nam. Critics proclaimed that recent academic reforms had failed or at least were not meeting prevalent needs. Although college board scores indicated that the public schools of the 1960s produced students with comparatively better skills in science and mathematics, questions were raised about the relevance of the curriculum, attitudes produced, individual needs of students, and the role of schools in social change.

In the 1970s, dissatisfaction permeated the social order and the grim realities facing the nation created a diversity of new educational criticisms. Fear that a lasting peace might not be achieved in the world, loss of faith in government following the Watergate affair, and the prospects of unemployment in an economy marked by inflation and recession added to uncertainty about the future. People began to ask how children should be educated to cope with the energy crisis, ecology, the depletion of natural resources, urban congestion, rising crime, a world population explosion, and a changing job market. Others focused less on problem solving and economic survival and more upon the developmental, creative, and human needs of individual students. One group of critics concerned themselves with the way schools mold or shape students. They were sensitive and sympathetic to groups of children who to one degree or another are "victims" of society and therefore of the school system.

By 1980 the focus of criticism had taken a conservative turn. Distrust of big government and bureaucracy caused dissatisfaction with programs for social engineering, school integration, and efforts to aid the poor. Inflation fueled a demand for more job-related training, more efficient use of school time, and less busing for desegregation. A new wave of attacks on teaching the theory of evolution, sex education, and values clarification came from the so called "moral majority." Multicultural studies and bilingual education became less popular and there were new demands for accountability. The reputation of education declined as ACT scores continued to slide and many high school graduates proved unable to read beyond an elementary level. "Excellence" and a "return to basics" were the most popular slogans of the times.

Samuel Bowles and Herbert Gintis.   Among those who advocate radical school reform or argue that education cannot be improved without a far-reaching social revolution are Bowles and Gintis. Their book, *Schooling in Capitalist America,* called attention to hostility of the school toward the need of the individual for personal development. Like Paul Goodman, Edgar Friedenberg, Everett Reimer, and

Paolo Freire, these authors call for radical school reform. Bowles has questioned whether education has been of any real economic benefit to minority people, showing that the relative incomes of Blacks declined even when the absolute incomes improved. He has also been very critical of the way James Colemen analyzed his data in the *Coleman Report*. Like Ivan Illich, Bowles and Gintis take an extreme antischool position. They do not think the schools can be reformed without drastic alteration of the underlying social and economic forces.

George Dennison.   George Dennison established the first "street school," which was an alternative educational program for minority children from low-income families on New York's lower East Side. Half of his students came from public schools where they had been given labels such as "severe learning and behavior problems." In *The Lives of Children* (1969), Dennison tells about his experiences with these children, including the violence and obscenity inherent in the daily routines of the pupils. Relating his work with disturbed children to the views of A. S. Neill, John Dewey, Paul Goodman, and Leo Tolstoy, Dennison points up the needs of those who have been cast off by society or parents. His writings have gained the attention of educators and social reformers sensitive to the depth of individual problems that plague the lives and experiences of many children in the modern world.

John Holt.   An experienced teacher on both the elementary and secondary levels, Holt began expressing himself to other educators in 1964 when he wrote *How Children Fail*. He urged teachers to focus on children and their individual needs rather than upon the formal ingestion of a rigid curriculum. Calling attention to the ominous relationship between the fear and expectation of failing and actual failure, Holt showed how teachers often contribute to a self-fulfilling prophesy. He supports a child-centered approach in which each pupil can develop his or her own activities and abilities at his or her own speed. In other books, *What Do I do Monday?* (1970) and *Freedom and Beyond* (1972), Holt offered practical suggestions to teachers about how to keep interest alive in schools and what can be done to encourage each student to reach his or her maximum potential.

Ivan Illich.   Any educator who has not heard of Ivan Illich is isolated indeed! In *Deschooling Society* (1971), Illich not only denounced compulsory education but also called upon modern nations like the United States to give up their public systems of education.

Illich's background is somewhat different from that of most other educational critics. He was a Catholic priest in New York City, Puerto Rico, and South America until he resigned in 1961 to found the Intercultural Center for Documentation in Cuernavaca, Mexico. As a result of his experiences in Latin America, Illich concluded that mass education has detrimental effects upon poor people. For example, he says that to go to school in Mexico for two or three years and then drop out is worse than not attending school at all. Dropping out makes one a failure in the eyes of society and the learning gained probably is of no use to a poor laboring man. Illich feels that the right of the individual to learn is actually hindered by compulsory attendance and mass education. Schools are used as screening devices to sift out the gifted few or justify the existence of high schools and colleges for the children of the wealthy and powerful. Illich thinks it is not feasible to create schools which will actually meet the educational needs of the masses. Education is the responsibility of society and must not be delegated to schools, which are operated by governments for the benefit of the few. He contends that the disadvantaged would have a better chance if the bond between education and schooling was completely severed. By deschooling society, there would no longer be power or prestige associated with staying in school a long time or acquiring a degree. Probably no one, including Illich, really expects that the United States will abandon its public schools. His criticism is important because it calls attention to the fact that education may benefit one class of society at the expense of others, and that the values fostered by public schools are not necessarily those of greatest use for the survival of the individual and the well-being of the people.

Another group of modern educational critics believes that compulsory public education is detrimental to the purpose and process of learning. Some critics call for an end to "schooling" as a means of social control and value formation.

Herbert Kohl.   As a result of his first teaching experience with Black sixth graders in East Harlem, Herbert Kohl wrote *36 Children* (1967), which tells how he created a curriculum from his students' experiences and his own imagination. Holding that the standard school curriculum prevents communication between teacher and student, Kohl claimed success in combining creativity and relevant experiences with academic achievement. A more recent book, *The Open Classroom*, is presented as a "handbook for teachers who want to work in an open environment." Kohl has become a leader among teachers and parents who want to foster better community participation in education and he has worked with various systems in the creation of alternative schools.

Jonathan Kozol.   Unlike Kohl, Jonathan Kozol was dismissed as a substitute teacher in a Boston elementary school for deviation from the established curriculum. Concerned about his sincere efforts to communicate with lower-class Black students, Kozol shocked the nation with his book *Death at an Early Age: The Destruction of the Hearts and Minds of Negro Children in the Boston Public Schools* (1967). More than a critic of school programs, Kozol is politically sensitive to problems such as minority rights, bureaucratic manipulation by school boards, and the insensitivity of the public to the needs of some groups of children. In 1972 he wrote *Free Schools* and became interested in the efforts to develop meaningful learning programs for children with backgrounds culturally different from those of the majority. Kozol currently writes for educational journals and gives speeches, such as the highly publicized one at the NEA Convention in 1973 which called attention to the inadequate programs he sees in American schools.

Theodore Roszak.   It may be fairly said that Theodore Roszak is spokesman for the "counterculture," which is a world view that pugnaciously criticizes "establishment" ways of conducting society and its agencies. Roszak came to the attention of the public with *The Making of a Counter Culture* (1969), *Where the Wastelands End* (1972), and *A Man for Tomorrow's World* (1970). A history professor, Roszak has had a considerable effect on curriculum development and has addressed groups such as the Association for Supervision and Curriculum Development. He totally rejects compulsory education, which he considers "a product of the rigid social orthodoxy of industrial society." He represents a considerable number of social critics who are disenchanted with modern industrial society and its institutions. Roszak advised students to escape from the restrictions and conformity of modern public schools.

Some educational critics do not take extreme positions, but promote their own ideas while taking issue both with existing school practices and the views of other critics. Writers of this sort include Paul Goodman and Charles Silberman.

Charles Silberman.   Charles Silberman believes the school system has some merit. At the same time he opposes the views of those who wish to eliminate schools entirely and those who advocate a child-centered theme. Silberman believes that there is a need for centrality of purpose and a clear educational philosophy in American schools. He attributes failure in recent curriculum reform movements to the fact that educators have not understood the issues that perplexed the progressive education movement or the problems of educating the child for the modern society. Like Goodman, Silberman is an established journalist and a respected scholar. *Crisis in the Classroom* is the best known statement of his educational criticism and it has been widely read since its publication in 1970. Both Silberman and Kozol warn educators to be wary of past errors. They suggest that we use history as a guide—sifting through past experience to eliminate what is obsolete and ineffective and retain what is beneficial.

Critics with Other Viewpoints.   While no complete enumeration of modern educational critics is possible here, some of those with special interests or points of view should be mentioned. Sylvia Ashton-Warner, who wrote *Teacher* (1963) and *Teacher in America* (1972), is concerned with the meaning of equality and authority in education. Joseph Featherstone's *Schools Where Children Learn* (1971) warns about "faddishness" and raises the question of whether schools can build a more equal society. The problem of relevance is of concern to George Leonard who wrote *Education and Ecstasy*. *Teaching as a Subversive Activity* by Neil Postman and Charles Weingartner deals both with relevance and with communication. William Glasser's *Schools Without Failure* and Sunny Decker's *An Empty Spoon* are other examples of the same theme.

     Those who claim the schools have not been interested in humanistic psychology include Abraham Maslow and Carl Rogers. Another psychologist, Jerome S. Bruner, believes that too much emphasis has been placed upon the structure of knowledge within the disciplines and not enough concern given to structure in the context of learning and problem solving. Jean Piaget holds that learning takes place at various levels or stages of development which depend upon both maturation and experience. He feels that too little attention has been given to the process of learning and too much to the content.

     The wide range of criticisms of American education is not surprising in a rapidly changing, pluralistic, dynamic, and democratic culture. Some critics operate from a scholarly base within the profession, some represent philosophical causes, some are concerned about the role of the school in social change, and others attack education for its support of social values. So long as education is not an exact science and the American society is dynamic and open, criticism may be expected to continue. The problem for the professional educator is understanding exactly what the critics are saying and selecting the best ideas from a host of suggested alternatives.

The School as Agency for Social Action.   The role of the school in social change is a philosophical issue, as Theodore Brameld and his critics are quick to point out. So many programs have developed in recent years which seem to use education as a social institution for cultural change, that the problem of purpose and function of schools has received new attention.

As James S. Coleman and Edgar Z. Friedenberg have insisted, demands and challenges for the adolescent members of modern society are very great. The impact of social change on the adolescent, pressures on middle-class teenagers, and the problem of youth values in an open society are major concerns for schools. Superimposed upon this are the special problems of low-income students, the children of the urban poor and the youth from Black, Indian, or Mexican-American families. These students have more than their share of educational difficulties and are more apt to drop out of school. Various attempts to compensate for cultural disadvantages and meet the needs of all children and adolescents have been tried.

Ever since the Wechsler Scales for measuring adult intelligence were invented and the Army Alpha and Beta tests were given in World War I, mass testing to establish norms has been used in the United States. Many educators fear that both individual and group intelligence tests are misused in schools, but the first great objection to grouping or categorizing students by test scores came from those who charged cultural bias. It was argued that merely being from a middle-class White environment gave students an unfair advantage on instruments for measuring ability. Efforts to construct culture-fair tests were followed by attempts to remove racism and sexism from textbooks. Most American public school texts before 1960 made Black and other minority people "invisible" and fostered definite sex roles for youngsters.

Project Head Start, Vista, Job Corps, Teacher Corps, and Upward Bound are federally funded projects to help disadvantaged students. Job Corps centers were established to teach vocational skills to high school dropouts. Upward Bound attempted to prepare disadvantaged youth for success in college. Other programs used federal funds for more teachers, buildings, and equipment where there were concentrations of low-income or minority children.

The issue of federal projects is still undecided. Supporters of the programs say that gains were made by the disadvantaged as a result of their development and that no harm was done to other students. They call for more money and an extension of the programs on all levels. Others claim that the schools should not be involved in attempts to equalize differences or change society through social action programs. The *Coleman Report* and Illich's *Deschooling Society*, and the work of Christopher Jenks indicate that these programs made very little lasting difference. Illich does not believe that it is possible for government-sponsored school programs to compensate for cultural differences.

Superimposed upon the issues concerning the role of the government in aiding the culturally different were more emotional ones concerning race, heredity, and intelligence. In 1969, psychologist Arthur Jensen published an article in the *Harvard Educational Review* which suggested that Blacks average about 15 points below Whites on IQ tests. The writings of William Shockley also supported an inferior position for Blacks. Jensen tried to point out that his data was not a basis for judging the intellectual capacity of any individual, but there were strong criticisms of his work. Charges of racism and the use of Jensen's studies to prove that integration must fail only further clouded the issue. Authors on both sides allowed their emotions to rule their logic.

ACCOUNTABILITY

In this section we will treat the modern issue centering on how schools should be held accountable for what they do (or fail to do) and related problems that have to do with the responsibility of educators to the public. As we have seen, many critics of American schools believe that teachers are not pursuing the right methods, curriculum objectives, or educational aims. Others feel that while the goals may be clear, education lacks efficiency in accomplishing those goals. The parents are very much concerned because of decline in measures of achievement such as ACT scores and the constant accusation that "Johnny can't read." Others attack the schools for failure to meet the needs of the culturally different, the non-English speaker, and the exceptional child.

The idea that schools and educators should be responsible for their actions is not new in American education. Annual reports of Horace Mann and the journal articles by Henry Barnard carried criticisms of inadequate or mistaken pedagogical efforts. The means by which teachers are trained has been under fire since the development of normal schools and university departments of education. As early as 1898, the American Association of Manufacturers charged the schools with "repressive brain stuffing," "dulling the intellect," and failing to provide youth with the skills needed to enter the job market. The business community ever since has taken issue with educators over the curriculum and the degree of concentration on courses needed for preparing an effective work force. Educators have also attacked each other as in the rejection of the Herbartian lock-step methods by the progressives and the subsequent rejection of the progressive program by William Bagley and the essentialists. Perhaps the main difference between the past and the present is that today attacks are more widespread and rapid, due to modern communications and the mass media.

American public schools experience periods of ebb and flow both in the interest expressed by the public and in public pressure. Following 1970, criticism of schools and teaching was linked to demands for accountability. The basic concept comes from the field of management and it is intended to hold someone responsible for performing according to terms previously agreed upon. While serving as secretary of defense, Robert MacNamara brought the unrelenting evaluative practices of business to government through his program planning and budgeting system. In education, the founding of the accountability movement is usually credited to the works of Leon Lessinger (*Every Kid a Winner: Accountability in Education*, 1970). The sudden popularity of the concept of accountability can be traced to growing dissatisfaction with the quality of schools, a feeling that school people were closing ranks against public criticism, and the ever increasing pressure for more tax dollars to finance education. Many educators have been quite negative about accountability and the issues surrounding it continue to be argued in the 1980s.

As a theoretical concept, few would quarrel with accountability. Teachers obviously need to be responsible for what they do and the educational profession does not object to evaluation. Teachers do object to the idea that they are guilty of something and must be punished, or to the negative presumption that legislation is needed to make them do their jobs. More significant, questions occur to which no one seems to have the answers. Who is accountable? If the student fails to learn is that always to be blamed on the teacher and not on the student or the parents? There is massive evidence that schools are responsible for only a part of the child's learning and teachers for an even smaller part. For what are teachers accountable? Information and skills which can be examined on tests surely do not represent total learning. Incidental, collateral or attitudinal learnings are not capable of being organized into objective sequences and are hard to test. Most accountability tests measure only a very limited part of what the student actually learns. John Goodlad had pointed out that timeworn instruments of assessment and archaic criteria for evaluation are poor means for measuring pupil achievement. To whom are educators accountable? The answer to this would seem to be the clients, (students, parents, and taxpayers) but if teachers have had no role in determining educational policy, accountability is unfair. Often the criteria for accountability is determined by state or federal officials with no input from the local community. If teachers are treated as mere employees and not consulted about issues or practices in the schools, they can hardly be held accountable as professionals.

In the past, reputations of teachers were built on some estimate of what constituted "good" teacher behavior. Keeping order in the classroom and grading each student fairly were examples of such behavior. In recent years the measure of good teaching has shifted to the ability of the teacher to produce specific behavioral changes in learners. California's Stull Act requires that the competence of teachers be measured at least in part by the performance of students. This implies that when students do not learn, for whatever reason, the fault is to be placed on certified personnel. Some critics see this an analogous to the ancient practice of paying physicians only if the patient recovers. Accountability has also been tested in the courts. In 1976, the San Francisco Unified School District was sued by a student who had been allowed to graduate from high school although he was unable to read at sixth-grade level. Lawyers for the plaintiff argued that the school personnel were negligent in failing to detect and correct his learning problem. In *Donohue v. Copiague*, a student charged a New York school with failure to cope with his learning disabilities. The plaintiffs were not successful in these cases but the idea of holding teachers accountable to society for the quality and quantity of educational results has clearly been established. Courts in New York and Iowa have reaffirmed that teachers cannot be held liable for poor student performance but the public demand for accountability has not diminished.

In the 1970s, many states passed laws for accountability. Some require the assessment of students on specific tests while others are broad and vague. Seven states involved in the Cooperative Accountability Project require some sort of evaluation but specific measures are determined locally. Some educators fear that business-industrial models of accountability threaten teachers with punitive and often inoperable directives. Others see the schools becoming more rigid and authoritatian with emphasis placed on improvement of test performance and nothing else. Sociologist Robert Havinghurst cautions against a simple form of accountability that makes teachers totally responsible while taking no account of other forces in the learning environment. Both the NEA and the National Commission on Teacher Education and Professional Standards have called accountability unprofessional, inhumane, and arbitrary unless the standards and methods of measurement are developed by the profession itself. These organizations are especially opposed to laws which require the application of business and commercial instruments to education. The American Federation of Teachers has taken an even stronger stand, linking accountability laws to "school-haters" who are looking for scapegoats to blame for social failures.

Competency Tests for Teachers.   Along with accountability, the public has become concerned with weeding out teachers who are poorly prepared or incompetent. Colleges of education are no longer trusted to train teachers or to recommend certification without some external evidence of skills and knowledge of subject matter. Prior to 1978 when Florida passed a bill requiring a comprehensive written examination before certification, three states required beginning teachers to pass the National Teacher Examination. Georgia, New York, Oklahoma, and Wisconsin had plans for some form of competency testing by 1981 and several other states were considering such requirements. After 1978 when the Supreme Court ruled that the NTE was not discriminatory (although more Blacks failed it than Whites), other states began to use it. It seems likely that some form of minimum competency test will be required for all beginning teachers in the nation before the end of the century.

Some school districts require new teachers to pass their own tests before they are hired. The Dallas Independent School District had high failure (about half) when tenth-grade verbal and quantitative ability tests were given as a prerequisite to teaching. This alarming rate has done little to enhance the public view of institutions which train teachers. It should be pointed out however, that these tests measure knowledge of subject matter and not skills in teaching. If colleges and universities are to be held accountable, the academic departments that teach mathematics and geography are more vulnerable than colleges or departments of education. It is not clear that superior knowledge of subject matter necessarily makes a superior teacher but the public has a right to demand that teachers are minimally competent in basic subjects. President Albert Shanker of the AFT favors entry level testing of teacher candidates on the grounds that an improved profession will result. Both the AFT and the NEA oppose tests for teachers already in service.

Since 1970, the public demand for accountability has grown. Interest in voucher plans, cost-effectiveness, community control, and the curriculum has contributed to demands for assessment of teacher performance. More basic concerns revolve around the steady decline in ACT scores and the question of, "why Johnny can't read?" Most states have passed laws requiring some form of accountability or are planning for such legislation. Holding a teacher responsible for student performance when the teacher does not make school policy and when other factors (including the attitude and ability of the student) may account for inadequate performance is a major issue. Accountability tests are inadequate if they measure only limited aspects of education such as skill in mathematics, and more comprehensive tests are difficult to construct. It has not been determined if tests should be criterion-referenced, norm-referenced or both. Teacher candidates are now required to pass minimum competency tests in many states before they can be certified. There are questions about the effectiveness of such tests in predicting success in the classroom and some concerns about the effect on the projected future shortage of teachers.

Curriculum Concerns.   The entire body of subjects or courses offered in the program of a school is the curriculum. Historically, one of the best ways to understand what a school system tried to accomplish is to study its curriculum. District schools in Colonial New England taught religion, reading, and writing, while the Latin grammar schools concentrated on Latin, Greek, and theology. The use of a core curriculum and the involvement of students in the selection of courses from a wide spectrum of possibilities was a characteristic of progressive schools. In the 1950s, Sputnik and the NDEA produced a discipline-centered curriculum stressing science, mathematics, and foreign languages. With the civil rights movement and a demand for equal educational opportunity came a child-centered program with emphasis placed on ethical, social, and multicultural subjects. This was followed by a "back to basics" movement with more formalized instruction and strict accountability. Within a period of only thirty years, popularity has shifted from Deweyian progressives, to strict academicians, to social reconstructionists, to conservative essentialists. The 1980s and 1990s promise to be filled with conflicting demands for different curricular choices. While the debate goes on, teachers and administrators are faced with making curriculum choices and building appropriate programs. Given some basic assumptions about purposes, it is possible to develop a logical and consistent curriculum. In the past, such tasks were undertaken by the central administration or by local or state boards, but now many schools and individual teachers have considerable freedom in curriculum matters. The selection of materials and the stress placed upon certain concepts or examples have a profound effect on the school curriculum. A teacher who feels that ecology should be included in the work of the student can provide ecological materials in a variety of related subjects ranging from biology to civics.

A vast body of literature has grown up around the problem of curriculum development. It should be remembered that curriculum choices can never be made in isolation and that the needs and wishes of the public must always be weighed against the teacher's perception of the needs of the child.

Since the middle of the 1960s, two schools of thought have dominated the controversy over curriculum organization and content. One of these is the free, open, child-centered, humanistic, and socially oriented movement. The theory behind this movement is grounded in the work of John Dewey, A. S. Neill, the social reconstructionists, and humanistic-existentialistic authors. The opposite movement calls for standardized subject matter, no-nonsense basic education, high academic standards, and discipline oriented schools. The philosophical foundation for this position reaches back to Plato and has been supported by twentieth-century perennialists and essentialists.

Modern spokesmen for the first movement include Edgar Friedenberg, Paul Goodman, John Holt, Herbert Kohl and Charles Silberman. They oppose the conformity and docility characteristic of the subject-centered school. Accusing traditional schools of indifference to social issues and a meaningless curriculum, these authors demand relevant programs geared to the actual needs and desires of students. For them, the content of the curriculum is less important than the process used and the degree to which the learner is able to relate to the school activities. This means that much of the content of the curriculum must be taken from experiences in the life of the student. The school should deal with social issues, materials drawn from the mass media, and problems of the local community. Sex and drug education are included in the curriculum along with human relations and programs designed to help students understand the racially and culturally different. Calling for free and open education, these authors emphasize the development of self-concept, problem solving the ability to make reasonable choices, and humanistic attitudes. They understand the need for basic skills like reading but they have no interest in filling the mind of the student with lots of facts or in "mastering" specific subjects. They wish to foster a positive attitude toward learning and practical skills for dealing with other people and the outside world.

Holding the opposite position are authors like Jacques Barzun, Arthur Bestor, Clifton Fadiman, Robert Hutchins, and James Koerner. Their point of view is similar to that expressed by James Conant and Admiral Rickover after Sputnik, that the schools must concentrate on producing subject matter experts and superior scholars to lead the technological society. Koerner has been a spokesman for the Council for Basic Education which opposes the "soft" pedagogy of progressive education and demands a return to "solid" academic subjects. The Council argues against student input into the curriculum, saying that the adults know best what children should study. This is also the position of Hutchins who wants a curriculum composed of those aspects of the culture that have been subjected to the greatest amount of sophistication and refinement (the classics, mathematics, and science). Bestor believes that the function of the school is the teaching of intellectual disciplines, not teaching about current social problems or adjusting students to different cultural groups. This group opposes social engineering in education and bending the curriculum to make it relevant to the student. By 1980 the Council for Basic Education and the "back to basics" movement had gained vast public support, partly from parents disappointed with the level of information and skills learned by their children in public schools and partly from the "moral majority" which is opposed to all open, humanistic, child-centered, life adjustment programs. In calling for a return to fundamentals and a curriculum of basic studies, Barzun has said, "Nonsense is at the heart of those proposals that would replace definable subject matter with vague activities copied from 'life' or with courses organized around 'problems' or 'attitudes'."

Curriculum Innovations and Methods. A number of emergent trends have provided persuasive arguments to broaden the public school curriculum. It is not the case that all schools have adopted new subjects, but sufficient demand has been expressed to make them important in the field of curriculum development. They reflect an interest in interdisciplinary approaches to schooling as well as a thrust toward individualization and relevance.

1. Career education is an expression of discontent with the old division between vocational and academic programs. With emphasis on the functional value of career planning for all students, this program claims to be part of general education. On the theory that almost all students will enter some sort of work in the future, career education emphasizes occupational training, career information and guidance, and the involvement of business and community groups. The aim is to make career education available to all students and not just to those in vocational or industrial programs.

2. Consumer education is now part of the social studies curriculum in many schools. The pressures of inflation and the need of all people to make wise choices in purchasing makes consumer education valuable. Courses are often included as part of economics, or career education, but sometimes consumer education is taughts as a separate course.

3. Environmental education reflects a public concern with energy, pollution, ecology, and depletion of natural resources. Population pressures on the natural environment have created a demand for better understanding of environmental issues. Many schools attempt to build environmental content into standard courses in geography and the sciences.

4. Ethnic and multicultural educational offerings have grown rapidly since the Black revolution and the emergence of interest in ethnic identity. Some states require schools to include courses in ethnic studies or cultural pluralism and most have policy statements on the subject. The need for identity and recognition of minorities and ethnic groups is clear. Ethnic education is designed to enhance self-esteem of culturally different students and to promote understanding by majority students.

5. Education dealing with drug and alcohol abuse is an expanding program. Because of the widespread problem of abuse and addiction, public demand for such education has been strong. Coordinated programs with law enforcement agencies, community health projects, and former drug abusers are often found. The major criticism of these programs comes from those who do not feel that they are well taught and effective.

6. Sex education was placed in the school curriculum because of high rates of illegitimacy, venereal disease among students, the national increase in divorce, and massive evidence that students are sexually active. The sensitive nature of the subject and the belief by many that the school has no business dealing with matters of sex has created considerable controversy over this subject, Yet the evidence is clear that students are not getting information about sex from their parents, religious institutions, or peers. The number of unwed teen-age mothers is increasing at an alarming rate and very few sexually active students use contraceptives. The traditional units on repro-duction in biology classes are hopelessly inadequate and now are supplemented with programs on dating, marriage, parenthood, child care, health, and social responsibility.

While not strictly adding to the curriculum, numerous modifica-tions have been undertaken which alter certain subjects. Courses in mathematics have been changed to allow for metric conversion. Although using the metric system is voluntary, it is expected that mathematical skill in metrics will be needed in the future. Handheld calculators are now part of the equipment of many students and are as common as the slates of the nineteenth century. Teachers have had to adjust to giving less time to practice in manual calculation and more to problems in which electronic calculators are used. Com-puters are rapidly becoming available in classrooms across the na-tion. Language and techniques for using mini computers is included in many courses in science and mathematics at all levels.

The curriculum can never be totally divorced from methods. The same subject matter used for a lecture and in discovery learning will produce very different results in students. As a general rule, con-servatives are more comfortable with time-honored methods such as lecture, textbook assignments, homework, standardized tests, and library reports. Liberals tend to promote laboratory methods such as discovery learning, problem solving, and inquiry learning. The activity curriculum and the child-centered curriculum are not popu-lar with the "back to basics" movement although individualized in-struction may be used by both liberals and conservatives. Computer-assisted instruction is acceptable to the subject-matter curriculum advocates so long as it does not stray from the subject. Team teaching and flexible scheduling are most often found in schools with a pro-gressive orientation. The activity-centered curriculum which began with William H. Kilpartick in the 1920s centers on life experiences such as field trips, group projects, social enterprises, and local cen-ters of interest. Some modern schools support an activity curriculum by working with community groups, social agencies, and governmental institutions. The activity curriculum requires extensive student and community participation.

Competency Based Training and Performance Contracting.   Just as competency based teacher education has become popular, there is a demand that public school students show evidence of mastery of fundamental subjects. The move to place greater emphasis on reading, writing, and mathematics in elementary schools and on English, science, history, and mathematics in secondary schools supports minimum competency testing. Some schools have contracted with private firms to produce specific behavior in specified areas of learning. Such performance contracting (as in Texarkana in 1972) has produced disappointing results but it is clear that the public demands improvement in the informational levels and skills of students. The pros and cons of testing for minimum competency are much the same as the arguments over accountability.

Demands for stress on basic education and an end to "frills" call for testing students to make sure that they have at least the minimum requirements for each course. Those favoring competency testing want an end to social promotion. They believe no student should graduate from high school without demonstrating proficiency in reading, oral and written communication, and mathematics. Part of the interest in private education comes from the belief that public schools are soft on the fundamentals and try to provide a curriculum that is too broad. "Project 81" in Pennsylvania is an example of a state-wide attempt to insure that all students meet graduation requirements as measured by competency tests. Florida also is a leader in adopting tests for minimum competency. It is argued that merely accumulating the necessary credits is not enough and that testing for knowledge of course content must be universal. Those favoring minimum competency testing usually stress patriotism, strict discipline, homework, dress codes, and teacher-directed activities. They are against innovations in the curriculum, electives, and such "frills" as sex education.

Arguments against competency testing are both theoretical and practical. Many educators oppose a narrow curriculum with no electives. They feel that such programs lack interest and relevance to the needs of students. Those who favor problem solving and inquiry as methods doubt that the tests used are adequate. They say that eliminating the new math, linguistic approaches to grammar, and humanistic studies means a return to the nineteenth century. There are also charges that tests are culturally biased against minorities and ethnic groups. Some believe that it is unfair to prevent a student from graduating because the school has been unable to develop his or her skills. Many argue that the minimum competency tests are directed toward mechanical skills and the memorization of information. They say competency programs detract from higher skills such as reading for comprehension and logical thinking. Only those things which can be easily tested are given emphasis, making the curriculum rigid, narrow, unimaginative, and dull.

Of course, some schools and teachers use contracting with individual students as an instructional method. Giving a grade for specific performance is most often used in schools with a progressive orientation but it is not different in concept from requiring specific competency for graduation, demanded by essentialists. Whatever the arguments, minimum competency testing seemed to be winning public support in the early 1980s.

Educating the Exceptional Child.   In the twentieth century, vast gains were made in the diagnosis and treatment of students with special problems. Starting with programs for the deaf and the blind, educational institutions developed a variety of effective methods for educating the exceptional child. New facilities for the handicapped were built, including ramps and restrooms to accommodate students in wheelchairs. The Rehabilitation Act of 1973 prohibits discrimination against the handicapped by failure to provide reasonable facilities and access. Obvious physical and mental handicaps have been understood and dealt with in education for many years, although with varying degrees of success. Learning specialists trained to work with various learning disabilities have been in the schools only for a little over a decade. Programs for the mentally retarded and the trainable mentally handicapped were made to identify and help students with less pronounced difficulties. The gifted and talented were ignored by many schools on the grounds that they would learn in spite of the system. Even today, numerous school systems are just starting special programs for the gifted.

A major issue concerning special students centers on Public Law 94-142. In hearings for this law (passed in 1975) it was pointed out that one-and three quarters-million handicapped children were excluded from school and another four million were not receiving full educational services. The law required that each exceptional learner be placed in the least restrictive environment in which his or her educational needs could be satisfactorily served. This meant that children who previously spent their entire in-school time in special classes would be mainstreamed. Handicapped children must spend at least part of the day in classes with nonhandicapped students. The intent of P. L. 94-142 was to remove the stigma attached to special students, to improve social relationships, to provide nonhandicapped learning models, to allow for a richer and more competetive environment, and to learn to live in the real world outside of the school. Other reasons included allowing more students to be served, providing more cost-effective education, and decentralizing services to reduce transportation costs.

An Individualized Education Program (IEP) is required for all mainstreamed exceptional children. This is a plan for education cooperatively prepared by parents, teachers, and school officials. It covers the content, objectives, means of implementation, and evaluation of each student's program. Usually this plan is drafted by the classroom teacher and modified by parents and learning specialists. An IEP may not be altered without the consent of the child's review committee.

There is no question about the benefit of mainstreaming to the exceptional child. If all children were in small classes and if good cooperation always existed between the learning specialist and the regular teacher, there might be no controversy. This is not the case. Regular classroom teachers often feel that they are not prepared and do not have the time to work well with the handicapped. Making and reviewing an IEP for each child requires much time and energy that might be devoted to other tasks. The teachers often feel that they must give most of their time to the special learners while these students are present in the classroom. Parents of nonexceptional children often complain that their children are getting less attention as a result of mainstreaming. Others say that the presence of handicapped students for a large portion of the day reduces the level of expectation and takes away from excellence. Sometimes the classroom teacher feels that he or she must work harder than the learning specialist and negative feelings result. Although colleges of education usually require a course in special education, many classroom teachers do not feel able to meet the needs of exceptional children. It is not always clear just what responsibilities belong to the learning specialist and what ones to the classroom teacher, especially when the specialist is functioning as an observer to review the effectiveness of the program. Mainstreaming seems to be working well in a number of school systems but there is a good deal of criticism and public acceptance is mixed.

Some of those who oppose mainstreaming of the handicapped support programs for gifted and talented youngsters. Demands for academic rigor, excellence, and intellectual development were loud in the era of the cold war and Sputnik. James Conant argued in The American High School Today that the academically talented student was not being sufficiently challenged. John Gardner pointed out that excellence is needed not just in scientists and engineers, but also in teachers, scholars, professional people, and social leaders. The White House Conference of 1955 stressed the development of the abilities of especially bright children. Science, mathematics, and foreign languages were considered the major areas of needed excellence.

Following the NDEA, interest in the gifted began to shift toward a better understanding of the exceptionally bright student. It was pointed out that many of the most able students found school boring and a waste of time. Tests of intelligence failed to reveal special qualities such as creative ability. It was found that gifted and talented students often felt socially isolated from other students and sometimes had difficulty in adjusting to group norms. By the 1970s demands were growing for special programs for all gifted and talented students. Limititions of money slowed the development of these but legislation was passed which required that special offerings be made available for the gifted. Gifted and talented students must also be mainstreamed, but there is less controversy over this. Most teachers find having the gifted in their classes part of the day much less stressful than dealing with the handicapped. It is expected that all schools will provide programs for the gifted and talented by the end of the 1980s. Interest in the academically talented has increased since former U. S. Commissioner Sidney Marland submitted a report to Congress in 1972 which recommended better education for the capable student. Nevertheless, low funding and a lack of trained teachers for the gifted have caused programs to lag far behind the level provided for "the handicapped."

Voucher Plans.   The voucher system is a plan for financing schools with tax money but with parents in control of that money. A voucher is a certificate issued to parents. The parents give the voucher to a school of their choice and the school exchanges the voucher for payment by the government. The system was studied at Harvard University in the 1960s. Voucher plans were tried in the South after 1954 as a means of supporting segregated schools, but these were found unconstitutional. Some states have attempted to use a voucher system for supporting parochial schools, and cases are still pending on their legal status. Modern proposals for voucher plans guard against racial discrimination or the use of taxes to supplement tuition at expensive private schools.

Proponents argue that parents could have a choice as to what schools their children attend. They say the schools would become more competitive and establish many alternatives in curriculum and methods. They point out that without the voucher system, only those wealthy enough to pay tuition can select schools for their children, while the poor must accept whatever the local public schools offer. Properly regulated, a voucher system could bring innovation and reform to schools and give parents much more control over the education of their children. These arguments are especially strong in California where a large segment of the population is supporting a law requiring the state adopt the voucher system

Many public school people and organizations such as the AFT are opposed to the voucher system. They believe that the schools would become more segregated with middle-class parents selecting one type while the poor and minorities would be concentrated in others. Competition between schools would foster publicity seeking and teachers would try to be popular rather than professional. Many believe that the system would be unworkable and that it might destroy public education in the United States.

Multicultural and Bilingual Education.   Issues over the inclusion of multicultural studies in the curriculum and providing primary instruction in a language other than English developed in the 1970s and continued into the 1980s. The United States is made up of a large number of people with diverse cultural backgrounds. In addition to a substantial Black minority, Hispanics, Native Americans. certain European minorities, and Orientals are part of the American population. Some members of these groups have been assimilated into the mainstream of the culture but others maintain an ethnic identification and may be regarded as subcultures.

Historically, education has been used as an instrument for bringing foreigners into the national culture. Early arguments for public schools stressed the need to Americanize the immigrants and to make sure that all children learned to speak English. Although this "melting pot ideal" did not result in uniform cultural patterns, the dominant "Anglo" protestant group managed to require conformity to its language, cultural preferences, and value orientation. Schools not only reflected middle-class interests, they also showed a decided preference for White, Anglo-Saxon, "establishment"norms. Of course assimilation did not include Blacks, Indians, and Hispanics who were segregated and not allowed to fully participate in the majority society. The civil rights movement called attention to discrimination against minority and ethnic groups. Blacks were the first to demand equality of opportunity, with Hispanics and Native Americans soon following. As part of the minority revolution, pride in ethnic culture and ethnic identification increased. The unique contributions of minorities to language, art, food, entertainment, and sports were emphasized, together with ethnic histories and distinctive cultural patterns. This increasing ethnic identification led to the concept of cultural pluralism and a growing respect for the contributions made by each ethnic group and minority. Schools began offering programs in cultural awareness and specialized courses like Black history and Hispanic studies. Multicultural education was also seen as a means of reducing prejudice through better understanding.

Many schools in America have incorporated elements of multiculturalism in existing programs. Units dealing with Eskimos and Indians have been part of the curriculum for years. Textbooks have been rewritten so that Black and Hispanic models are used along with those from the dominant culture. Attention is given to special events such as Native American week or Hispanic heritage week. Where large numbers of minority children are in attendance, whole courses in ethnic studies or cultural pluralism are sometimes offered. Colleges that train teachers try to encourage the teaching of values which support cultural diversity, ethnic awareness, the exploration of alternative life styles, and an understanding of cultural pluralism. Professional groups, state departments of education, and local curriculum committees are developing methods for multicultural emphasis in all public school classrooms.

Bilingual and bicultural education grew out of the problems non-English speaking and limited-English speaking children were having in schools where primary instruction was in English. Before the civil rights movement, most states required that public school instruction be given only in English. In the 1960s attention was called to the large number of students who failed or who dropped out of school because the instruction was in a language foreign to them. This was especially the case in Texas where many Spanish-speaking students entered schools in which teachers spoke no Spanish. In 1968 the Bilingual Education Act was passed and appropriations of nearly $160-million for bilingual programs were made by 1979. This act calls for instruction in two languages for children whose native tongue is other than English. Projects using various Native American and Asian languages were created but most bilingual instruction is in English and Spanish. Support for bilingual education also came from a Supreme Court case in 1974. In *Lau v. Nichols* the Court held that schools must take steps to aid students who find the educational experiences "wholly incomprehensible" because they do not understand English. This case stands even though federal funding for bilingual programs was reduced in the budget cuts of the Reagan administration.

Minority and culturally different students often suffer from educational disabilities related to their cultural backgrounds. Studies of Native American children have shown that some Indian youngsters are taught to be quiet in the presence of elders and that their primary learning patterns are very different from those used in most classrooms. While Black English is not one of the bilingual programs, students used to speaking a Black dialect often have trouble acquiring language skills in standard English. Educators are beginning to understand that different instructional approaches are needed with different racial and ethnic groups.

Opposition to bilingual and multicultural education is widespread. Obviously the "back to basics" people are against spending time in pluralistic or multicultural studies when that time might be used for fundamental courses. Conservatives regard such studies as another "frill" which should be eliminated from the basic curriculum. Others argue that the multicultural movement tends to promote cultural, social, and economic separation. They want the schools to emphasize the core values of the whole culture and to assimilate the culturally different into the American mainstream. Some feel that bilingual programs allow children to maintain their first language and discourage the use of English by allowing them to function in school with another language. The idea of a large region of the United States where Spanish is the primary language is considered harmful to national unity by this group. It is feared that the curriculum will be fragmented by attempts to include cultural diversity and cultural pluralism. Educators like Harry Broudy believe that large amounts of material on ethnic diversity tend to "trivialize" the curriculum and may be used to justify a poor quality education for disadvantaged students. Stress on ethnic and cultural differences may lead to cultural separation and have a disunifying effect on the body politic. This seems especially important when educators are trying to find ways to support the values at the core of the democratic society. Americans generally are beginning to doubt that the goals of equal educational opportunity can be achieved through schooling and there is now much opposition to spending money for social engineering or for ethnic studies. Yet educators realize that American society is based on the principle of equality and that it is improper to force every child into a mode of behavior determined by the norms of the majority.

In this chapter we have discussed issues, court cases, and critics recent enough to be considered contemporary. In every case, there is a connection or a relationship to earlier critical writers, litigation, or educational arguments. Nothing which is at issue in modern American education is without historical foundation. The argument over whether the federal government had the right to establish land grant colleges under the Morrill Act of 1862 bears some similarity to the current question of what role federal government should take in public school matters. The caustic criticism of all public institutions including schools which is found in *Deschooling Society* is not so far removed from the attack on schools in *Emile*. Rousseau and Illich are separated by the centuries but the positions they represent are much the same. The appeal to the courts made by the citizens of Kalamazoo in the 1870s is an example of the same means used for resolving an educational issue that we find in modern school desegregation cases. It is also true that those aspects of education which are important enough to stir public debate and emotion seldom end at a given point in time. They become the trends which are our best guides for anticipating the educational future.

BIBLIOGRAPHY

Bloom, Benjamin. *All Our Children Learning.* New York: McGraw-Hill, 1980.

Bowles, Samuel, and Herbert Gintis. *Schooling in Capitalist America.* New York: Basic Books, 1976.

Cordasco, Francesco. *Bilingual Schooling in the United States: A Sourcebook for Educational Personnel.* New York: McGraw-Hill, 1976.

Ellis, Arthur, John Cogan, and Kenneth Howey. *Introduction to the Foundations of Education.* Englewood Cliffs, N. J.: Prentice-Hall, 1981.

Hewett, Frank, and Steven Forness. *Education of Exceptional Learners.* Boston: Allyn and Bacon, 1977.

Jones, R.L., ed. *Mainstreaming and the Minority Child.* Reston, Va.: Council for Exceptional Children, 1976.

Noll, James. *Taking Sides: Clashing Views on Controversial Educational Issues.* Guilford, Connecticut: Duskin, 1980.

Ornstein, Allan, and Daniel Levine. *An Introduction to the Foundations of Education,* 2nd. ed. Boston: Houghton Mifflin, 1981.

Pratte, Richard. *Pluralism in Education.* Springfield, Ill.: Charles C. Thomas, 1979.

Wise, Arthur, *The Bureaucratization of the American Classroom.* Berkeley, Cal.: University of California Press, 1979.

From Now to Then: Education in the Future

8

History has its own intrinsic value but most of us are interested in the past because of its practical value in understanding the present and its ability to suggest the probable course of future events. Teachers must of necessity be oriented toward the future. Children now entering kindergarten may reasonably be expected to be alive and active in the middle of the twenty-first century. Colleges that train teachers are currently working with teacher candidates who will directly influence the citizens of the twenty-second century. In a period of very slow cultural change such as the Middle Ages, significant spans of time were important but not critical. Today with accelerating invention in many fields, the explosion of research and knowledge, careening technology, electronic communications networks, and computers, the rate of change does indeed approach future shock. If the twenty-first century is as different from the twentieth as the twentieth was from the nineteenth, children entrusted to the care of educators may expect changes that stagger the imagination. All indications point to an even faster rate of change and not even an economic depression would reverse the trend. It should be obvious that the existing school program with a curriculum derived largely from the past is inadequate to meet the future needs of children. Because we cannot know the future in advance, it is neces-

Industrial Era	Computer Age	Information Age
1969	1970	1980
Apollo	Toffler's	World Wide
Moon	Future Shock	Telecommunications
Landing		Networks
	Transistor	
First Generation	Computer	Mini-Computer
Vacuum Tube		in Homes
Computer		

sary that we prepare future citizens for as wide a variety of alternatives as possible. It is extremely difficult to give future generations the skills and information (to say nothing of the attitudes and values) they will require for future survival but anticipation of events to come seems fundamental to the attempt. The worst we can do is to send students into the next century armed only with an education based on the ideals and needs of nineteenth-century agrarian America. It is said that education always looks to the past and that invention in the schools comes slowly but it is imperative that teachers become students of the future and that they do their utmost to give students the best tools possible for coping with a variety of probable futures.

On first reflection, history may seem an odd means for approaching the future. Further analysis will show that past recorded events do shed light on how human beings expected things to go, how things actually did go, and what consequences followed. The television series *Connections* is an example of the way one scientific discovery led to another until the whole shape of technology and even of human society was drastically altered in unexpected ways. An illustration is the invention of the chimney during an unusually cold period in the twelfth century which made it possible to heat numerous rooms on more than one floor. One result was a dramatic change in architecture because buildings no longer had to be built around one fireplace with a smoke hole in the roof. An educational example is furnished by the social revolution which took place in Athens during the fifth century B. C. A new class of rich men emerged who made their money from banking, shipping, and the manufacture of goods for export. These men wanted to obtain an education for their sons similar to that provided for the young men from the old aristocratic families. For this purpose they hired migrant teachers called Sophists such as Protagoras, Gorgias and Antiphon. The Sophists were skilled at teaching oratory and grammar, but they also criticized conventional morality, religion, and law. They taught practical ways of getting ahead in the world and clever

Post-Industrial Age	2000	2001	Communications Era

	2000	2005	2015	2030
Socialization and Basic Learning Through Home Computers and TV	Genetic Engineering Common	Automated Highways	Human Travel by Light Beam	Mind to Mind Communication
1990		2012	2020	
All Students Skilled in Computer Languages		Drugs for Raising Intelligence	World Wide Guaranteed Minimum Income	

means for evading rules. The Sophists drastically changed the values and norms of Athenian society and eventually altered the entire social order.

History may also be used as an instrument for analyzing and evaluating major forces or trends in the culture with the purpose of anticipating the future. Robert Heilbroner has done exactly that in his books *The Future As History* (1959) and *An Inquiry into the Human Prospect* (1975). In the first book, Heilbroner looked at longstanding trends in American culture as a means of defining the crucial problems that must be resolved if a viable future is to be achieved. He made no effort to play the role of prophet but gave detailed accounts of the revolutions in the twentieth century to show what must occur if liberal society is to survive. The second book treats the global situation in a similar way. Heilbroner looks at world economic trends, the challenges to political democracy, exploding population, environmental destruction, and obliterative weaponry. His conclusion is that neither industrial capitalism or Marxist socialism in their present forms have the necessary strength to avoid global catastrophe. While he is pessimistic about what is happening in the modern world, Heilbroner uses history as a tool to spell out exactly what we must do if the consequences of our past activities are not to result in disaster. Many futuristic writers use history as an instrument for examining societal propensities and suggesting alternatives.

History is filled with examples of attempts to foretell the future. Some of the earliest legends and artifacts deal with predicting things to come and rationalizing the plausibility of those predictions. The difficulty is that forecasting the future has seldom proved accurate and predictions which did come true were rarely accepted more widely than those which failed. One of the major difficulties is a human tendency to assume that the future will only be an extension of the present. Those without an appreciation of history believe that the future will consist of a massive dose of today. This is a serious error in a period of dramatic and accelerating change as futurists are fond of pointing out. In general, the record of forecasting future events is not a good one, partly because changes in behavior and values of people are not so easy to predict as weather patterns or oil production. As Harry Broudy puts it: Human behavior cannot be extrapolated in any simple linear fashion. We can extrapolate the increasing need for energy by using the current rates of use as a base. But we cannot predict that the demand for energy, as measured by the demand for air conditioning, electrical heating, and household appliances will increase at the same rate as it has in the last decade.

Many of those who claim to be futurists draw an analogy between well-established scientific or materialistic trends and what they believe will be the life conditions of the future. These extrapolists usually have the support of those in control of wealth and power who desire and expect that known general tendencies will merely accelerate. They ignore the possibility of radical change in values, social behaviors or attitudes. Herbert Spencer's doctrine of inevitable progress and the steady advance of technology leading to a utopian world for man was so popular and so widely accepted that few took seriously the dystopian predictions of H. G. Wells. Yet Wells, in such books as The Time Machine, War of the Worlds, and The Shape of Things to Come, anticipated world war, space travel, and the breakdown of the social order. Like Jules Verne before him, Wells made predictions that turned out to be far more accurate than those of his more "respectable" comtemporaries. The same can be said for Huxley in Brave New World and Orwell in 1984. We must conclude that science and the most sober human reasoning are conditioned to look only at the immediate past for causes of human problems. Human intellect and judgment are not well-adapted to interpreting the behavior of social systems, anticipating radical changes in values or understanding that existing governments are inadequate to manage the affairs of men in the modern world. One reason for this is that training has become so sophisticated and therefore so specialized that very few are educated broadly enough to see the whole picture. Futurism centers upon the interrelationship of human activities, the wide range of possible alternatives for human action and the opportunities for consciously altering or inventing the future.

It must also be understood that intellectual activity does not always merely follow change in the materialistic and technological spheres. Ideas, such as those of the world's great religious leaders, have the power to change not only values but also priorities and views of the good life. Those who have really changed the world are the thinkers who have challenged basic theories, beliefs, values, and myths. Rousseau, Marx, Darwin, and Freud are examples of such thinkers.

Educators must be students of the future if they are to make any real progress in meeting the needs of students in the world of tomorrow. Scholars in many fields are speculating about the future and examining trends in the current world. While much of the futuristic writing sounds a warning about what may happen, some of the work is optimistic in tone. The ancient Chinese wrote the word "crisis" as a combination of the symbols for "danger" and "opportunity". Teachers must not forget that a period of rapid change presents both a challenge and a chance for achievement at a higher level. Fortunately, people in education have a lot of support in dealing with the future. Although writing about the future has a tradition going back to Plato's Republic, modern futurists are armed with sophisticated techniques and massive statistical data. They are legion in number and they represent a wide spectrum of disciplines and nationalities.

THE FUTURES MOVEMENT

Ever since Alvin Toffler published *Future Shock*, laymen in America have been becoming aware of what experts in certain fields have known for decades—that the rate of change in modern society is rapidly accelerating. A new group of scientists and authors, known generally as futurists, have taken issue with the standard assumptions implicit and explicit in modern civilization. They question the idea of progress leading to ever-greater production of goods, the expenditures of enormous quantities of energy, the rapid depletion of the nonrenewable natural resources, and the development of a world-wide market for materialistic consumer's goods. Futurists build on the social theories of Karl Marx, Karl Mannheim, Pitirim Sorokin, Oswald Spengler, and Arnold Toynbee, among others. They are aware of the culture lag theory, which suggests that human beings cannot cope with the shattering stress and disorganization that results when materialistic invention comes too rapidly for social adjustment. Problems such as the exploding world population, the threat of nuclear war, pollution, runaway technology, the knowledge explosion, and environmental destruction, cause many futurists to doubt the survival of civilization and its institutions, unless radical adjustments can be quickly made.

In *Cybernation: the Silent Revolution*, Donald N. Michael shows how poorly prepared modern men are for the revolution now in progress. Kenneth Boulding refers to the automation-biological revolution as "The Great Transition" and ranks it as significant on human growth and development as the discovery of agriculture or the industrial revolution. In *The Coming of Post-Industrial Society*, Daniel Bell forecasts the most radical changes which have ever faced the human race. In *Overskill*, Eugene Schwartz argues that the present trend toward increased technological and materialistic expansion cannot be maintained. Lester Brown illustrates the growing economic gap between the rich and poor in *World Without Borders*. He points out that the whole world is becoming poverty stricken in terms of the earth's total ability to sustain life and predicts that a stable world order depends on meeting the basic needs of all people. Radical economists like John Kenneth Galbraith and Robert Theobald maintain that the present socio-economic system in the industrial nations like Japan, West Germany, and the United States cannot insure survival. In *The Prometheus Project*, Gerald Fineberg calls for a new and revolutionary set of long-range social goals while Donella Meadows insists that for future survival there must be limits to growth. John R. Platt believes that a science for human survival is needed to examine social and individual priorities.

Some futurists see man as an endangered species clinging precariously to a life-support system which his own actions may destroy. Others are concerned about efforts to maintain wealth and privilege in an overpopulated world, where equality of distribution of resources is badly needed. Barry Commoner believes that our technology is responsible for deterioration in the quality of the environment and that a new and better technology is needed to prevent massive biological degradation. Almost all see overgrowth, increased industrialization, urbanization, unemployment, psychological alienation, environmental destruction, polarization of rich and poor, expansion of the population, and demands for resources beyond the capacity of the earth to provide them, as major problems of the present and the future.

Most futurists are painfully aware of the danger of prediction and the terrible record of forecasting human events previous intellectuals have had. Still, most of our basic institutions and beliefs depend upon the assumption that things will remain pretty much as they are, an assumption which plainly runs contrary to fact. Electronic media and the invention of the computer have joined to produce an explosion of information unlike anything previously experienced by man. New knowledge can be quickly disseminated and applied to tasks that stagger the imagination, such as landing human beings safely on the moon. Each new technical development creates new possibilities for invention and the rapid exchange of ideas, plans, and programs, which grow at an exponential rate. Linking information systems and machines creates cybernation. The possibility of a highly refined automated, cybernated system of production is now very real. There are also very great breakthroughs in areas of science such as biology and genetics, the results of which are not yet clear, but certainly highly significant. Every day much more is learned about human behavior and the learning process.

Futurists use different terms to refer to the transformation now taking place. The unknown state into which we are passing is labeled "post-industrial, post-civilized, automated, cybernated, super-industrial, information-era, communications-era" and the like. Futuristic writers do not agree on exactly what form the great revolution will take, but they agree that it is already in process. The transformation offers great hope for achieving a higher level of human potential and "inventing the future"; however it also poses the danger that people will be unable to adjust rapidly enough to change. Obviously, futurists have little faith that education can be guided by ideas of the past, such as the collection of classics known as the Great Books of the Western World.

METHODS OF FUTURES RESEARCH

Futures research is concerned with collecting information and developing the processes by which alternatives are determined and policy is made in a variety of disciplines. It concentrates on anticipated developments, the probability that various events will occur in a given time period, and the consequences of alternatives. Much attention is given to the impact of one event upon another and the way two or more events may interact to change future conditions. Futures research is action-oriented and realistic rather than utopian. It assumes that human action can and should make a difference in increasing or decreasing the probability of various possible futures. It concerns itself with conceptualizing and inventing the future by examining the consequences of various plans of action *before* they become tomorrow's reality.

Delphi.   The delphi technique is a means of forecasting based on the consensus of a group of specialists or experts. Its methodology involves first the selection of knowledgable people in a given field or problem area. Each member of the group is asked to render forecasts individually. After all forecasts are collected, the results of the total survey are returned to each member of the group. Members may then revise their earlier forecasts or explain their reasons for not being in consensus with the other members. The process of collecting and distributing the survey results is carried out until each member understands all other positions and all have reached final conclusions on their individual positions. Lonsdale concluded that the delphi technique provides for a convergence of forecasts and their defense as well as the defended minority positions.

Cross-Impact Matrix.   This is a refinement of the delphi technique which purports to determine the impact of future events upon each other. A delphi procedure can be used to measure the relationships between forecasted events. A computer analysis of the matrix can also be used to develop a set of probabilities for a complex set of events.

Digital computers, which have the capability of solving hundreds of equations within short periods of time, provide the researcher with the means for dynamic systems modeling. Mathematical simulation through computer analysis can facilitate knowledge about inherent lags between normative and exploratory forecasts. The computer is an important instrument for analysis of the cross-impact of events and dynamic modeling. It is a learning tool as Jerry Debenham asserts in describing his computerized game, SAFE (Simulating Alternative Futures in Education). The computer, however, can only simulate a system to the extent that operating equations accurately describe behaviors in the real system. Theobald stresses that "the computer is a very good servant and a very bad master."

Simulation-Gaming.   Simulation and gaming processes encompass a broad range of methodologies. They usually involve an analysis of alternative future systems. They may be confined to particular fields of futurist interests using the computer (as described above) or they may involve more simplistic models such as three-dimensional (pencil and paper) games and experience compression techniques (brain storming). The simulation may also involve a cross-impact analysis such as George Koehler's game, Futuribles, which provides participants with 288 possible futures in areas such as education, religion, energy, government, transportation, and the like.

Perspective Trees.   In this process, the researcher first examines the forces of change (rather than solutions to problems) within a given parameter. Second, a list is devised containing broad categories (poverty, health, war) as well as specific categories (government regulations, subcultures). Next, numerous relations or perspective trees are produced. This can be initiated, for example, with the following questions: What deterministic forecasts are related? Relationships may then become trees or partial trees. While perspective trees do not provide a whole method for forecasting, they are instrumental in the planning process. They are especially helpful when used in conjunction with the delphi technique, trend extrapolation or computerized cross-impact analysis.

Trend Extrapolation.   This technique entails an analysis of past and present trends in order to predict future trends. The central thesis is one of continuity; future trends will resemble past behaviors. A major problem in trend extrapolation is the selection of parameters. First, parameters are quantifiable at best. A subjective analysis of trends does not satisfy this methodology. Second, parameters must be selected which provide sufficient historical data. Third, regularity of patterns must be established. Fourth, the researcher should determine the interaction of past trends and changes in relationships between past and present parameters. Trend extrapolation may be used as a method itself or it may be incorporated into other methods. Extrapolation assumes no discontinuity with the past and is widely used by business, industry and government.

Scenario Concepts.   A scenario is usually a study of possible futures. Scenario conceptualization of the future is often limited by its subjective, nonquantitative format. It does provide, however, a creative means for analyzing futuribles without dependence upon past projections. This method is particularly important in the realm of social values. It is extremely difficult to model a hierarchical social system and to forecast value changes. Scenario conceptualizing facilitates a profile of social thresholds and provides descriptions of possible alternatives which oblige an individual to examine goals and priorities. The writing of scenarios is not only a research method, it is one of the best ways for students to learn how to deal with the future. The construction and evaluation of scenarios has become one of the most common classroom activities in future courses.

SCHOOLS OF FUTURISTIC THOUGHT

Because of the diversity of futures theories, it is helpful to divide them into groups according to general principles and shared beliefs. Just as in philosophy, there is some overlap and a few individuals do not fit well into any given category. Nevertheless, some system of classification is essential for treating assumptions and selecting the positions from which a futuristic philosophy of education may be constructed. (The divisions used here were suggested by Betty Barclay Franks and Mary Kay Howard.)

Optimistic Extrapolists.   As the name implies, Optimistic Extrapolists are hopeful about the future and often accuse critical theorists (like Robert Heilbroner) of crying "Wolf." One of the best known representatives of this group is Herman Kahn of the Hudson Institute. Kahn predicts a future society where technology has provided people with all possible comforts and leisure time. Support for Kahn and the Hudson Institute comes from business and government. Optimistic Extrapolists analyze existing trends and attempt to forecast future needs and markets. Members of this group assume that we will get the technological inventions to resolve such major problems as the energy crisis and that we will get them in time to avoid catastrophe. Kahn and his colleague Bruce-Briggs say that there is no such thing as pollution—only resources which we have not yet learned to recycle. Extrapolists use think tanks to study trends and to propose alternative courses of action related to specific problems in industry. They have pioneered new methods of research such as delphi, computer-assisted trend analysis, and the cross-impact matrix.

In opposition to the limited growth advocates, Optimistic Extrapolists see growth and technological development as natural and good for the whole world. They believe that we will discover new resources and learn how to better utilize existing ones so that there will be ample support for a high quality of life, even for people in underdeveloped nations. This optimism is reflected in Daniel Bell's *The Coming of Post-Industrial Society.* Other examples of the position are found in Olaf Helmer's *Social Technology,* and *The Image of the Future* by Fred Polak. The educational need of the future will be more and better trained scientists, engineers, and planners. Optimistic Extrapolists do not predict social revolution but they do think the developed industrial nations must provide leadership for a stable high-technology future world.

Future Constructors.   These futurists often have experience and training in science or engineering. They use laboratory experiments and empirical data for proving the points they wish to make. Future constructors plan to control the future and education will play a major role in bringing about the society they prescribe. One of the best statements of how this might be accomplished is found in B. F. Skinner's *Walden II*. Future Constructors believe that people can be educated to cooperate with planners and to make whatever adjustments are required for survival. They feel that future events cannot be left to mere chance or to individual wishes but must be designed for optimum benefit of all people. They say we must make better use of technology and do more with fewer resources. The future will most certainly not take care of itself, but planning, limiting growth, and social engineering can lead to the construction of a better future for all. Many writers in this group feel that very little progress has been made toward planning the future and that time is running out. As R. Buckminister Fuller puts it, we must choose either utopia or oblivion.

Donald N. Michael warns in *The Unprepared Society* that people are not ready for the onslaught of the future but he argues that utopia is possible through careful planning. He understands that a complete break with the past is impossible but human activities can be controlled and the future can be altered in a positive way. Social and technological engineering make it possible to carefully design and to control both the physical and psychological environments. Learning to do more with less will provide an ample supply of scarce natural resources to sustain life. Even biological and genetic engineering must be used for the optimum chances of survival. Constructors wish to produce a future that provides human satisfaction, some degree of choice, and well-adjusted individuals. Of course this implies that major social, economic and environmental problems can be resolved. This is possible only if the best trained planners and engineers are given the power to alter many of the priorities of the present industrial era. John R. Platt makes the point very well in his book *The Step To Man* and in an article in *The Science Teacher* called "Science for Human Survival."

Systems Futurists.   The popularity of general systems theory is reflected by those futurists who see the world as a series of interrelated systems. They point out that change in one area will often create vast and unexpected results in another. Systems Futurists believe that our resources are finite on the "spaceship" earth and that we must use them carefully. Members of this group use computer models to study the interaction of such variables as population growth, resource allocation, food supply, land use, and industrial growth. They believe that human survival depends upon a change of attitude among the peoples of the planet who must now recognize the necessity of living within certain constraints. Systems Futurists insist that growth can be organic and differentiated so that each part fits into and contributes to the whole. Allowing total freedom for materialistic growth and industrial development without considering the consequences to resources, levels of pollution, impact on the poor, or global stability is dangerous to survival. These futurists want to work closely with leaders in government and business to make them aware of thinking globally and adopting a systems approach to planning the social and economic future. Systems futurists are opposed to what Thorstein Veblen called "conspicuous consumption." They believe that education must provide experiences in holistic problem solving and stress the need to limit demand for scarce resources.

Lester R. Brown's books *World Without Borders* and *The Twenty-Ninth Day* are examples of treating demography, agriculture, and economics on a global scale. The "limits to growth" theory of Dennis and Donella Meadows reflects systems thinking. Jan Tinbergen is typical of the systems theorists associated with the Club of Rome. Hazel Henderson's *An End To Economics* and Ervin Laszlo's *The Systems View of the World* are statements of the position of systems futurists.

Participatory Futurists.   Numerous futurists, especially those with backgrounds in the social sciences and economics, fall into the category of Participatory Futurists. They agree with John Dewey that all mature human beings should participate in the decisions that affect them. In *Alternatives For America II*, Robert Theobald stresses the need for free access to unbiased information, open communication, dialogue, and authority based on use rather than status. Participatory Futurists want to examine all available alternatives in order to bring about consensus on plans of action. This may require the altering of the economic system, educating for problem solving, more cooperative styles of life, and abandoning values of the industrial era. These futurists prefer to work for change within the system but they are ready to form "ad-hoc" groups to overcome red tape, bureaucratic roadblocks, or archaic rules. They believe that all the people working together can act to control technology and justly allocate scarce resources. Economic growth should not be freely allowed without the input of all those who will benefit or be harmed by it. People must decide how much of anything (energy, automobiles, styrofoam cups) is enough and be guided by the principle of "enoughness."

In *The Everyman Project*, Robert Jungk speaks of forming communication networks to foster social responsibility. Alvin Toffler pointed out in *Future Shock* that the accelerating rate of change makes it dangerous to rely on past experience or modes of thought. In *The Third Wave*, Toffler calls for decentralizing authority and solving most problems at the local or community level. Like other Participatory Futurists, Toffler recognizes the existence of tremendous problems but he is convinced that all the people working together can resolve them. Of course, future planning and anticipatory democracy require a high degree of honesty, humility, and love. Education must play the important role of teaching people how to communicate, cooperate, choose wisely, and cope with rapid change. Schools must provide unlimited information and methods to evaluate and use that information. Techniques for group problem solving and group consensus would be emphasized by Participatory Futurists.

Evolutionary Futurists.   Emphasis on moral and spiritual values rather than on technological growth is characteristic of Evolutionary Futurists. They view the future with optimism because materialism and the rapid consumption of vital resources will be replaced by a new consciousness and more humane lifestyles. Evolutionary Futurists have roots in the past, especially in classical literature. Some of the concepts fostered by this group can be found in Maria Montessori's *The Absorbent Mind*. These futurists envision a world in which human beings undergo a transformation to a higher form of spiritual awareness and achieve integration of body, mind, and spirit. Living in harmony with themselves and the universe is their goal. They believe that leadership should be in the hands of those people who demonstrate a strong sense of moral and ethical responsibility. Evolutionary Futurists oppose unchecked economic growth which fosters exploitation and the accumulation of wealth. Technology, they believe, should be under control so that neither the natural nor the human environment will be harmed. The evolutionary transformation in progress is not physical or biological but involves freeing the mind and transcending materialistic preoccupations. Evolutionary Futurists see the past, present, and future as a continuum. They seek to live in harmony with themselves and the cosmos.

Willis Harman's *An Incomplete Guide to the Future* and E. F. Shumacher's *A Guide for the Perplexed* are typical of the works of these futurists. They are concerned about improving the quality of human life on earth. They believe that natural and human resources are gifts which must be used with wisdom. Education should foster a strong sense of moral and ethical responsibility. John Lilly in *The Center of the Cyclone* deals with the problem of individuals getting in touch with themselves and developing community consciousness. Education is the means by which wisdom and spiritual values are acquired. Schools should be used to discipline the mind and aid understanding of the broad range of alternatives open to everyone. Mass media values, keeping up with the Joneses, and specialized job training are just the opposite of what the Evolutionary Futurists want. They are interested in general education for moral development which would include the classical wisdom of ages past.

Humanistic Futurists.   George Leonard's classic *Education and Ecstasy* is a statement of many of the beliefs of the Humanistic Futurists. These people believe that the actions we undertake now create or invent the future. Humanistic Futurists believe that modern society places too much emphasis on role playing, competition, status, and materialistic success. This has distorted human nature and makes it difficult to pass from the industrial era into an age of awareness. People must remove their masks, become more sensitive to others, and learn compassion. Leonard feels that until people are more aware of their own bodies, feelings, and intellects, they cannot live fully in the present or create an adequate future. All of us need to deal honestly with our own emotions and discover what is of real value in life.

Transpersonal Education: A Curriculum for Feeling and Being, edited by Gay Hendricks and James Fadiman, suggests the kind of schooling Humanistic Futurists desire. They want to see the earth kept beautiful and safe to stimulate joy in living. This requires better protection of the environment and limits to economic growth. Teachers should be co-learners and role models in an open, trusting, sensitive learning situation. Learning must be an integral part of the total human experience and students must get in touch with their own emotional being. In addition to creating sensitive and compassionate human beings, this group wants to challenge the values of the current industrial age. Unlimited growth, economic expansion, more technology, and the sacrifice of natural beauty to commercial interests are opposed by Humanistic Futurists. They believe that future problems can best be solved by well-adjusted people who enjoy life and each other. They want us to husband our resources and distribute them more evenly. They are concerned about preserving the natural environment for future generations. Humanists believe we have moved too far toward the kind of world described in Orwell's

1984 and Huxley's *Brave New World*. In order for each person to achieve his or her full potential, the highly technological structured world of business and industry must be abandoned. Affective learning is as important as cognitive learning. The study of alternative lifestyles, dream sharing, and sensory awareness activities would be part of the curriculum. This is the theme of Bob Samples' *The Metamorphic Mind: A Celebration of Creative Consciousness*.

Visionaries and Radicals.   Two smaller groups with quite different conceptions of the future are the Visionary Futurists and the Radical Futurists. Those who fall into the Visionary category refuse to be bound by the constraints of common-sense reality. They stress imagination for freeing people from the shackles of the past and enabling them to leap into a new era. They envision a future in which a complete transformation of human nature will occur and universal consciousness will develop. They believe Jules Verne and H. G. Wells were able to anticipate future events because their imaginations were unlimited. The idea that intelligence and awareness may transcend known human capacity is used in television programs like *Star Trek* and in the books of Arthur Clarke, Harlan Ellison, and Kurt Vonnegut, Jr.

A leading Visionary Spokesman is F. M. Esfandiary. In *Optimism One* and *Up-Wingers*, he argues that such problems as resource allocation, energy, world peace, and pollution are irrelevant. By attaining cosmic awareness, new generations will have the whole universe at their disposal and decisions will be made by all humanity through an instantaneous universal referendum. Adrian Berry in *The Next Thousand Years: A Vision of Man's Future in the Universe*, speaks of electronic brain stimulation and expanding human horizons through linking the brain to computers. Those who do not share these optimistic views are not considered futurists at all by the Visionary Futurists.

The best known book by a Radical Futurist is Illich's *Deschooling Society*. Illich, like Paul Goodman, Arthur Waskow and Everett Reimer, believes schools foster bad social values and that they cannot be reformed. Radicals want to overthrow the existing power structure and drastically alter society to gain personal freedom and insure the well-being of future generations. They think the past is repressive and should be forgotten. Distrusting all forms of authority, Radical Futurists view economic growth as just another form of exploitation. They say individuals must be freed from the burdens of economic and governmental oppression. For them, technology is to be feared when it is in the hands of a power elite. For the Radical Futurists, each person must live the future now and make his or her own personal choices in spite of institutions like schools which try to restrict individual freedom.

IMPLICATIONS FOR EDUCATIONAL THEORY

A great deal of the history of American education is the history of conflict over future aims and goals. When Comenius wrote about his concept of pansophia and his belief that human beings could better themselves through schooling, he was preparing for a better future. Locke, Rousseau, Pestalozzi, and Herbart concerned themselves with the kind of education that they thought would bring about a utopian society. Most speculative plans for educational reform have been directed toward the kind of world that would be free of the problems and weaknesses of the present. Those who wrote plans for a national system of education in 1795 and Jefferson's plan for public education in Virginia were also futuristic in the sense that they aimed at producing a better society and a more democratic one in years to come.

It is easy to trace elements of futurism in the educational theory of John Dewey. His pragmatic philosophy centered on the question of how we can know and control the world. Dewey created an educational theory to meet the needs of a growing, dynamic, urban, industrial society which was in constant flux. His principle of the continuous reconstruction of human experience in the light of new learning is one commonly found among futuristic writers. The idea of making a better society through the schools is central to social reconstructionists who followed Dewey.

Seeking agreement among the various modern schools of futurism is an exercise in futility. The optimistic forecasts of Herman Kahn have little in common with the Illich's radical demand for deschooling society or the cosmic consciousness of Esfandiary and the Visionaries. On the other hand, Evolutionary and Humanistic Futurists are quite similar in their views of human nature and of the kind of future society they would like to create. Systems Futurists and Future Constructors share many assumptions and seek similar goals. Participatory Futurists draw upon the work of many of the other divisions in order to reconstruct society and achieve survival with maximum realization of human potential. Educational theory can benefit from a serious consideration of those futures concepts shared by leading authors in schools of futurism who are interested in altering education.

The futures field has been heavily influenced by economics and sociology but it is interdisciplinary and broadly based. No adequate theory of education for the future can ignore the wide range of forces that influence the human condition. Marshall McLuhan has attacked the "fragmented unrelation" of the industrial era school curricula and pointed out that any subject studied in depth at once relates to other subjects. A futuristic educational philosophy must be global, open, synergetic, interdisciplinary and oriented toward cultural synthesis.

Americans and citizens of the other industrial nations appear to be caught up in the pursuit of hedonism and what Veblen called "conspicuous consumption." Little effort is made to understand the past or to trace roots of the culture so that people seldom appreciate their cultural heritage. Looking with apprehension at the future, many opt for a life centered in the present and pursue the immediate gratification of desires. Following the crowd to materialistic values and situational ethics as fostered by the mass media and commercial advertising is a poor approach to the future. Those with no sense of the past cannot locate themselves in historical perspective or live vicariously through their posterity. This is not to say that the future should be approached by way of a rear view mirror image of the past. A traditional mind set and the uncritical acceptance of earlier values may prevent us from accepting change or making the best choices among alternatives. Values of the Puritan ethic are not helpful in guiding the use of leisure time nor can we expect an optimum future to be shaped by the ideals of the industrial era. Education must encourage the study and the use of the past to take maximum advantage of collective human experience but it must not allow the future to be subsumed under the values of the past or the present.

An accelerating rate of technological change together with the emergence of new problems in the adaptive nonmaterial culture is accepted as a fact of life by most futurists. There are disagreements about limiting technological growth and about the kinds of technology that may be most important for the good life of the future but very few advocate a "back to nature" movement or a smashing of machines as the Luddites tried to do in the nineteenth century. Rapid change and invention will almost certainly continue unless there is a total breakdown of civilization resulting in a new dark age or total annihilation. Certainly the knowledge explosion and the growth of electronic communications networks will have a major impact on education. If learning is to be an instrument for survival, it must prepare people to understand and control technological change. Change for its own sake or for mere economic growth is not necessarily healthy but many of the most important problems require a technological solution and little progress can be expected unless people have access to new information and the tools for using it. The great task for educational theory is clearing the way for social inventions that will match expansion in technology and keep up with rapid change.

Many serious scholars including Robert Heilbroner and Cristopher Lasch are not at all convinced that a Malthusian apocalypse or a nuclear holocaust can be prevented. Nevertheless, any hope for inventing the future by human action is predicated upon the assumption that people can understand and control the forces which shape their world. In the past, people beset by obscure problems and difficulties often adopted the "whatever will be will be" attitude and abandoned faith in human capacity. This "failure of nerve" which has occurred periodically in human history makes planning impossible and abandons reason for fate. Even when problems appear to be insurmountable, educators must have faith in the ability of human intelligence to comprehend the world and to control the destiny of man. The belief that wisdom and rational action cannot alter the future is a self-fulfilling prophesy which education must combat.

There is a tendency for writers in futurism, especially science fiction arthors and utopian novelists, to suggest desirable goals without saying how these goals are to be achieved. Futurism in educational theory will do well to consider John Dewey's argument that means and ends can never be separated and that the ends do not justify the means. Goals, ends, and aims in future education must be evaluated not only on the basis of their desirability but also on the criterion of the possibilities for implementation. Simple solutions to complex problems often have side effects that are as bad or worse than the original problems. It must be remembered that nothing is done in a vacuum and what is involved in getting from here to there is just as important as the goal identified as "there." In society and education, as in ecology and economics, any change or alteration will have widespread and often unpredicted effects beyond the primary area in which the change takes place.

The schools of futurism are not in agreement on an ultimate educational aim in a fixed or cosmic sense, but the goal of human survival with maximum realization of potential is common to all. Maximum realization of the human potential cannot be achieved unless people work together to resolve the really crucial problems such as preventing nuclear war, protecting the natural environment, and meeting the basic needs of all people for scarce resources. Solving basic problems is necessary but not sufficient for realization of the human potential. There must also be the opportunity to achieve the good life, the life of greatest value. This, in turn, implies the availability of alternatives and the ability to choose. Schools often set arbitrary limits to choice and inhibit creativity. Limits are also set by society in that models are taken from the industrial era with its emphasis on materialism, production, exploitation, and growth. It is incumbent upon future educational theorists to make sure that education clearly delineates the problems, provides learners with necessary tools and information, and encourages the selection of sane alternatives. Every educational plan for the future must show that it enhances the chances for human survival and the quality of life.

CHARACTERISTICS OF FUTURISTIC EDUCATION

Some leading educational futurists have suggested specific changes in order to help bring about a viable future for the citizens of tomorrow. While these alternatives are speculative, they do address the problem of the inadequacy of existing bureaucratic schools to meet the needs of the next century. Their purpose is to criticize certain characteristics and practices in current educational institutions and to offer possible substitute practices more likely to meet future requirements.

Replacing Linear with Synergetic Processes.   Institutions are established to meet certain human needs. They are apt, however, to become self-sustaining bureaucracies with goals of self-aggrandizement and immortality. The school, like most bureaucracies, has a dominant nonhuman priority—its own survival. The objectives of the institution are necessarily more important than individual objectives. . . . It is possible to change this aim of permanence by changing two other essential characteristics of the bureaucracy—its linear design and division of labor.

American institutions have been, by Theobald's analysis, successful in the recent past by concentrating on major goals while ignoring secondary and tertiary consequences. This, he specifies, is a consequence of linear design. He cites seven inherent weaknesses which are

characteristic of linear organizations. They are most applicable to
the school.

1. The school can only receive information that it is designed to
   receive. This requires that information must be adjusted to
   the classification system. Schools are primarily designed to
   receive state-approved textbools. Information must conform
   to specialized courses. Teachers cannot easily provide new
   materials because of the cost and time involved.
2. Linear organizations can only make linear decisions. This implies that educators must extend existing patterns. Administrators cannot make decisions from the perspective of students or teachers.
3. Linear institutions are easily overloaded. Teachers often have
   too many students, activities, and information to process in
   short periods of time. Decisions become difficult to adminis-
   ter properly.
4. Linear organization people tend to be promoted until they
   reach a level of incompetence. In education, upward mobility
   requires many teachers to become administrators.
5. Linear organizations are capable of reproducing. This is especially true in higher education as departments attempt to gain
   strength through numbers.
6. Linear organizations tend to repress unfavorable information.
   Educators rarely pass unfavorable information up or down
   the organizational hierarchy since it may reflect upon an individual's competence.
7. Linear organizations are only capable of controlling people
   who wish to be controlled.

A synergetic system is proposed as an alternative to linear organization. In its early stages, it is perceived as an "ad-hocracy", which
is Toffler's term for the creation of task forces which move within
bureaucracies to complete temporary tasks. In a more advanced
stage, this would be replaced by what Theobald labels "consentives." Consentives already exist in the form of buyers' cooperatives,
community ecology groups, and Nader's Raiders. In education, the
alternative of a synergetic, process-oriented organization first requires a distinction between training and education.

Education is More Than Training. The educational system is designed to carry out a process of training. Training perpetuates existing information and reinforces current trends. It is usually a
memorization/regurgitation, short-term, method of learning.

Whenever, for example, students are expected to memorize the presidents of the United States, they are being trained. Few graduates can define and give one example of a gerund even though most of them were provided with this training through several years of middle school. The true purpose of education, however, is to study the principles operant within an activity in order to facilitate new questions and new answers. In essence, education requires an environment in which students are not asked questions for which the answers are known; if the questions involve predetermined conclusions, the process is training.

Both education and training should be provided in the school. There are, obviously, skills such as typewriting, bookkeeping, and welding in which many students would choose to be trained. The problem is that training has dominated the curriculum. It is suggested that many school problems are attributable to students' growing resistance to training. Even on college campuses many students are questioning the assumptions inherent in the present social system. For them, learning through training is not "relevent" because it does not provide an atmosphere for re-examination of society's priorities, classifications, habits, and values. Although training was an asset to the industrial revolution, the emerging communications era requires an educational system which will enhance the development of new values and behavior patterns. This will entail changes in classroom control. Training results primarily in a teacher-centered classroom while education facilitates a student-centered environment. Both applications are responsive to authoritarian methods.

Structural Authority v. Sapiential Authority.   Structural authority provided an important rationale in the industrial-era world view. Railroads were built, assembly lines were developed, and warfare was accomplished through the principle of structural authority. This authority, which is derived from one's position or rank, is the dominant pattern in educational institutions. The organizing prerequisite of the school is one whereby professors "teach" and the students "learn." Under the auspices of structural authority, the student is expected to accept the information, assume that it is correct, ingurgitate it as accurately as possible, and regurgitate all information deemed significant by the teacher. The critical factor is that the authority of the teacher is established by position rather than competency.

Sapiental authority, a term developed by Robert Theobald and Tom Paterson, is proposed as a future alternative form of authority. Sapiental authority is not based upon title or rank. It depends upon no sanctions from governments, schools or other institutions. Rather, sapiental authority is based upon the possession of information, knowledge or ideas which find support among others. A model for this exists today in the learned societies and professions. When a paper is read or a thesis is presented, it is accepted or rejected by those most knowledgable about the field and one's institutional position does not protect one's words from peers' scrutiny. A major qualification of sapiential authority is that all participants have the opportunity for critical analysis of any given piece of information. This authority is derived through group consensus and a recognition of those who can claim to know, because of the extent and depth of their work.

Many people fear that the breakdown of structural authority will result in chaos. Some want to return to earlier conditions as a psychological rejection of change. There are also those in every organization who have been promoted beyond their level of competence and fear any attack on structural authority because it threatens their security. Schools, like other bureaucratic institutions, use structural authority to protect incompetent individuals and useless regulations. Even though sapiential authority has not yet received serious attention, it is a necessary part of education for future survival. One qualification is necessary: this authority should not be interpreted as license or made to support the belief that any idea is just as valid as any other. But the problems of the present and the future are so vast and so difficult that every individual's best contributions are needed. Education must, therefore, provide conditions that allow for perception of sapiential authority by each individual and for development of each individual's full potential.

School Learning/Life-Long Learning.   The schools of the industrial age have become so specialized that there is no longer room in the curriculum for developing a broad understanding of the world. In his book *Overskill*, Eugene Schwartz shows that specialization is self-defeating. Civilization cannot be saved by a group of highly trained specialists who do not understand other fields.

Technology for the information age requires experts but there are many places in modern society where specialized information and skills can be obtained. In order to facilitate life-long learning, the school must focus on more education (rather than training) and sapiential authority instead of rigid structure. There must be an atmosphere conducive to interdisciplinary studies and humanistic values. Modern world problems are interrelated and their solution depends upon what Fuller calls a concept of synergy. He means that the unique behavior of whole systems cannot be predicted by any behaviors of their component functions taken separately.

As Dewey often said, school should not be separate from the community and the child need not be in conflict with the curriculum. Dichotomies between theory and practice or between idealistic and technical subjects may become academic as learning is understood to be a life-long practice. The mass media is already engaged in education. Xerox has an educational program which is almost of university status and many corporations train their own computer operators. Adult and continuing education will surely grow. So long as the concept of reaching a certain educational plateau (such as high school graduation) and then ending education to enter the work force remains in vogue, specialized training will remain paramount. We are, however, entering a learning society and an age of information. People must now expect that they will go on learning throughout life, not only as preparation for earning a living but also for avocations and leisure activities. Preparation for a life of learning should replace the idea of terminal schooling in the theory and practice of education.

An End to Zero Sum Games.   Educational institutions rely primarily upon the use of positive and negative sanctions which result in an "I win—you lose" competitive structure. Grading practices often lead to sorting children into success groups and failure groups. Educators talk about cooperation but enforce competition between students. As John Goodlad has pointed out, grades in school are good predictors of further success in school but not good predictors of success in jobs or in life. Good workers, compassionate human beings, caring parents, and concerned citizens are not made by winning high grades in a competitive school environment. Winners tend to be disproportionately middle-class, White, and affluent. Of course, the winners are also losers because they have been taught to perpetuate competition in work and in world affairs. This is a zero sum game in which everyone eventually will lose. The ecological crisis is one physical representation of this problem. Competitive attitudes put stress on limited natural resources and endanger wildlife. They are no longer useful in giant industrial cooperations that control goods and manage markets.

Learning how to cooperate is a future survival skill which educational institutions must now begin to practice and to teach. Students trained as passive, noninvolved spectators in the classrooms are not apt to be involved in cooperative activities outside. The mass media (especially the medium of television) also tend to promote isolation, noninvolvement, and spectatorism. School activities need to be made more cooperative and action-oriented with all students emotionally involved. Education involves change and the school situation must promote change in the learner. A passive attitude does not promote change and neither does competition. At the very least, students must be prepared to risk their prejudices if learning is to take place. If education is the process that changes the learner, the traditional school environment will simply not do. Within the existing school system, the competitive environment has precluded all efforts of teaching cooperation. In the future, it may be possible for educators to teach a healthy competitive perspective within a cooperative framework. At present, schools pick up competitive attitudes to control and manipulate children.

The Future School: A Problem Analysis/Resource Distribution Center.   In the future, educational institutions at all levels must become resource centers for the distribution and creation of unbiased information. Universities have long been expected to achieve this goal on a national and international basis. The linking of telecommunications and computers makes vast quantities of information available to any group or individual. Data banks for information may now be found in schools and even in many homes. Obviously schools will need to stop concentrating on the memorization of bits of information and start stressing how to find and use information. The process of comparing conflicting accounts of events and evaluating the validity of available data must take a much more important role in education. The research function of determining whether or not information can be trusted can no longer be left to universities alone. Each future citizen must have unbiased data upon which to make vital decisions and the skills of judging information must be taught early in life. It should be pointed out that critical viewing is also a survival skill since a great deal of our knowledge about the world comes to us through television. Raw data and unorganized information are not very useful in solving problems. Knowing how to quickly find and systematize information will surely become a vital part of tomorrow's education. Even when it is identified and organized, information is not knowledge and knowledge is not wisdom. Students must learn to make evaluative judgments, to analyze, clarify, generalize, and understand.

Much that passes for education today is of little value in helping students learn to solve problems. Giving information to the pupil is an inadequate means of producing self-directed scholars and future citizens. The questions for which answers are unknown are the most significant ones. Theobald's contention that everything already discovered should be called training and the term education should be used only for unresolved issues has implications for problem analysis centers. Future problems will certainly require input from individuals with different backgrounds and training, therefore students need to learn how to cooperate to reach consensus. Inquiry, discovery, and scientific methods of learning must take precedence over lectures, reading texts, and selecting answers from multiple-choice tests. The problem analysis/resource distribution centers can be modeled on some of the best of existing practices and earlier experiments such as those of the progressives. It is not necessary to invent a totally new process but merely to change the focus of education from the acquisition of information to the application of data to problem situations in a cooperative and action-oriented environment.

FUTURES CURRICULUM

Professional educators are not waiting for futures programs to gain acceptance in all schools before taking action. The popularity of the annual meeting of the Education Section of the World Futures Society, attended by hundreds of classroom teachers, attests to the interest many have in futurism. While formal courses in futurism are most often found only at university level, thousands of teachers incorporate elements of futures studies into the classes they normally offer. Communications networks and publications exist to promote various methods and materials used in the futures education movement. Some universities such as the University of Massachusetts and the University of Houston at Clear Lake City offer degree programs in futurism. Such universities also conduct courses and workshops for teachers interested in giving a futures focus to the subjects they teach. Some of the characteristics of futures programs in elementary and secondary schools are as follows:

Interdisciplinary Approach.   Futurism in education is not confined to any single discipline or subject area. Indeed, the overarching feature of treating the future in the curriculum is the interdisciplinary focus. The idea of a core curriculum as invented by Herbart and used by the progressives is central to futurism. Relating history to sociology and economics, or stressing the connections between biology, psychology, and ecology are common practices. A characteristic of futures is that the impact of one field of human endeavor on another is studied. The symbiotic relationship of plants and animals living in the same environments or the impact economic development may have on natural ecological balance is analyzed. The word "synergy" describes the change that altering one aspect of world may have on another. Synergetic, symbiotic, integrated, holistic, core, interdisciplinary studies are found in the futures curriculum. It is believed that the narrow boundaries of disciplines and narrow specialization may interfere with the complete understanding of an issue. Future problem solvers must be able to bring together information from a variety of subject areas if their solutions are to be viable.

Problem Analysis Focus.   Most futures courses attempt to help students analyze the problems around them. To say that things cost more because of inflation or that food is scarce in Africa because the soil is thin represents inadequate understanding. In order to solve problems and to select wisely between alternative futures, it is necessary to distinguish between probable causes and glib explanations. Futures courses are known for probing deeply to find the underlying causes of difficulties, especially social ones. When the reasons for failure in some human endeavors are understood, students are in a better position to evaluate possible, probable, and preferable futures. The study of trends and probable projections is strengthened if students have learned to be critical and to search for reasons when things do not go as expected. Inventing the future is not mere speculation about personal and societal preferences, it involves being realistic, critical, analytic, and careful. Futures courses also stress the power of the individual and the group to alter the future. The notion that "whatever will be will be" and the belief that human action can make no difference in the course of human events is not accepted. Fatalism is replaced with a pro-active orientation and a belief that many alternative futures are possible. Participation, involvement, creativity, and choosing are stressed by futurists as ways of getting people to take the initiative instead of waiting for the future to shock them.

Faith in Human Ability to Control the Future.   In spite of the critical and analytic aspects of futures courses, the field is generally optimistic. Obviously the world is in crisis and the possibility of such a catastrophe as thermonuclear war is real, but futurists believe that the major dilemmas with which societies are faced are capable of being solved. There is considerable skepticism about the viability of current technological solutions to global problems but futuristic literature is not highly pessimistic. Futurism stresses the power that well educated citizens have in controlling their own lives and tends to support the belief that human action can prevent the apocalyptic end of civilization. Stress is placed on the notion that what we do today will determine the shape of the future. While some attention is given to forecasting coming events, futures courses attempt to develop insight into the major current problems in an effort to show what must be done to prevent disaster and insure a desirable tomorrow

Open-Ended, Inquiry Based Methodology.   Futures courses attempt to avoid the mere imposing of facts and information on students. Much of the curricula is hypothetical, especially where possible and probable alternative futures are concerned. Evaluation of student written scenarios and classroom delphi polling are often used. Schools usually do not have access to sophisticated instruments such as the computer-based cross-impact matrix, but students can be involved in trend extrapolation, modeling, and various kinds of futures games. Teachers attempt to avoid authority relationships or any attempt to dictate the right answer but they try to promote logical thinking and careful analysis by students. The teacher as facilitator promotes problem solving, informed speculation, creative imagination, and systematic thinking. Student involvement does not mean that one future alternative is just as good as another or that the courses have no intellectual rigor. Students are encouraged to project themselves into a variety of probable future situations and to think logically about the problems and opportunities such situations might create. The use of science fiction literature, exploratory predictions, attitude surveys, and brainstorming techniques is common. A major goal is creating individuals who will be more likely to manage their own future in a pro-active way.

Value Teaching in Futuristics.   A strong value component is found in most futures courses. Values usually emerge whenever alternative futures are considered because of the nature of the choices students must make. For example, continued economic growth produces pollution, the destruction of natural resources, urban congestion, and materialism. If these by-products of expansion are to be avoided, future citizens must be willing to live on a lower standard or to adopt other styles of life. The question of whether or not affluence brings about the good life can hardly be considered without challenging cherished values. Futurism requires students to constantly re-examine adherence to the values of the current industrial era. Concepts like simple living, appropriate technology, environmental protection, zero population growth, and world political stability imply serious reconstruction of personal and societal values.

FUTURE TRENDS

While we cannot be certain about what will take place in the immediate future and long range forecasts are always risky, there are certain trends in American education that seem likely to continue and some world-wide forecasts can be made with a high degree of probability that they will occur. Of course, any real major change such as a new technique of learning or a war would alter trends in a dramatic way. If some degree of stability continues in the next decades the following educational speculations seem safe:

1. Education will become life long and will continue throughout the year. The present nine-month school will be replaced by learning opportunities available at any time. Mass media and home based mini computers will be used as educational aids for the very young. Adults will not finish school but will continue to learn throughout life. It will be necessary to retrain constantly in order to keep up with changes in various fields. Cycles of learning and work will replace the present pattern of school first and work later. Learning for life and leisure will be more important than job training.

2. As new ways of obtaining an education emerge, the old system of semester terms and units of credit will be altered. Means will be found to certify that the learner has the necessary level of skill and information to enter a new learning environment without showing academic credentials. Since much of the learning will be fostered by industry or given in courses, transcripts will be less significant.

3. The curriculum will be very much enlarged to include new discoveries, leisure and avocational skills, travel, human values, group therapy, and psychological guidance. The idea of a curriculum as broad as life itself which Comenius suggested, will finally become a reality. There will be nothing which cannot be formally studied if the students are interested.

4. Fewer classroom teachers will be needed but there will be an increase in the number of people engaged in teaching and learning.

Long years of training may be required before a person is allowed to manage a future learning environment. However, much learning will be informal and life long so that the distinction between the teacher and the taught will erode away. Learning facilitators will perform a variety of functions and educational centers will have differentiated staffing. Computers and teaching machines will carry on many teaching tasks but specialists will be available to help with any learning disability and to stimulate students.

5. There will be less competition, less standardization, less grouping by ability, and less pressure on the student. More attention will be given to growing, developing, problem solving, communication, and personal goals. Since learning will be an activity for life, knowing how to learn in an efficient and joyful way will be a very highly prized future skill.

6. Age specific compulsory learning institutions called schools will be replaced by a variety of diversified learning environments. Young people will be able to take responsibility for their own learning at a much earlier age. It will be common to find children and senior citizens in the same learning situations. A learning *society* will emerge, which means that most people will spend a great deal of every day of their lives in some kind of learning environment.

7. Technology will make possible many new educational possibilities. Telecommunications and computers will make information available to everyone. People will be able to link themselves electronically with others who are interested in the subjects they wish to study and to contact the best known experts in the field. Chemical and electronic learning aids including brain stimulation will be used to help concentration and eliminate learning blocks. The skill required to quickly find and evaluate *any* information on *any* subject will become as common as reading is today. New companies will develop which will produce and market educational materials as well as entertainment computers and a myriad of new communication networks.

8. Education will stress the understanding of the forces in the environment that must be controlled in order to insure the maximum realization of human potential and the good life. Problem-solving centers will emerge and students will become skilled at finding alternative solutions to all major difficulties. Greater attention will be given to world understanding and to the issues that involve all of the people on earth. All major new developments in the world (and perhaps in space) will immediately take a place in the curriculum. At the same time, much educational activity will occur with small interest groups or it will be directed toward the solution of commun-

ity problems. The ability to analyze data, to think in a systematic way, and to be realistic about the possibilities of the future will be skills everyone will need to develop.

As this book has tried to point out, the past, present, and future are always related. A real understanding of what has happened in American education and why it happened is essential for guiding action now and for inventing the future. As Lasch argued in *The Culture of Narcissisism*, those without an appreciation of history have no interest in the future because they live only for the present. Our hedonistic culture may stress the importance of living now and letting tomorrow take care of itself but such an attitude is devastating to the teaching profession. Educators must be future oriented if they are to prepare students for a world of tomorrow which surely will be vastly different from today. The background of historical understanding and the appreciation of issues and conflicts of the past provides the best foundation we can have for predicting trends and preparing for a viable future. Perhaps the most important use of history is that it shows us how far short of our own traditions we have fallen and stimulates us to strive for a higher realization of our individual and collective potential in the world of the future.

BIBLIOGRAPHY

Bowman, Jim, Fred Kierstead, Chris Dede and John Pulliam. *The Far Side of the Future: Social Problems and Educational Reconstruction.* Washington: World Future Society, 1978.

Botkin, James, Mahdielmanojra and Mircea Malitza. *No Limits to Learning: Bridging the Human Gap.* New York: Pergamon Press, 1979.

Bright, James. *Practical Technology Forecasting.* New York: Industrial Management Center, 1978.

Brown, Lester. *The Twenty-Ninth Day.* New York: W.W. Norton, 1978.

Hipple, Theodore, ed. *The Futures of Education 1975–2000.* Santa Monica, Cal: Goodyear, 1974.

Kierstead, Fred, Jim Bowman, and Christopher Dede, eds. *Educational Futures: Sourcebook I.* Washington: World Future Society, 1979.

Pulliam, John, and Jim Bowman. *Educational Futurism: In Pursuance of Survival.* Norman, Okla: University of Oklahoma Press, 1974.

Rubin, Louis, ed. *The Future of Education: Perspectives on Tomorrow's Schooling.* Boston: Allyn & Bacon, 1975.

Toffler, Alvin, ed. *Learning for Tomorrow.* New York: Random House, 1974.

Toffler, Alvin. *The Third Wave.* New York: Morrow, 1980.

World Future Society, ed. *The Future, A Guide to Information Sources.* Washington: World Future Society, 1979.

General Bibliography

Bailyn, Bernard. *Education in Forming of American Society*. Chapel Hill, N.C.: University of North Carolina Press, 1960. 147 pp. This is a critical essay on American history of education from the cultural standpoint. It surveys the main themes of educational history yet to be written. There is a useful evaluation of earlier movements in American cultural history, such as Puritanism, philanthropy, race relations, and the growth of sectarianism.

Butts, Freeman, *The Education of the West: A Formative Chapter in the History of Civilization*. New York: McGraw-Hill, 1933. A very sound general history by one of the best known American educational historians.

Butts, Freeman. *Public Education in the United States: From Revolution to Reform*. New York: Holt, Rinehart and Winston, 1978. The work is outstanding for its detail and depth of study. It is the best account of legislation and court cases in recent years.

Commager, Henry Steele, ed. *Documents of American History*. New York: Appleton-Century-Crofts, 1963. 739 pp., including index. Contains 665 noteworthy documents, significant in the shaping of American history. Documents pertinent to education are included.

Cremin, Lawrence. *The Wonderful World of Ellwood Patterson Cubberly: An Essay on the Historiography of American Education*. New York: Columbia University Teachers College, Bureau of Publications, no date. This is an interesting and delightful treatment of the first great American educational historian by a leading modern scholar in the same field.

Cremin, Lawrence. *Public Education*. New York: Basic Books, 1976. This is a treatment of the history of American education with attention given to public policy, the emerging role of government, and the issues over control of schools.

Curti, Merle. *The Social Ideas of American Educators*. Patterson, N.J.: Pageant Books, 1959. 613 pp., including index. Contents: Part I, (1) Colonial Survivals and Revolutionary Promises, 1620-1820, (2) New Conflicts and a New Solution 1800-1860, (3) Education and Social Reform: Horace Mann, (4) Henry Barnard, (5) The Education of Women, followed by a summary of Part I; Part II, (6) The School and the Triumph of Business Enterprise, 1860-1914, (7) Education in the South, (8) The Black Man's Place: Booker T. Washington, 1856-1916, (9) William T. Harris, The Conservator, 1835-1908, (10) Bishop Spalding, Catholic Educator, 1840-1916, (11) Francis Wayland Parker, Democrat, 1837-1902, (12) G. Stanley Hall, Evolutionist, 1846-1924, (13) William James, Individualist, 1842-1910, (14) Edward Lee Thorndike, Scientist, 1874-1949, (15) John Dewey, 1859-1952, (16) Post-War Patterns. A conclusion and bibliographical notes follow and there is a treatment of recent educational history. This book provides an excellent social understanding of American educational development. Also useful is Curti's *The Growth of American Thought*. New York: Harper & Row, 1951.

Curtis, Stanley J. and M.E.A. Boultwood. *A Short History of Educational Ideas*, 3d ed. London: University Tutorial Press Ltd., 1964. 615 pp., including index. This is a standard text in Western educational history, paying considerable attention to American education and American educational leaders. Helpful bibliographical information is given at the end of each chapter.

Dworkin, Martin. *Dewey on Education*. New York: Columbia University Teacher's College Press, 1959. This is the best quick reference to the work of Dewey for those who do not wish to use Dewey's own books. Also suggested is Dewey's own *Democracy and Education*. New York: Macmillan, 1916.

Good, Harry, and James Teller. *A History of American Education*. 3rd ed. New York: Macmillan, 1973. This is a detailed history of American education complete with index and extensive bibliography. It is especially useful for the period prior to the twentieth century.

Johanningmeier, Erwin. *Americans and Their Schools*. Chicago: Rand McNally, 1980. This is a superior new text which is both very detailed and interesting. It would be an excellent choice for a text in a graduate level history of American education course. Johanningmeier is an interesting author to read and he puts to rest a number of common myths about education in this nation.

Karier, Clarence J. *Shaping the American Educational State, 1900 to the Present*. New York: Free Press, 1975. This is a collection of essays and documents on the most important forces at work in developing the modern American educational system. Karier deals with issues and problems as well as ideas and movements.

Knight, Edgar W. *Fifty Years of American Education*. New York: Ronald Press, 1952. 484 pp., including index. Other standard works on the subject by the same author include: *A Documentary History of Education in the South Before 1860*. Chapel Hill: University of North Carolina Press, 1949. And *Education in the United States*. Boston: Ginn, 1951.

Mayer, Frederick. *American Ideas and Education*. Columbus, Ohio: Charles E. Merrill, 1964. Mayer's book is an intellectual and social history of American education which is especially useful for the student of ideas, attitudes, movements, and people. Mayer includes a large number of quotations from the leaders with whom he deals.

Meyer, Adolphe E. *The Educational History of the American People*. 2d ed. New York: McGraw-Hill, 1967. This very readable text presents the material in a refreshing way. It does assume some basic knowledge of American history on the part of the student.

Monroe, Paul, ed. *A Cyclopedia of Education*. New York: Macmillan, 1911-1913. Five volumes, including illustrations, charts, diagrams, and references. This monumental work is dated, but still the only one of its kind and a valuable source of information. A revised edition is in progress which will include modern material.

Mulhern, James. *A History of Education*. 2d ed. New York: Ronald Press, 1959. Parts IV and V contain a wealth of material pertaining to the growth of and the changes in the American educational system.

Perkinson, Henry. *Since Socrates: Studies in the History of Western Educational Thought*. New York: Longman, 1980. Perkinson gives a fresh account of the development of educational thought in the western world, with stress placed on intellectual and cultural history.

Perkinson, Henry. *Two Hundred Years of American Educational Thought*. New York: McKay, 1976. This book contains one of the best accounts of the critics of American education to be found anywhere in the literature.

Potter, Robert E. *The Stream of American Education*. New York: American Book, 1967. 522 pp., including a list of sources and index. Potter's book is one of the most complete single volume treatments of American education available. It is especially useful for the study of current educational issues and problems.

Power, Edward J. *Main Currents in the History of Education*. New York: McGraw-Hill, 1962. A useful general treatment of major American educational ideas.

Pratte, Richard. *Ideology and Education*. New York: Wiley, 1977. This is a useful account of the theories and philosophies of education. It treats individual thinkers and the social conditions that contributed to their ideas.

Rusk, Robert and James Scotland. *Doctrines of the Great Educators*. New York: St. Martin's Press, 1979. A new account of the contribution to education made by those who really changed the basic conceptions about education.

Thayer, V. T. *Formative Ideas in American Education.* New York: Dodd, Mead, 1965. Professor Thayer presents the philosophic views and changing theories held by leading educators in the United States. The detail in which significant ideas are presented makes Thayer very good reading for serious educators.

Tyack, David B., ed. *Turning Points in American Educational History.* Waltham, Mass.: Blaisdell, 1967. Some of the most significant writings and documents in the history of American education are presented with introductions by the author. This is a well-selected collection of the most significant materials relating to the subject of schooling in America.

Warren, Donald, ed. *History, Education, and Public Policy.* Berkeley, Cal. McCutchan, 1978. This collection of essays and documents gives a clear account of the way education and public policy in the United States are related.

Glossary

Academic Freedom. The liberty of teachers and scholars to pursue scholarly questions without fear of control or chastisement by administrative personnel of educational or governmental institutions.

Academy. An American secondary school of the colonial and early national era which stressed practical subjects like bookkeeping rather than the classics.

Accountability. The requirement that schools be responsible to the public for how well students do. This is done by testing of the students.

Activity Curriculum. A school program or curriculum chosen by the students themselves with the guidance from the teacher. The activity curriculum was used in some schools associated with progressive education.

Apperceptive Mass. The term used by the philosopher-psychologist Herbart to describe interlocking related or associated ideas in the subconscious part of the mind.

Associationism. The school of psychology which holds that learning should emphasize the relationships of concepts or ideas. Herbart was an associationist in this sense.

Bargaining, Collective. A provison for negotiating with a school board by which teachers are represented not as individuals but as a group. A union or a professional organization may be the bargaining agency.

Behaviorism. A school of psychology started by John B. Watson in 1912 which assumes nothing about people or animals and bases its conclusions entirely upon the observed reactions or "behavior" of subjects when they are exposed to a given stimulus.

Child-centered School. A school in which the primary concern is with developing the whole child rather than with subject matter. John Dewey and the progressive educators developed child-centered schools in which they tried to follow the natural needs, interests, and abilities of children.

Child Study Movement. The scientific study of the nature of children and learning, started about 1900 by G. Stanley Hall.

Common School. A school for all of the people. In the United States, free, public, elementary schools were the first "common" schools, but the term is now applied also to public high schools.

Compensatory Education. Systematic efforts to overcome problems of the culturally different student as with Head Start or bilingual teaching.

Competency-based Teacher Education. A requirement that teachers demonstrate minimum competency in the subjects they will teach before they are certified. Competency testing of students to see how well they can perform is now often required before graduation.

Comprehensive High School. A secondary school which attempts to cater to the needs of all students by offering more than one course of specialization in its program. Comprehensive high schools usually have a college preparatory course and one or more scientific or vocational courses which are terminal.

Compulsory Education. School attendance which is required by law on the theory that it is for the benefit of the commonwealth to educate all the people. Today, the practice is under attack by critics.

Core Curriculum. A program in which the different subjects of the curriculum are related to a central group of studies. History and geography are combined into the social studies core. Modern core curriculums often relate foreign languages with other subjects.

Dame School. A low-level primary school in the colonial and early national periods usually conducted by an untrained woman in her own home. Dame school teachers taught only the bare fundamentals for which they received small fees or presents.

De facto Segregation. A condition of segregation or separation of races into different schools caused by district boundaries which include children from only one race in a given school. This differs from segregation de jure which is a legal requirement for segregated schools (illegal since 1954).

Deism. The belief, held by many liberal colonial leaders, that God created the world and then withdrew to let it operate according to natural law. This means than man is on his own because God does not interfere with the affairs of men.

Developmental Stage. The theory that learning depends upon the maturity of the learner, and that it is necessary to reach a certain level of development (physical or mental or both) before certain kinds of learning can take place.

District System. A scheme of school organization, originating in Massachusetts, in which the local geographical unit or district is the legal authority for a school or schools. Modern districts, within state systems, are the legal areas covered by the services of a given school or schools.

Early Childhood Education. Any systematic effort to teach a child before the normal period of schooling begins. Froebel and Montessori were pioneers in the field. Project Head Start is a modern example of early childhood education.

Empirical Principle. The belief, as expressed by John Locke, that the measure of the truth of an idea is its comparison with common-sense reality. Many nonempirical theories hold that truth is tested by logic, revelation, or innate feelings.

The Enlightenment. A pattern of thought which protested against authority in religious and secular life. The Enlightenment stressed science, reason, and the dignity of all men, and it helped to create the shift of thought which made the American Revolution possible.

Essentialism. An educational theory which is a protest against progressive education and consists of an effort to identify the most important practical skills which are then taught to children as the basic or essential subjects.

Experimental Schools. Schools in which new methods or materials are tried in an effort to select the best. Experimental schools may be conducted by universities, school systems, or private groups. Normally, careful records are kept in order to measure the progress of pupils using a new curriculum or technique against those using more established ones.

Faculty Psychology. The belief, which was the basic psychology of educators in the nineteenth century, that the mind is divided into separate faculties or powers like willing, memory, and reasoning. Exercise of the faculties was supposed to strengthen the mind; thus the study of Latin grammar would transfer to or improve the ability to use logic.

General Education. Education which is not specialized and which is designed for general living or good citizenship rather than preparation for a vocation. There is an issue over just what should be included in general education as well as how many years should be devoted to it.

Graded School System. A division of schools into groups of students according to the curriculum or the ages of pupils as in the six elementary grades. Early schools were not graded and a substantial number of modern elementary schools are experimenting with nongraded systems, although grading is still the common practice.

Great Awakening. A religious revival in colonial America which was responsible for the creation of many schools and church-related colleges. Jonathan Edwards is credited with starting the Great Awakening among Puritans about 1733.

Herbartian Method. The formal system of presenting subject matter to students by the American followers of Herbart, using the five formal steps of preparation, presentation, association, generalization, and application.

Hornbook. A single printed page containing the alphabet, syllables, a prayer, and other simple words which was used in colonial times as the beginner's first book or pre-primer. Hornbooks were attached to a wooden paddle for ease in carrying and covered with a thin sheet of transparent horn for protection.

Humanism. A movement to attain knowledge of life and institutions through the study of the Latin and Greek classical authors. Humanism influenced the American colonies and had a profound effect on the development of American schools. Modern humanism is concerned with the needs and values of people.

Idealism. A major school of philosophy which holds that only ideas are real and that objects cannot exist outside some mind. Idealism was used by Berkeley to signify the opposite of realism. Jonathan Edwards and W. T. Harris were American idealists who influenced education.

In-Service Training. Continuing education for teachers who are actually teaching or in service. Such training may be conducted in a school as a workshop or extension course, or teachers may attend classes in a university at night or in vacation periods.

Intelligent Quotient (IQ). A number which is obtained by dividing mental age (found by a standard or normal test) by chronological age. Intelligence Quotients are widely used for placing children in school programs, although they are by no means perfect measurements.

Involuntary Segregation. Forced separation of students on the basis of race, color, or creed. Racial segregation may not be required by law in the United States since the Supreme Court decision in the Brown Case of 1954.

Kindergarten. A "garden of children" or an institution where small children may grow and develop. The term was coined by Froebel who began the first schools for children aged four, five, and six years. Kindergartens appeared in America about the time of the Civil War and are now schools for five-year-olds.

Knowledge Revolution. The tremendous explosion of information in almost every field, which makes it difficult for scholars to be aware of the new knowledge discovered in their own and related fields. The knowledge revolution is accompanied by a vast increase in sources of information, especially computers.

Laissez faire. The idea, based on Adam Smith's *Wealth of Nations*, that the government should not interfere in any way with the laws of supply and demand. *Laissez faire* theory holds that the best government is one which governs least.

Land-grant College. Colleges or universities founded or supported by a gift of public land. Many American agricultural and mechanical colleges were established by the Morrill Land-Grant Act of 1862.

Latin Grammar School. A classical secondary school with a curriculum consisting largely of Latin and Greek, the purpose of which was preparation for college.

Lock-step. A rigid or uniform organization and curriculum in which each grade or course is the foundation for each higher grade or course and there is no flexibility. The influence of the American Herbartianists led to the lock-step in our public schools after 1890.

Mainstreaming. The process, required by Public Law 94–142 of placing exceptional learners in the least restrictive learning environment. This means that handicapped students spend at least part of each day in a "normal" classroom.

Mental Discipline. A theory, associated with faculty psychology and transfer of training, which holds that the mind must be disciplined or exercised through drill, memorization, and the study of difficult subjects.

Middle School. A modern school organizational plan. Middle schools may be imposed between elementary and junior high schools or they replace them. A 4-4-4 plan uses the term "middle school" for the middle four years.

Modular System. Flexible schedule in a school, organized around modules of time (usually 15 minutes each) to allow for different time periods for various subjects and individual needs.

Monitorial Schools. Schools developed by Joseph Lancaster and Andrew Bell in which one teacher taught a number of bright students or monitors who, in turn, taught other groups of children. Monitorial schools were brought to America in the early national period in an attempt to provide cheap charity education for poor students.

Multi-track System. The educational program, found in Europe and in the American colonies, which provided one kind of education for the wealthy elite and another kind for the ordinary people.

Naturalism. In philosophy, the belief that the world contains only forces which require no supernatural explanation. In education, the belief that children should be free to follow their own interests, desires, and needs. Rousseau was a naturalist in education.

Nongraded School. A school which is not divided into specific grades for each age group. Nongraded schools may have children grouped according to social needs, ability, or progress, or not grouped at all.

Normal School. An American teacher-training school or college. Nineteenth-century normal schools were often two-year institutions on about the same level as high schools. Modern teacher-training colleges are four-year institutions and many offer graduate training.

Object Lessons. Teaching by means of objects and activities rather than through abstract symbols and words. The object lesson of the Swiss educator Pestalozzi was first introduced in America at the Oswego Normal School by Edward Sheldon in 1850.

Old Field School. A colonial educational institution developed in Virginia by families who would cooperate to build an elementary school on one of the fallow "old fields." These schools were the counterparts of district schools in New England.

Open Classroom. A modern educational innovation in which self-contained classrooms are replaced with an open plan with individualized instruction and freedom for the child to move about the school.

Pedagogy. The scientific study of education, or the curriculum of teacher-training institutions with regard to how to teach.

Perennialism. A term used by Theodore Brameld to describe a position which opposes pragmatism and progressivism, and which looks toward a restoration of the absolute or ultimate value system of ages past. Robert Hutchins and many Catholic educators may be described as perennialists.

Pragmatism. The school of philosophy which holds that only the practical results of a belief give it meaning and that arguments which have no practical consequence are meaningless. Charles Peirce coined the term and John Dewey is a good example of a pragmatist in education.

Programmed Learning. Any learning device which may be used by a student in such a way that a reaction to his activities is immediately supplied. These range from simple, printed notebooks to computer-assisted instruction, and the learner is not dependent upon a teacher in order to progress.

Progressive Educators. A term applied to a group of educators who objected to subject-centered schools, followed the philosophy of John Dewey, and applied the doctrines of Rousseau, Pestalozzi, and Froebel to education. Francis W. Parker was an early progressive, but the term is usually associated with members of the Progressive Education Association which was founded in 1918.

Project Method. The method of William H. Kilpatrick and his followers. Any learning activities in which pupils have an opportunity to choose, direct, or plan their own work under conditions similar to those of real life.

Rate Bill. A scheme for supporting schools that was a transition from fees to tax-support. Each child was charged a rate or graduated amount for his schooling, according to what his parents were able to afford.

Sapiential Authority. A term used by futurists like Theobald to mean authority based in truth or use value of information rather than upon status or position.

Scientific or Sense Realism. An effort to relate education to the "real" or common-sense world, which was started by scientific thinkers like Copernicus, Galileo, and Bacon. John Locke and Benjamin Franklin were scientific realists who influenced American schools.

Sectarianism. A term which refers to religious denominations. Early schools were under the control of particular church groups or sects until the Bill of Rights required that public schools be secular because of separation of church and state in America.

Secularism. The principle of religious freedom applied in such a way that the sphere of influence of religious groups or religious leaders does not extend to public institutions like the schools.

Single-track System. An educational program in which all the students have the same kind of educational opportunity, rather than one school system for the elite and another for the masses.

Social Darwinism. The theory of evolution applied to society rather than to biology. Social evolution was used by Sumner and Spencer to justify the existing social conditions and the concentration of wealth in the hands of the few.

Social Reconstruction. The belief that society can be made over or changed. Some social reconstructionists in education have held that the schools can reconstruct society, while Theodore Brameld believes that schools should have some role in social change.

Special Education. A school program designed for the child who is exceptional; that is, either gifted or below normal in ability. The study of exceptional children is now well established and most American school systems have special education classes.

Subject-centered School or Curriculum. The traditional educational program which is organized around subject matter or around major concepts in the organized fields of knowledge or disciplines. This is in opposition to the child-centered curriculum which emphasizes individual differences, needs, and interests of children.

Sunday School. A movement started by Robert Raikes in England and transferred to the United States in the early 1800s, which attempted to teach the fundamentals to children who worked in factories all week.

Tabula Rasa. As used by John Locke, the theory that children have no innate ideas at birth, and that the mind comes to be furnished with ideas through the sense organs or sensation. All learning comes through experience, and the mind is blank at birth.

Team Teaching. A plan by which several teachers, organized into a team with a leader, provide the instruction for a larger group of children than would usually be found in a self-contained classroom. Team members may handle classes together, or one member may teach a large number of children while the others work with individuals.

Terminal Education. Education or schooling which is not designed to lead to further or higher schooling. Vocational programs in high schools which lead directly to jobs rather than to college are examples of terminal education.

Theocracy. Civil and political power vested in the same person or group. Separation of church and state in America is guaranteed by the Bill or Rights, but the early New England governments were theocracies.

Transfer of Training. The theory, associated with faculty psychology and mental discipline, that learning one subject will aid, or transfer to, the study of another subject.

Utilitarianism. In education, the doctrine that the school curriculum should be governed by its usefulness for vocational success or public utility.

Vocational Education. Training which is intended to prepare the student for a particular job or to give a basic skill needed in several vocations.

Voluntary Segregation. The practice of establishing a school or other institution which is not for the use of the general public but which is under the control of a specific group. Parochial and private schools are examples of voluntary segregation.

Index